# THE
# PARLEMENT OF THE
# THRE AGES

EARLY ENGLISH TEXT SOCIETY

No. 246

1959 (reprinted 1967)

PRICE 40s.

*Oxford University Press, Ely House, London W. 1*
GLASGOW  NEW YORK  TORONTO  MELBOURNE  WELLINGTON
CAPE TOWN  SALISBURY  IBADAN  NAIROBI  LUSAKA  ADDIS ABABA
BOMBAY  CALCUTTA  MADRAS  KARACHI  LAHORE  DACCA
KUALA LUMPUR  HONG KONG  TOKYO

British Museum Addit. MS. 31042, f. 176
Thornton text ll. 593 ff.

British Museum Addit. MS. 33994, f. 25v
Ware text ll. 592ff.

# THE
# PARLEMENT OF THE
# THRE AGES

EDITED BY
M. Y. OFFORD

*Published for*
THE EARLY ENGLISH TEXT SOCIETY
*by the*
OXFORD UNIVERSITY PRESS
LONDON  NEW YORK  TORONTO

# OXFORD
UNIVERSITY PRESS

Great Clarendon Street, Oxford OX2 6DP
United Kingdom

Oxford University Press is a department of the University of Oxford.
It furthers the University's objective of excellence in research, scholarship,
and education by publishing worldwide. Oxford is a registered trade mark of
Oxford University Press in the UK and in certain other countries

© The Early English Text Society 1959

The moral rights of the authors have been asserted

Database right Oxford University Press (maker)

First Edition published in 1959
Reprinted 1967, 1997

All rights reserved. No part of this publication may be reproduced,
stored in a retrieval system, or transmitted, in any form or by any means,
without the prior permission in writing of Oxford University Press,
or as expressly permitted by law, or under terms agreed with the appropriate
reprographics rights organization. Enquiries concerning reproduction
outside the scope of the above should be sent to the Rights Department,
Oxford University Press, at the address above

You must not circulate this book in any other form
and you must impose this same condition on any acquirer

Published in the United States of America by Oxford University Press
198 Madison Avenue, New York, NY 10016, United States of America

British Library Cataloguing in Publication Data
Data available

Library of Congress Cataloging in Publication Data
Data available

Original Series, 246

ISBN 978-0-19-722246-1

TO
THE MEMORY OF
DOROTHY EVERETT

# PREFACE

PRELIMINARY studies of *The Parlement of the Thre Ages*, for a thesis prepared under the guidance of the late Miss Dorothy Everett at Lady Margaret Hall, convinced the present editor that the poem well merited a fuller apparatus than lay within the scope of Sir Israel Gollancz's edition in 1915 for his series of *Select Early English Poems*.

I owe my thanks to all those who have helped me in preparing this edition. To Miss Everett I am especially indebted for the help she gave so generously in the earlier stages of this work; her advice and stimulus were invaluable. I am indebted also to Dr. Mabel Day for reading my typescript in its original form, for many helpful comments, and for advice in reducing and reshaping the edition; to Professor Angus McIntosh for some useful suggestions; to Mr. R. W. Burchfield for help in preparing the edition for the press; and to Members of the Council of the Early English Text Society for their advice and criticism during the various stages of the production of this book.

To the Trustees of the British Museum I am obliged for permission to print the two versions of the poem and to reproduce the plates which form the frontispiece.

M. Y. O.

*Harrow Weald*
*April* 1959

# CONTENTS

BRITISH MUSEUM ADDIT. MS. 31042, f. 176 AND
ADDIT. MS. 33994, f. 25$^v$     *Frontispiece*

## INTRODUCTION
The Manuscripts and Texts of the Poem     xi
Language:
    Phonology     xvii
    Accidence     xxii
    Dialect     xxiv
Vocabulary     xxvi
Metre     xxix
Alliteration     xxxi
Relation to other Alliterative Poems; Date and Authorship     xxxiii
Sources and Analogues:
    The Dream Setting and the Debate     xxxix
    The Nine Worthies     xl
The Style of the Poem     xlii

## SELECT BIBLIOGRAPHY     xliv

## TEXT
    Thornton     1
    Ware     9

## ABBREVIATIONS OF TITLES     34

## NOTES     35

## GLOSSARY     71

## INDEX OF NAMES     98

# INTRODUCTION

## THE MANUSCRIPTS AND TEXTS OF THE POEM

*Manuscripts.* There are extant only two manuscripts of *The Parlement of the Thre Ages*: one contains a full version of the poem and one is incomplete, lacking ll. 1–225. The complete version is contained in one of the English miscellanies compiled in the middle of the fifteenth century by the Yorkshireman Robert Thornton.[1] This collection, which was acquired by the British Museum in 1879, is numbered Additional MS. 31042; it will be referred to in this edition as T. The incomplete version was discovered by Sir Israel Gollancz, who identified some pages at the end of a miscellany assembled by Sir James Ware (1594–1666) as part of *The Parlement of the Thre Ages*. The manuscript was acquired by the British Museum in 1891, and numbered Additional MS. 33994, ff. 19–26; it will be denoted by W in this edition.

*Editions of the Poem.* The only previous editions have been those by Sir Israel Gollancz: for the Roxburghe Club in 1897, where both texts are printed, together with *Wynnere and Wastoure*; and for the series *Select Early English Poems* in 1915, where only the Thornton text is printed, with a list of some variant readings from Ware.

*Thornton MS.* This manuscript is a fifteenth-century quarto volume; it contains 181 paper leaves measuring 10¾ by 8 in., and four vellum fly-leaves (from a fifteenth-century Breviary), which may have formed part of the original binding. There are twenty-six items in the collection, which comprises mainly English poems, romances, and religious pieces. The most interesting of these items from a literary point of view are 'The Segge of Ierusalem', 'The Sege of Melayne', 'Þe Romance of Duke Rowlande and of Sir Ottuell of Spayne', the poem now known as 'The Quatrefoil of Love' (it is not given a title), and 'The Parlement of the Thre

---

[1] He is thought to have been a native of East Newton, near Pickering, in Yorkshire; for an account of the evidence for this identification, see the Introduction to *The 'Liber de Diversis Medicinis'*, ed. Margaret Sinclair Ogden, E.E.T.S., o.s. 207 (1938).

*Introduction*

Ages' and 'Wynnere and Wastoure', which are the last two items.[1] The *Parlement* begins on f. 169ʳ and *Wynnere and Wastoure* on f. 176ᵛ. The name of the compiler appears twice: at the end of the third item, 'The Passion of Our Lord', before the Latin colophon, is a partly defaced signature 'R. Thornton', and the colophon of the fourth item, 'The Segge of Ierusalem', reads 'Explicit la sege de Ierusalem. R. [apparently Thornton, partly altered to another name which is hard to decipher] dictus, qui scripsit sit benedictus. Amen.' Exactly how long this miscellany remained with the Thornton family is not known, but at the top of f. 49ʳ, in a hand which is probably of the second half of the sixteenth century, is written 'John Nettletons boke'; and the surname 'Nettylton' appears three times in the right-hand margin, and 'Netylton' is scrawled at the foot of the centre margin, on f. 139ᵛ. This is presumably the John Nettleton of Hutton Cranswick in the East Riding of Yorkshire, whose name occurs in a list, thought to have been compiled in about 1565, of owners of medieval manuscripts.[2]

The script of the miscellany is a book hand of the mid-fifteenth century, small and rather cramped, but usually clear and consistent. The *Parlement* is written as verse, in single columns with about forty verse-lines to a page. There is no spacing between the sections, but the poem opens, and each new section begins, with a large rubricated capital letter. In the margin beside each such capital is a lightly written small guide-letter. Ordinary capitals are used throughout the text; often, though not always, at the beginning of a metrical line, and within the line sometimes inconsistently with modern practice. On ff. 174ᵛ and 175ʳ the scribe or illuminator (who may have been the same person) has partly rubricated some of the small capitals, usually by filling in a centre stroke with red. Double *f* is used for capital *F*, as is usual at this date. No distinction is made between *I* and *J*. There is no punctuation, either within or at the end of lines.[3]

---

[1] For a full list of the items in this collection, interesting as revealing the literary tastes of a fifteenth-century compiler, see the *Catalogue of Additions to the MSS. in the British Museum 1876–81*, 148–51.

[2] See C. E. Wright in *The English Library before 1700* (London, 1958), 157–8 and 173, notes 24 and 25.

[3] Except that there appears to be a stop after *I* in 295.

## Introduction

The Thornton scribe conforms with the usual fifteenth-century practice in his abbreviations and contractions: þ<sup>u</sup> and w<sup>t</sup> are often written for *þou* and *with*; *þe* is often written *þ<sup>e</sup>*. Marks of abbreviation used are: the usual signs for *-er*, *-ur*, *-us*; for *-rum*; for *Sir*, and for *ser-*; for *pri-*, *pre-*; for *pro-*; for *per-*, *par-*. The omission of a nasal consonant is marked by a stroke over the preceding vowel, as in *hȳ*. The general mark of contraction is a slightly hooked curve (*om̃ia*). Final *-n* nearly always, and final *-m* often, has a curled stroke, which was originally a mark of abbreviation;[1] but in this text, as often in English documents written during the fifteenth century, it probably has no significance.[2] Double *l* is generally crossed,[3] and *h* sometimes,[4] but here again the stroke seems to have no significance. Another abbreviation mark often used in this text is a slightly curved and sometimes hooked stroke above a letter or group of letters, usually in the neighbourhood of *-n-* or *-m-*; it occurs twice over *-p*, in *wirchip̂* 175, 276. In words containing medial *-n-* or *-m-*, it occurs generally over the nasal and the letter preceding and following, and since it is seldom clear how or whether the stroke should be expanded, it has been ignored in the text of this edition. Full examples of words over which it occurs are as follows: the names *Cassãnder, Corborãnt, Fesõme, Frãnce*, where it may indicate *-u-*; perhaps *-e-* in *blossõms, corbỹns, maydẽns*, and *-e-* or *-u-* in *burgõns, caprõns* (twice), *fawkõns, Indyãns*; it may indicate doubling of the consonant in *sõne* 'sun' (twice), and in *sal-ĩeme, wãne*; it must be redundant in *berỹne, cõmes* (four times), *coũntours, gãmnes, kyngdõmes* (twice), *Londõne, neũened, nỹne* (twice), *opỹnede, Sampsõne, sõne* 'son' twice, and 'soon'. Probably this stroke was often added mechanically even when the word was not abbreviated, or the scribe in expanding a contraction may sometimes have copied the contraction sign too.

---

[1] Johnson and Jenkinson in *English Court Hand*, i. 70, suggest that these final flourishes 'may be due to an instinctive feeling in scribes accustomed to write Latin that *n*, and some other consonants, could not be right as terminations'.

[2] e.g. in the first 100 lines of the poem all words ending in *-n* or *-m* have the curled stroke except the following: *in* 1, &c. (throughout), *hym* 34 (twice), 35, 45, 54, 58, 60, 61, 63, 66 (twice), 70, 81, *than* 86.

[3] In the first 100 lines, uncrossed *ll* occurs in *hillys* 17, *stilly* 41, *hallede* 53, *fellys* 59, *fallen* 65, *felle* 77, *pullede* 84, *alle* 92. In all other instances, *ll* is crossed.   [4] In the first 100 lines, *h* is crossed in *dreghe* 3, *thurgh* 56, 91.

## Introduction

**Ware MS.** MS. Additional 33994 was formerly part of the library of Sir James Ware, the Irish antiquary and historian, who died in 1666. It is a small quarto volume containing twenty-six paper leaves which range in date from the fifteenth to the seventeenth century. The leaves vary slightly in size, and all appear to have been cut to fit the binding; those containing the *Parlement* measure roughly 7 by 5¼ in. This little collection contains four rather oddly assorted items: a short treatise in Latin on the history of the Irish language; notes in Spanish on the early church history of Ireland; a printed treatise 'De officio Admirallitatis Anglie', translated from French by Thomas Rowghton de Rowghton; and on f. 19$^r$, the fragment of the *Parlement* beginning 'Than fauconers ful frely foundyn hem aftur'. This is followed in the same hand by a list headed 'Distretacio Rerum',[1] reminiscent of the catalogue of terms which includes 'a Gagle of gees' in the *Boke of Saint Albans*. Sir James Ware probably acquired the English manuscript on one of his visits to England, where he is known to have examined several libraries, including the Bodleian.

The fragment is written in a bold and usually clear hand; probably of the end, certainly of the latter half, of the fifteenth century. It is arranged in single columns with about twenty-eight verse-lines to a page, and with a space before each new section of the poem. Each section opens with a large flourished capital, not coloured, and in the right-hand margin the name of the speaker, or the main subject of a section, is written in a tall, flourished script, probably by the same copyist.[2] In some places these names have been cut off when the pages were trimmed to fit the binding, but as far as they can be read they are printed in the footnotes to the text in this edition.

As in T, *I* and *J* are not distinguished, and *ff* is used for *F*. Each line begins with a capital, and within the line capitals are often used inconsistently with modern practice. In this text, however, there is a considerable amount of punctuation, with full stops and

---

[1] 'An heerd of hertis.      An Iye of Fesauntz.
   An heerd of dere.       A Covy of partrikes.
   An herd of Cranes.      A Bevy of ladyes.
   An heerd of Curlues.    A Beve of quayles.
   An herd of Wrennes.     A Bevy of Roes.'

[2] This is evident when the flourishes of the capitals are compared.

## Introduction

what may be intended as commas,[1] at the end of lines; and stops are sometimes used within the line to mark a speech-pause, as in 235 after *chefly*, 392 after *love*, and 489 after *see*. (Occasionally, as in 488 after *Dragon*, 630 after *many*, they do not correspond with the caesura of the line.) The punctuation at the end of lines does not generally correspond with modern practice.

Most of the remarks about abbreviations and contractions in T apply here also. The only differences worth noting are as follows: the contraction ę for -*es* or -*is*[2] is used very often; a stroke curving upwards and to the left from -*m* and -*n* occasionally,[3] and frequently from -*r* (as in *to gidr* 600: see Frontispiece, Addit. MS. 33994), appears to indicate final -*e*, and has been expanded thus in the present text; the usual Latin contraction 9 for *con* is found in 9*teyn̄* 307. The scribe of this text is particularly fond of the stroke of abbreviation —: in words ending in, or containing, *h*, *th*, or *ht* it is extremely common, as a stroke through the *h*: sometimes it may be the scribe's concession to a final -*e* in the text from which he is copying, but sometimes it is obviously redundant, as in *fouḡhten* (twice), *hiḡhe* (once), *knyḡhtes* (three times). Over *p* this stroke occurs only twice, in *yep̄* 270, *Penelop̄* 628. In connexion with *n*, *m* it is used to a considerable extent: occasionally to supply the nasal, as in *hȳ*, sometimes perhaps to indicate final -*e*, as in *yern̄*, &c., or -*nn* as in *down̄* or -*en* as in *awn̄*, *own̄*. But on the whole this mark, like the curved stroke in T, seems to have been used mechanically rather than significantly. It has been ignored in the text of this edition, except where it supplies the nasal, as in *hȳ*.

*The relationship between the two texts*. Very little can be deduced about the manuscript history of the text. It is unlikely that T is a direct copy of the original version: the mixed appearance of the

---

[1] The scribe sometimes, but inconsistently, uses what look like commas but may be only flourished stops. Sometimes (occasionally but perhaps accidentally in requirement with the sense) he has no punctuation; occasionally he uses a faint slanting stroke, alone or with a stop; occasionally, as in 296, 443, a comma and a stop together, and once (302) all three. These details have not been reproduced in the text of this edition.

[2] The scribe varies between -*es* and -*is* when this ending is not contracted; it has been expanded throughout to -*es* in this edition.

[3] The curled stroke of -*m*, -*n* (see p. xiii), to be distinguished from this strong upward curve, occurs only once, in *fongyn* 572.

## Introduction

language suggests some scribal alteration, probably by more than one scribe, even though the poet's own dialect may have admitted a variety of forms; and some irregularities in the alliteration (see pp. xxxi–xxxii) may be scribal. On the other hand, the text contains few obscurities, and does not give the impression of having passed through many hands before it reached the scribe of T, so it may not be far removed from the original.

T and W are obviously not closely connected, but there are a few indications that they may be descended indirectly from a common original (which was perhaps not far removed from the author's copy). Thus, both texts show that an adjective may have dropped out after *Pantasilia* in 325, and in 486 *athell* may have dropped out before *kyng*; but these slips—if they are slips and not intended to be ax/ax lines—could have been made independently. More suggestive, perhaps, is that in 347 both texts have *t* in a word which derives presumably from OF. *Arcage*; and both have the form *Candore* for 'Candace' in 627, though it is curious that W has *Cadace* in 396. Other indications depend on the rather doubtful assumption of regular alliteration in the original. Thus in 300, both texts have *first(e)* where a 'regular' line would have *areste* or *erste*; in 371 *kynges* (*kinges*), where *beryns* (*bernes*) would give an aa/ax line; and similar emendations could be made in 555, 621. But since it is by no means certain that the poet himself did not admit some 'irregularly' alliterating lines, this evidence should not be pressed.[1]

Clearly W is not directly descended from T: this is evident from the wide divergences in readings[2] (often unintelligible corruptions in W), the transposition of lines,[3] and the gaps in the text.[4] Moreover, W preserves fewer of the old constructions,[5] some of the rarer or older words have been replaced by more familiar ones,[6]

---

[1] For other instances of 'irregular' lines, see 'Alliteration', 4, p. xxxi.

[2] As in ll. 245, 367, 386, 499, 502, 661, and others.

[3] Cf. ll. 253-4 in the two versions, and textual note on W 360.

[4] Lines 328, 461, 503, 504, 602, 604, 605, 626, 638, and 657 are missing in W.

[5] e.g. T has *hym to fote* 490, beside W *to his fote*; T has *by hym one* 599 beside W *by his one*.

[6] e.g. in 245 T has *be-dagged*, W *dragild*; T *digges*, W *dikes*; 278 T *makande*, W *make*; 286 T *sowed*, W *sighed*; 313 T *tulke*, W *toure*; 429 T *radde*, W *feerde*; 482 T *blyot*, W *billet*; 661 T *schurtted*, W *serchid*.

*Introduction*

and names are often corrupt beyond recognition.[1] Thus W appears to be a considerably later version, and may be several times removed from the original.

*New readings.* A collation of the texts in Sir Israel Gollancz's editions with the two manuscripts has yielded a large number of new readings in both texts, the most important of which are the following, in T: 71 *brede* for Gollancz's reading *brode*; 164 *hopynge* for *hapynge*; 234 *quyrres* for *quysses*; 275 *es* for *as*; 539 *Nioles* for *Naoles*; 648 *ȝe þat* for *þat ȝe*.

LANGUAGE

(A survey of the points of chief interest in the language of this text, particularly in relation to its dialect; examples from W are quoted only when they differ notably from T. Phonetic symbols used are those recognized by the I.P.A. Line references for the forms cited will be found in the Glossary. Abbreviations: see p. 71. For abbreviations of titles, see p. 34.)

*Phonology*

Vowels

1. OE. ă/ŏ or ON. ă before nasals: generally ă (or ā in an open syllable), but sometimes ŏ: *kane, man, name, schame*; *o* in *from(e), homelyde*; before *-nk*, once *bonke*; *blonke, donkede*.
2. OE. a/o before nasal in lengthening groups wavers between *a* and *o* (thus probably slack [ɔ:] from *and* > *ānd* > *ǭnd*, rather than tense [o:] from *and* > *ŏnd* > *ǭnd*). Examples: always *and*, but *hande(s), honde(s)* six times each; always *londe(s), longe*. W has a similar variation.
3. OF. *a* before nasal+cons.: generally *au* (occasionally *aw*): *braunches, daunsen, pawnche*. Undiphthongized forms occur in, for example, *angelles, besanttes, romance, ensample, chambirs*.
4. OE. ǣ is generally *a*: *aftir, sadde*; presumably *ā* in an open syllable: *athell, watirs*. In *feste* 91, the *e* may be from ON. *festa*, but see L. Morsbach, *ME. Gramm.*, § 87, Anm. 2. *Gryse* 8, OE. *græs*,

[1] e.g. in 301 T has *Troygens*, W *trochis*; 347 T *of Artage*, W *of heritage*; 356 T *Fozome*, W *his fomen*; T *Fozayne*, W *fighon*; 476 T *fytz*, W *fight*; 522 T *of Iene*, W *þe sayn*; 573 T *Nerbone*, W *Norburgh*.

xvii

## Introduction

may be an alternative form of *gres(e)*, OSwed. *grœs*: see K. Luick, *Hist. Gramm. der eng. Sprache*, § 382, 2 and Anm. 3.

5. (i) OE. *ǣ+g* is nearly always *ai, ay*: *faire, sayde* (but once *seyde*† 173).

(ii) OE. *ǣ+h* is diphthongized to *au* in *laughte, raughte*.

6. OE. *ǣ* before *l*+cons.: (i) unlengthened: regularly *a*, as in *alle, halfues*. The *au* (probably scribal) in *haulse* 90, *haulle* 253 indicates the diphthongal stage of late ME. *ă* followed by *l*.

(ii) Lengthened, before *l*+*d*: *a*, or with normal rounding *o* [ɔ:] is the rule: *aldeste*,[1] *Olde, halde, holde, halden, holden*; *o* forms are the more common.

(iii) Before *l*+cons., with mutation: *e* in *elde, eldeste* (cf. *aldeste*, above, and footnote). There are no *i*-, *y*- forms.

7. Late OE. *ǣ* before *r*+cons. is generally *a*: *armes* 113, 247, *harde*; *e* in *berde(s), ferne*.[2] *Byrdes* (W 482) may indicate a pronunciation with short [i].

8. OE. or ON. *ĕ* is normally *e* (presumably [ɛ:] in an open syllable, as in *dreped, freke*), but *ĕ* has been raised to *i* in *riste*, which seems to be a N. form,[3] and perhaps in *triste*.[4] Cf. *priste* 618, *pristly* 241 (OF. *prest*).

9. OE., ON., or OF. *i* normally remains, but lowering to *ĕ* has occurred in *reches, threuen*, and in *sterapis* (? OE. *ī* > late OE. *ī*, shortened in ME. in the trisyllabic pl. form). For the change of *ĭ* to *ĕ*, which is quite common in late ME. (especially during the fifteenth century in the N., where it is commonest), see Morsbach, op. cit., § 115, 2 and Anm. 2. (This change is to be distinguished from the earlier lengthening and lowering of *ĭ* to *ē* (presumably [e:]) which has occurred in, for example, *mekill*, perhaps in *deden*,[5] and probably also in the F. loan-words *peteuosely, reuere, disfegurede*.)

10. OE. *ȳ* is generally *i, y*, but sometimes *u, e*. Examples: *clyp, kysse, fiste, synn*; *cruche, lure, schutt* (W has *burde* 390

---

[1] M. S. Serjeantson in *RES*. iii (1927), 331, suggests that *aldeste* 'may represent the West Midland *i*-mutation of *æl*+cons., but is perhaps a new formation from *ald*'.
[2] See R. Jordan, *Handbuch der me. Gramm*. i, § 59, a and b.
[3] See Luick, op. cit., § 379.
[4] If this derives from ON. *treysta*: see Glossary.
[5] See Morsbach, § 130, Anm. 6.

## Introduction

beside *byrd* 453, and *dud* 'did' 557, 570); *belde, mery, werdes* (W has *beldid* 662, *lere* 323).

11. OE. *ǣ*¹ (non-WS. *ē*) and *ǣ*² appear as *e*; there are no rhymes to give evidence of the tense or slack pronunciation of these vowels, but the spelling *ee* sometimes found in W (*feerde* 429, *meene* 530) probably indicates [e:]. Shortenings from *ǣ*² appear in *any, lady. Are* (conj.), *ar(e)ste*, may represent a shortening (? in ONth.) of OE. *ǣr* > *ǣr* > *ar*, or may have been influenced by ON. *ár*.

12. OE. and ON. *ā* is generally rounded to *o* [ɔ:]: *bone(s), bothe, mo, rode*; but it is spelt *a* in *athes* 499, *gane* 460. In words with OE. *ā* followed by OE. *g* or *w*, *a* is more common: *awnn* (eight times), *ownn* (twice); *knowe* 168, *knawen* 458; but *soule* (three times) beside *saule* (once). For 'rode', W has *rode* (twice) but also *raied* 562, *rayed* 514, forms characteristic of Sc. rather than N. texts: cf. *raid* 'rode' in Barbour's *Bruce*. (The spelling *ai(y)* arose presumably because the ME. diphthong *ai* and ME. *ā* were levelled under one sound, ? [ɛ:], later [e:].)

13. OE. *ō* is generally *o*, but sometimes *u*: as in *gud(e)* adj. (seven times), *gude* n. (six times). (Cf. *tuke* 313, 569, beside *toke* 79.) W has *gode* (once *good*), *toke*. (Presumably *u* was a phonetic spelling, but not used consistently: *o* and *u* may both have indicated a sound approximating to French or German [y:].) T has also *-ew-* in *bewes* 662 (W *bowes*), OE. *bōgas*; *-ew-* may represent a diphthong [iu],¹ with the first element unrounded, from an earlier [üu]; see Luick, op. cit., § 406. Luick notes that the spelling *-ew-* < OE. *-ōg-* appears from the fifteenth century on, so the form in T may be scribal. Cf. also *bewells* 69 (OF. *bouel*).

14. OE. *ĕa+-i, -j* appears as *e*, presumably [e:]: *elde* (see 6, iii), *ferde* 330, *leue* 197. The *ee* in W *feerd* 330 probably indicates [e:]. The form *yeld*, W 283 (if not corrupt) does not necessarily suggest a S.E. scribe.²

15. OE. *ēag, ēah*: T has no *-ig, -ih* forms: *eghne, heghe, seghe*; W has *highe* 411, *sye* 512.

16. OE. *ĕo* appears as *e*: *beryn* (W *berne, beern*), *erthe*.
OE. *ēow* appears as *ew* in T: *hewe, trewe*. (W has the later spelling

[1] Cf. *Iewe* 426, &c. (OF. *giu(e)*).
[2] See H. C. Wyld, *History of Modern Colloquial English*, 308.

## Introduction

u(e :) hue, tru(e).) Ēow appears also as ou, ow in trouthe, trowede, presumably from OE. forms with shifted stress. There is, however, no trace in this text of OE. ēow > aw, au (trawe, trawþe, trauþe, &c.) as in the dialect of the *Gawain* group.

OE. eo in the group weor appears as e in werke(s), werlde; as i in wirchip(e); as o in worthen 461, &c. W has a in warkes 481, < OE. (Angl.) wærc; o in world, worship, worth.

### Vowels in Unstressed Syllables

1. T has the typically N. -yn in beryn; see Luick, op. cit., § 450.

2. -yn in verb-endings is fairly common in T, particularly between 220 and 245, and common in W (see 'Verbs', p. xxiii). W has -yn for -en fairly commonly in other words also: hevyn 320, selvyn 271.

3. W has -ur regularly for -er (T -ir, -er), as in aftur, wyntur; but no examples of -us, -ud for -es, -ed.

4. For the treatment of final -e (inflexional and orthographical), see under 'Metre'. It is spelt -ee in noblee 251, sondree 90.

### Consonants

1. OE. cw, OF. cu, qu, appears as qu (qw) in T: quelled, quene, qwene, querrye, quotes. W has quene, but whellid, whirry, &c. In some parts of the N. dialect qu < OE. cw and wh < OE. hw had apparently become identical in sound (presumably [χw]), so they were often interchanged in spelling, and were sometimes alliterated together: as (perhaps) in T *Whare . . . qwene* 626.[1] Qu in quo[p]es 233, quyppeys 234 (both alliterating with qu < cw, cu) also may = wh, but see Glossary. (The alliteration of wh and qu is found in other alliterative poems: occasionally in *Siege Jer.* and *Morte A.*, fairly often in *Wars Alex.*, and commonly in *Destr. Troy.*)[2]

2. OE. hw appears as wh in what(e), when, where; and as w in were 'where' 611, wiche 293, perhaps scribal errors. Wh appears to alliterate with w in 507 *wiste—werlde—where*, and perhaps in 293 *wiche—when—whate*. This seems inconsistent with the allitera-

---

[1] 'Whare es now Dame Dido was qwene of Cartage?' (The alternative would be 'Whare es now Dame Dido was qwene of Cartage'.) On the other hand, quene may alliterate with [k] in 627. Both pronunciations of qu may have been possible as a poetic licence, if not in the author's own dialect.

[2] See M. Day, *Siege Jer.* xi–xii.

## *Introduction*

tion of *wh* and *qu* (*qw*) mentioned above, but the pronunciation [w] as well as [χw] for *wh* may have been current in parts of the North Midlands.[1]

3. OE. *g*: T. has *g* in *gaffe, gouen, agayne*; probably [g], from ON. *gefa, i gegn*. W. has *yeve, yoven, ayayn*; probably [j], from the OE. forms.

4. OE. palatal *c*: T has *ch* in *seches, myche*; but *k* in *sekis, mekill*, perhaps owing to Scand. influence. (On the other hand, OE. *secst, secþ, miclan*, for example, would give *sek-, mik-* in ME. without Scand. influence.)

5. OE. *sc* is generally *sch* in T, always *sh* in W. *Sall* in T 168 may represent the N. tendency to reduce [ʃ] to [s] in unaccented words, but as it occurs only once, beside *schall(e)* twelve times, it may well be a scribal error.

6. OF. *ss* is *s(s)ch* in *bruschede, encrampeschet(t), floreschede, lessches*; *ss* in *lesses*. *S(s)ch* here may = [s], from the Central F. development of *-iss-*, as opposed to the Northern F. [ʃ]. This [s] in words derived from F. *-iss-* forms appears to be characteristic of the N. and Sc. dialects: see Luick, op. cit., § 732, 4. Since *sch* was often reduced to [s] in N. and Sc., converse spellings of *sch* for [s] (as *schir* 'sir', *schemit* 'seemed') are common; hence, probably, spellings like *lessches*. Similarly, OF. *s* is spelt *sch* in *Paresche* 305; and see note on *sowssches* 218. W has *ch* in *leches*, and cf. W *Marchel, parych* 'Paris', and T *perche* 'pierce', *Merchill*; in all these, *ch* probably = [s].

*Spelling*

There are no striking peculiarities of spelling in either manuscript, but a few points may be noted.

1. *ie* is occasionally used in T for OE. tense *ē*, as in *wielde, thies*, but perhaps [e:] had been raised to [i:] (in the scribe's pronunciation, at least), since *ie* is used also for OE. *ī* in *wies(e)ly, stiewarde[s]*.

2. *ȝ* is used only for the front spirant: *ȝates, ȝere, ȝonge*, &c.; W. has *y*: *yates*, &c., but once *ȝates* 575.

3. *g* is used for the back stop, as in *gud, grene*, &c., and for the affricate [dʒ] in some F. loan-words, as *gentill*; this alliterates

[1] The alliteration of *wh* with *w* as well as with *qu* is found occasionally in *Wars Alex., Destr. Troy, Morte A.*, and *Siege Jer.*

## Introduction

with $i = j$ in F. loan-words, *Iewe, iugge*, &c.; it is spelt *ientille* once in T, *Ientill* three times in W.

4. *gg* is used for the OE. affricate *cg*, as in *segge, rigge*, &c.

5. *gh* is used for the back spirant, as in *droghen, laghe*, &c.; W has *w*: *drowe, lawe*, &c. *gh* is used also for the back spirant from OE. *h*, as in *heghe, thurgh*, &c.; T has *-ow* once: *thorowe* 238.

6. Redundant mute *h* sometimes occurs initially: in T, *habade, habyde*; in W, *hay* for 'ay' 564, *hewe* for 'ewe' (OF. *eau*) 590; conversely, mute *h* is omitted in T *ayers* 577 (W *heyris*).

7. *s* voiced is written *z* in T *Sarazenes, philozophire*.

8. A double consonant fairly often occurs in T, in words in which the consonant was not doubled in OE. or OF.; this seems to occur particularly in words containing *t, n*, or *nt*, whether the vowel in the preceding syllable is short or long: *besanttes, profettis, lightten, whitte, awnn, bownn(e), rawnnsunte*, and with *s, nesse* 99, *sessede* 'seized' 419.[1]

9. In W only:
   (i) *ee* is sometimes used for tense $\bar{e}$: *beern* 391, *feere* 388, &c.
   (ii) *f* (alliterating with *f*) is once written *v*: *disvigured* 284.
   (iii) *v* is used for *w* in *vised* 451 (OE. *wisian*).
   (iv) *w* is used for OF. *ui*: *swid(e)* 382, 567.
   (v) *c* is used for *s* in *vncele* 438; conversely *s* is used for OF. *c* in *sesid* 'ceased' 286.

### Accidence

*Nouns*

The *-e* of the nom. s. is sometimes historical, as in *hunte, bagge, gome, sone* 'sun'; but often merely orthographical, as in *gryse, dewe, dragone, renke, segge*. See also under 'Metre', p. xxix.

*Adjectives*

There is little trace of inflexion. T generally has *-e* throughout s. and pl., weak and strong, even in adjectives which in OE. ended in a consonant; occasionally a distinction may survive, as in *Sir*

---

[1] This doubling may be a habit of the Thornton scribe: cf. WW. *henttis* 211, *ownn* 400; Qu. Love *withowtten* 58, *crownned* 199; and Morte A. *lyghttys* 251, *bownn* 1633, to mention a few examples taken at random from other poems in the Thornton MS.

## Introduction

*Gawayne the gude* 475 beside *gud Sir Gy* 528. In W the ending *-e* for adjectives which in OE. ended in a consonant is exceptional: *bold, blak, long,* &c.; but *Sir Gawayn þe gode, gode Sir Guy.*

### Pronouns

The most notable forms are: fem. s. *scho*, W *sho*; pl. *thay, thaire*, &c. (see Glossary); W has *they, ther(e), them*, &c., but twice *hir* and six times *hem* (all but three of the *h-* forms occur in the first seventeen lines of the fragment).

### Verbs

Infin.: generally ends in *-e*, but sometimes *-en*, occasionally *-yn*; nine forms have no *-e*, as *begynn, hent, sitt*, &c.; W has about twenty forms without final *-e*. There is no trace in either text of the suffixal *-i* of OE. class II weak verbs.

Pr. indic.: 1 s. has *-e*, or no ending; the N. ending *-is* occurs once in *sekis* 269, probably pr. 1 s. rather than imper.; 2 s. is generally *-es*; *-ys*, *-is* in *duellys* 175, *faris* 184; 3 s. is generally *-es*, but sometimes *-is*, *-ys*; W has also three *-ith* forms: *likith* 521, *sendith* 558, *takith* 556. Pl.: in T, mainly *-en*, but *-yn* forms occur between 220 and 245; *-es* three times (*brynges* 224, *hyghes* 213, *sowssches* 218); *-is* in *mendis* 146; *-on* in *nowmbron* 308; *-e* in *chefe* 243, *kane* 425, and always in the pl. of 'have': *hafe, haue*, &c.; W has a similar mixture of forms. Verb 'to be': T has s. *am—arte—es*, pl. *are* six times, *bene* eight times; W has s. *am—is*, pl. *ar, bene*, once *be*.

Imper.: s. *bye, make* 190, pl. *haues* 653, *makes* 290.

Pr. partic.: *gronande*, W *gronand* 343.

Subj.: pr. 3 s. *amende* 665, *dele* 664, *spede* 260, *tyde* 37; 1 pl. *flyte* 264, *iugge* 422; pt. 3 s. *see* 501; see also *be, haue* in Glossary.

Past tense: (1) Strong: 1 and 3 s. generally *-e*; pl. generally *-en*, but *-e* in *gane, ranne, wanne*; once *wonnen* pl. 463, W *wan*. Some verbs which in OE. were strong have now a weak pt. or pp.: e.g. *bewede, crepite, crept* (W *cropyn*), *fared, loutted*, &c.

(2) Weak: s. endings generally *-(e)de, -ed, -id* or *-te*; sometimes *-et(t)* in T (*assemblet, heryett, maket*, &c.); pl. in T often *-en* (*demden, ferden*, &c.), sometimes *-ed(e), -te* (*assegede, fologhed, wroghte*); *-yd* in *duellyd*. W generally has *-d, -t*, but *lovedyn* 612.

## Introduction

Pp.: (1) Strong: in T *-en*, except *layne, slayne*; W has *-en, -yn*; *-e* in *yeve* 575 beside *yoven* 398.

(2) Weak: in T *-ed* or (more often) *-(e)de*; *-et(t)* in *assommet, encrampeschett, heryet, -it* in *fadit*; *-te* in *refte*. W has *-d*, generally *-i(y)d*; *-t* in *reft*.

### Dialect

It seems fairly clear that the original dialect of the poem was N. Midland. How far the rather mixed appearance of the dialect in the texts as we have them is due to scribal corruption, and how far to a mixture of forms in the dialect itself, it is difficult to say. Certainly there has been scribal corruption, and especially in W some modernization, but the dialect itself probably was changing and beginning to admit forms from other dialects, particularly from the E. Midlands and S. Midlands. However, the evidence for the N. character of the language is clear enough, in both texts. Distinctively N. features (in the fourteenth century) are: *Vowels*, *a, ai* for OE. and ON. *ā* (see under 'Vowels', 6 (ii), 12); *u* for OE. *ō* (see 13); forms such as *are* 'before' (11), *gryse, riste* (4, 8), *beryn* (see 'Unstressed Syllables', 1). *Consonants*, alliteration of *wh* < OE. *hw* with *qu* < OE. *cw* (1); the *k* forms for OE. palatal *c* (4); *sall* for *schall* (5); the *s(s)ch* forms (6). *Accidence*, the pr. indic. forms in *-es, -is*, and *-es* in pl. imper.; pr. partic. in *-and*; weak pt. and pp. in *-et(t), -it*; strong pp. with no prefix and ending in *-en*; 3 s. *es* of verb 'to be'; the pron. *scho*. *Vocabulary*: this contains a fair number of words, both of native and of Norse origin, which appear to be distinctively N.: see pp. xxvii–xxviii.

Certain Midland characteristics make it unlikely that the poem was composed in the dialect of the extreme N. Some of these features may have been scribal, but taken as a whole they suggest the N. Midl. rather than the extreme N. dialect. The Midl. features are: the *o* forms (which are the more common) for OE. and ON. *ā*; *ch* for OE. palatal *c* ('Consonants', 4); possible alliteration of *wh* with *w* (2); the infinitives with *-n*, not always to avoid hiatus (e.g. *helpen* 227, *stillen* 268); the *-en, -yn* endings of the pr. indic. pl.; *from(e)* used beside *fro*; *to* rather than *till*, which occurs only once as prep. (52).

## Introduction

It is less easy to determine whether the dialect was originally NE. or NW. Midl.: the texts as we have them show both easterly and westerly features. The easterly (as opposed to westerly) characteristics are: *a* before *n*, *m* ('Vowels', 1); *i*, *y* for OE. $\check{y}$ (10); *e* for OE. *ĕo* (16); no *h*- forms in pronouns, apart from those in W. On the other hand, there are some notable westerly features: the *o* before *n*, *m* ('Vowels', 1): this rounding has been shown to be typically Western and traces of it in E. Midl. texts are rare; the *u*-forms for OE. $\check{y}$ (10); and the spelling *-ur* in unaccented syllables (*aftur*, &c.) in W may possibly be a westernism which has survived from the original.[1]

In the absence of rhymes and of internal evidence there can be no certainty as to the original dialect of the poem, but NW. Midl. is perhaps the most likely. The W. Midl. features are more likely to have been original than scribal: there is good evidence that many of the alliterative poems were originally written in the W. Midl., whereas none in the alliterative long line can be proved to have been of E. Midl. origin.[2] The dialect of *Parl.* agrees in several important points with that, for instance, of *Morte A.*, *Destr. Troy*, *Wars Alex.*, *St. Erkenwald*, and *Awntyrs*, all of which have been placed in the NW. Midl.[3] J. P. Oakden (op. cit., chap. 3) would place them in the extreme NW., near the Ribble valley. *Parl.* too, he thinks, was written in the NW., but the scribe was NE. Midl. It could indeed be suggested that the easterly features were traces of Robert Thornton's own dialect, since he probably came from east Yorkshire, but there is no need to assume that the E. Midl. features are all scribal; some of them may be due to the spreading of these forms westward during the fourteenth century, or to a growing familiarity with a literary 'standard'. M. S. Serjeantson (loc. cit. 331) suggests that the dialect of *Parl.* and *WW.* may represent that of the N. Central Midlands, possibly of

---

[1] M. S. Serjeantson (*Sir Gawain*, E.E.T.S., o.s. 210, p. liii) mentions 'the use of *-us*, *-ur*, etc. for *-es*, *-er*, etc. in unstressed syllables' as 'often regarded as typically West Midland'.

[2] In view of the close similarity of dialect between *Parl.* and *WW.*, it is significant that the author of *WW.* implies that he is a 'westren wy' (*WW.* 8-9).

[3] See, for example, M. S. Serjeantson, *RES.* iii. 54-67, &c., S. O. Andrew, ibid. iv. 418-23, and J. P. Oakden, *The Dialectal and Metrical Survey*, chap. 3.

## Introduction

Nottinghamshire. This county, however, is not quite northerly enough to account for the strong northern element in the language and vocabulary; Oakden may be nearer to the truth when he suggests an area 'not far away from the Ribble boundary'. The poet's dialect could have been that of the central or southern part of the West Riding of Yorkshire, but at this distance of time it is impossible to localize it exactly.

### VOCABULARY

The *Parlement*, like most of the ME. alliterative poems, has a rich and varied vocabulary. Alliterative verse demands an ample store of synonyms, and writers in the fourteenth century had a wide field from which to glean. Much of the 'word-hoard' of the Germanic poet was still familiar to those who liked to hear and compose their poetry in the ancient alliterative style; and in sharp contrast, there was an abundance of new French words for almost every sphere of activity and thought. Between these extremes was the writer's native dialect, with its own resources of vocabulary and its own peculiarities: the bulk of it Anglo-Saxon, but with many 'local' words and with its own share of borrowings from Scandinavian and French. The vocabulary of the alliterative poets is remarkable not only in its richness but also in its blending of the new and unusual with the ancient and traditional.

*Native Element*

(1) Words found chiefly in verse in OE. and in ME. chiefly in alliterative poetry of the fourteenth century: a striking number of synonyms for 'man' or 'knight' or 'people', as *beryn, douth, freke, gome, hathelle, lede, ledys, segge, wy*; and *blonke* 'steed', *here-wedys* 'armour' (*Beowulf* 1897).

(2) OE. words used in prose or verse which have become archaic and 'poetic' in ME.:[1] *axles* 'shoulders', *brande* 'sword', *borely* in the sense 'massive', *bryme* 'stream', *flode* 'waters', *were* 'man'; *bewes, bowes* 'goes' (OE. *būgan*), *dreped* 'slew', *foundes* 'hastens', *lengen* 'tarry'.

[1] See J. P. Oakden, *A Survey of the Traditions*, 183 ff.

## Introduction

(3) Local or dialectal words. There is rarely enough evidence to assign a ME. word to any particular locality within a small area, but certain words can be labelled 'Northern', since they do not occur (except in 'dialect', as in Chaucer's *Reeve's Tale*) outside the N. area in ME. An investigation into the possibilities of ME. word geography has been made by Rolf Kaiser,[1] who after examining numerous texts is able to present a long list of 'Nordwörter' and a shorter and more tentative list of 'Sudwörter'. Among the N. words of native origin in Kaiser's list[2] which occur in the *Parlement* are: *bodworde, brande, fatills, hathelle, hopynge* ('belief', without implication of 'desire'), *krage, threpe, whills*. To these may be added: *athes*, perhaps *by-dene, dede* 'death', *digges* 'ducks', *dowkynge, euerous, hurkles, keppyn, slome*, and perhaps *pufilis*.[3] Some words too, though widely distributed, appear in a distinctively N. form: such as *are, ar(e)ste, beryn, gryse, riste*. Words of Norse origin peculiar to the N. dialect will be mentioned below.

*Scandinavian Element*

There are about ninety-four words of certain, and about eighteen of possible, Scandinavian origin in the *Parlement*, and three native words whose sense has changed to that of their Scandinavian equivalent (*dremed, ferly, wandrynge*). Many of these words were in fairly general use by the fourteenth century: such as *angrye, croked, felowe, happen, legge, same, wronge*. A number of words, however, have an English equivalent in other parts of the country. Such are: *agayne* (cf. W *ayayn*), *feste, fro, gaffe, gouen* (cf. W *yeve, yoven*), *hauke, laupis* (in W), *laythe, rigge, skyftede, poghe*.

Some of these loan-words correspond to native terms like *blonke, segge*: that is, they are preserved mainly in N. alliterative verse, as additions to the store of synonyms. Such are: *carpe* and *kayre, tulke* and *renke*, probably *maye* 'maiden', and *thro(ly)*. Kaiser includes most of these in his list of N. words, and also *aughtilde, buskede, fell(ys), gete* 'to guard', *graythely, irkede, layke, naytly,*

[1] 'Zur Geographie des mittelenglischen Wortschatzes', *Palaestra*, 205 (Leipzig, 1937).
[2] A few words in Kaiser's list are not exclusively N.: e.g. *wird* (Parl. *werdes*), *wye* (Parl. *wy*).       [3] See note on 144, p. 45.

*Introduction*

*nayttede, radde, skayled* (but see Glossary), *wothe*;[1] to these may be added *donkede, hore* 'hair', *sowed* (probably Scandinavian), *syled* and perhaps *makande*, of which there is no other instance recorded in *OED*.

Other Scandinavian borrowings, not distinctively N. but uncommon in ME., are: *bole* 'tree-trunk', *coloppe, crab(tre), dreghe* adj., *lythe, mukkede, taytte(ly)*. Of *crab(tre), mukkede, OED*. records no instance before the fifteenth century, but *mok(e)re* 'to hoard' occurs in Chaucer.

*French Element*

There are numerous[2] distinct words of certain French origin in this poem. Many of these were in general circulation during the fourteenth century, such as *age, cite, dame, mercy, noble, romance, sir, table, vertu*. Descriptive passages in particular contain a high proportion of French terms, as in the fifteen lines describing Youth's attire, where we find as many as twenty-seven French words: *chaplet, chefe-lere, raylede*, &c. The hunting scenes too, as in several other ME. poems, contain numerous French terms, many of them from that technical vocabulary of sport with which it was a gentleman's duty to be familiar: *vnburneschede, feetur, ryalls, surryals, assommet, sowre, berselett, troches, assaye, herbere, sewet, nombles*. The vocabulary of hawking too, no less technical, is well displayed here: *lessches, caprons, towre, sowssches, tercelettes, laners, lanerettis, maulerdes, fawkons, heron, (to) sege, querrye, quyrres, ecchekkes, cowples, cowers, vertwells, luyre, spanyells*. (*Laners, lanerettis*, and *vertwells* are recorded here for the first time.) Such passages may be compared with the descriptions of hunting, equipment, and dress in *GGK., Awntyrs*, and other alliterative poems, and with the long account of the feast in *Morte A*. 176 ff. and in *WW*. 332 ff., where almost every item is mentioned or described in French terms: all these descriptions, which displayed the author's knowledge of gentlemanly pursuits and of fashion and courtly fare, would have been impossible without the resources of a French vocabulary.

[1] Kaiser includes some words in his list which do not seem to be exclusively N., such as (citing the forms as in *Parl.*): *gayn(ly), lythe, mensk(fully), rase, sere, taytte(ly), ȝete*.
[2] About 365 in all.

# Introduction

## Metre

It is assumed in this summary that the alliterative long line in ME. has developed naturally, with no break in the tradition, from the OE. long line, and that it had four or sometimes five, not seven, primary stresses.[1]

It is not proposed to discuss in detail here the question whether or not final -*e*, when justified historically,[2] was still pronounced at the time when the poem was composed, but the matter obviously needs some consideration in an account of the metre. Dr. M. Day[3] has made some investigations into the metre of the *Parlement* and *Wynnere and Wastoure* which are relevant here. She has examined lines in which final -*e* is not in question and compared them with lines into the scansion of which final -*e* within the line may enter. She finds that the great majority of lines in the first group contain a two-syllable mid-dip, but that in the second group, if final -*e* is sounded, the great majority show a three-syllable mid-dip. Since the lines in which final -*e* is not in question show such a high proportion of two-syllable dips, Dr. Day concludes that the second group also should be scanned with two- rather than three-syllable dips and thus that final -*e* within the line had lost its value. (But it may occasionally have been sounded for metrical reasons: as in 173b 'and seyde† [MS. seyden] theis wordes', where it is more reasonable to assume that the -*e* in *seyde* was sounded than that the line was defective.) It seems probable, however, that final -*e* was pronounced at the line-end, where (as Dr. Day points out) the high proportion of weak nouns and of dative cases seems too great not to be intentional, and suggests 'a distinct preference for feminine endings'. In the following notes, therefore, it is assumed that final etymological -*e* was generally not sounded within the line but was sounded at the end of the line.[4]

---

[1] See, among others, K. Luick in *Anglia* xi (1889), 392 ff.; W. E. Leonard in *Univ. of Wisconsin Studies in Eng. Lang. and Lit.* xi (1920), 58 ff.

[2] Many of the final -*e*'s in this text are not justified and may be scribal: e.g. the -*e* is unhistorical in *Maye, schotte, frome, one, gryse, dewe, cukkowe, daye* (from the first sixteen lines of the poem).

[3] In an unpublished paper to which she has kindly given me access.

[4] Except in originally trisyllabic words, e.g. the pt. 3 s. ending -*ede*.

## Introduction

Of the OE. types, A, B, and C still occur.[1] Examples of A: 5b, 11a. Sometimes this type ends in two unstressed syllables, a licence which was not admitted in OE.:[2] 244a, 287a. The A type is much more common in the second than in the first half-line, which tends to have B or A with anacrusis (discussed below).

The most usual OE. B type (x)x́x́ is not very common, e.g.: 32b. The type (x)x́xx́ (which Luick calls A1)[3] is extremely common, however, especially if -e is not sounded at the end of the first half-line. Examples: 3a, 6a, 144b.

The C type is less common than A or B. It occurs more often in the second than in the first half-line. Examples: 35b, 104a, 485b. With two unstressed syllables in the second dip: 16b.

The commonest metrical type is the AB or A with anacrusis, a rising-falling rhythm; already used in OE. but much less often than in the later verse. Examples: 2b, 267a. With two unstressed syllables (or possibly an unstress and a half-stress) in the second dip: 35a, 427a. With a one-syllable mid-dip, the type which Luick calls BC: 30b, 55b. Luick recognizes also a type ́xx́ (which he calls A2) and a type xx́́ (which he calls C1). There is no certain example in the *Parlement* of the type 'bléssid were Í' (quoted by Luick); in the following apparent instances, final -e (which is etymological) could have been omitted by the scribe: 72b, 232a, 538b. Similarly, most instances of xx́́ could be explained from the dropping of an -e(s) by the copyist: 130b, 196b, 406b, 445b. There are, however, two instances with unetymological -e comparable with the type 'þat he fóre wíth' quoted by Luick: 53b, 473b.

The *Parlement* has about sixty-two clear examples of 'extended', or three-stress, half-lines. Most of these occur in the first half-line; there are no certain examples in the second half-line, but possible instances are: 131, 176, 336, 344, 453, 479, 527, 529, 606, 627 and 652 (see 'Alliteration').

The three-lift A, or falling, type does not occur, but an A type with no final dip is not uncommon. Examples: 95a, 290a. With 'clashing' lifts: 119a, 281a. The AB, or A with anacrusis, is fairly

---

[1] Using the terminology of Sievers in the form generally adopted in discussions of OE. metre.

[2] The origin of this tendency is discussed by M. M. R. Stobie, *JEGP.* xxxix (1940), 327.

[3] See Luick, *Anglia* xi. 402–4, for his discussion of these types.

## Introduction

common. Examples: 50a, 223a. With 'clashing' lifts: 19a, 444a. By far the commonest three-lift line, however, is the B, or rising, type. Examples: 40a, 386a. With 'clashing' lifts: 111a, 203a.

Finally, it may be noted that some half-lines may still have had a recognized secondary stress after the two main stresses, as in the OE. D type. This seems to occur particularly, though not exclusively, in words of French origin. Examples: 121a, 283a, 568a, 607a, 200a, 220a, 264a.

### ALLITERATION

The following scheme is an analysis of the alliterative types in the T text of the *Parlement*:[1]

1. aa/ax. About 482 examples, approx. 72 per cent.: ll. 1, 2, 3, &c.
   aaa/ax. Examples: 19, 20, 40, 50,[2] 95, 97, &c. (36 in all).
   (a)aa/ax: 22, 58, 263, 269, 285, 293, 375, 388, 406, 465.
   aa/(a)ax: ? 627.
2. ax/ax: 181, 325, 478, 486, 499, 511, 548, 558,[3] 626.[4]
   ax/a(a)x: 527.
   aax/ax: 75, 99, 289, 408, 433, 443, 470, ? 512, 608.
   aa(x)/ax, where (x) may have a secondary stress: 18, 28, 46, 52, 65, 80, 93, &c. (about 52).
   (a)ax/ax: 37, 454.
   aax/xax ? 131.
3. ax/aa: 513.
   ax/(a)aa: 479.
   aax/aa: 295.
4. aa/xx: 106, 232, 238, ? 306,[5] 357, 405, 461, 497, 526, 546, 552, 555, 569, 570, 604, 621. (See notes on 232, 461, 497, and 546 for suggested emendations. In 106, 552, 555, 570, and 621

---

[1] See J. P. Oakden, *The Dialectal and Metrical Survey*, chap. 8. The above analysis differs in some points from Oakden's.
[2] Or perhaps abb/ax: the alliterating sounds are *gn-gr-gr-gn*.
[3] This will be an ab/ab line if *Merchill* is stressed on the *ch* (=[š]); see Language, 'Consonants', 6, p. xxi).
[4] Or possibly aa/bb: see Language, 'Consonants', 1, p. xx.
[5] Or possibly *als* should be stressed, making it an aa/ax line.

*Introduction*

also it would be possible to alter a word, but only drastic alteration could make 238, 357, 405, 526 and 604 into aa/ax lines, so the type may have been a recognized one.)
aaa/xx: 319, 371.
5. aa/xa: 184; 639 (Latin).
6. xa/xa: ? 338, ? 423.[1]
7. xa/ax: 132, 300, 379.
   xaa/ax: 152.
   axa/ax: 541.
   (a)xa/ax: 390.
8. aa/aa: 70, 383, ? 585 (cf. 4), 622, 651.
   aaa/aa: 111.
   (a)aa/aa: 610.
9. aa/bb: 113, 483.[2]
   aaa/bb: 382, 389.
10. aa/abb: 47, 332.[3]
    aa/bab: ? 344.
11. aab/ab: 359, 420, 425, 429, 561.
    (a)ab/ab: ? 619.
    abb/ba: 139, 206.
    ab/aab: 529.
12. aba/bax: ? 336, ? 453 (both might be aa/ax), ? 652.
(Lines 642, 645 and 647 are quotations in Latin.)

A few other features may be noted:
1. The alliteration in the *Parlement* is nearly always placed on a natural stress.[4] In this respect the *Parlement* differs from poems of the *Gawain* group and from *PP.*, *Alexander* A and B, and *Wm. P.*, in which naturally unstressed words such as prefixes, auxiliary verbs, prepositions, and conjunctions are often brought into the alliterative scheme.
2. Consonant groups. As in OE., certain groups of consonants

[1] If *as* is stressed, this will be an ab/ab line.
[2] Or perhaps this line should scan: And aúghtilde Sir Árthures bèrde / óne scholde bè.
[3] Or perhaps aa/bb: Aftir this Sír Alysáunder alle þe wórlde wánne.
[4] The only possible exceptions in *Parl.* are in 306, 423, where *als*, *as* may alliterate (see above, footnote 1, and p. xxxi, footnote 5). In *parfourme my profers* 205 the prefix is stressed, but it would have been pronounced so at the time. A few instances of unnatural stress occur in *WW.*: see pp. xxxiv–xxxv.

## Introduction

alliterate only with themselves: *sp* only with *sp*, *st* with *st*, and *sw* with *sw*; *sc*(*h*) generally with *sc*(*h*), but once with *s* (l. 4; cf. 585); *sl* generally with *sl*, but twice with *s* (70, 533). *Pr, tr, wr* alliterate only with themselves or with *p, t, w*. Other groups, such as *br, bl, fl, fr, gn, gr*, are not treated strictly as units. For the alliteration of *wh* and *qu, qw*, see under Language, 'Consonants', 1. Mute *h* in words of French origin alliterates with vowels, as in 74 *herbere—anone—aftir*.

3. Vocalic alliteration. There is no marked tendency in the *Parlement* to alliterate identical vowels in all of the alliterating words in a line: eight instances occur out of a total of forty-six lines with vocalic alliteration. The alliterating of two identical vowels in a line could hardly have been avoided in most cases.[1]

4. The use of identical alliteration in groups of two or three lines. How far this was a conscious device it is difficult to say;[2] in many instances it was probably accidental. The *Parlement* has thirty-five pairs of lines linked by identical alliteration: as in 30–31, 53–54, 55–56, 77–78. It has eight groups of 'threes': 144–6, 177–9, 238–40, 338–40, 369–71, 389–91, 500–2, 609–11.

5. The practice of 'allowing the last unalliterated stressed syllable in the long line to set the alliteration for the next line'[3] occurs most commonly with *s*, as in 161–2, 172–3, 194–5, 224–5, but is perhaps hardly worth considering as a conscious device;[4] in some cases, indeed, it would have been hard to avoid.

### RELATION TO OTHER ALLITERATIVE POEMS; DATE AND AUTHORSHIP

There are so many resemblances between the Middle English alliterative poems, not only in style and theme but in details of phraseology, that theories of common authorship have often been

---

[1] Oakden, op. cit. 52, mentions that the author of *Parl.* was 'in the habit of' alliterating identical vowels together. But there is little evidence in *Parl.* of conscious effort to alliterate on identical vowels.

[2] In *Morte A.* it is particularly noticeable and does seem to have been used consciously: e.g. 1523–30, 2755–65.

[3] Oakden, op. cit. 154.

[4] See W. W. Greg on this point, in 'The Continuity of Alliterative Tradition', *MLR.* xxvii (1932), 453–4.

## Introduction

advanced. But the poems usually contain little evidence of date, and it is often hard to decide between common authorship and close imitation, or to be sure in which order the borrowing went. Comparisons quoted in the Notes show that the *Parlement* has phrases, drawn probably from a traditional store, in common with many of the other alliterative poems, but that sometimes the parallel is close enough to suggest some interconnexion.

The question whether or not the *Parlement* and *Wynnere and Wastoure* are the work of one author has aroused some controversy, of which only a summary can be given here. Gollancz and Kölbing[1] thought that the poems were by one author, arguing chiefly from a comparison of language and metre; J. R. Hulbert,[2] however, pointed out that the two poems showed a marked difference in verbal inflexions, and J. M. Steadman, Jr.,[3] argued emphatically against unity of authorship, but without making any really convincing points.

A detailed investigation into the language and metre of the two poems was made by J. P. Oakden,[4] who concludes that both dialectally and metrically the poems are in close agreement. An independent examination of the language of both poems confirms Oakden's view. The only important differences are: *WW.* has *hire* 14 and perhaps *hir* 16,[5] but otherwise *thaire*, &c., as in *Parl.*; and the pr. indic. in *WW.* shows a fair number of *-st*, *-th* endings.[6] However, these verbal forms and *hir* for 'their' are the only features inconsistent with the N. Midl. character of the language in *WW.*, and may be scribal, like the three *-ith* endings and the *hem* and *hir* forms in the Ware text of *Parl.*[7]

With regard to alliteration, a few differences not mentioned by Oakden may be noted. *WW.* shows a slight tendency, found rarely if at all in *Parl.*,[8] to alliterate on an unstressed syllable, as in

[1] See *Eng. Studien* xxv (1898), 273 ff.
[2] In *Mod. Phil.* xviii (1920), 31–40.
[3] In *Mod. Phil.* xxi (1923), 7–13.
[4] See *RES*. x (1934), 200–2, and *The Dialectal and Metrical Survey*, 51–55, 182–4, and Appendix I, 3.   [5] This depends upon an emendation.
[6] For details, see J. R. Hulbert, loc. cit. 33.
[7] Ware 521, 556, 558; *hir* 237, 536, *hem* 226, &c. (six times).
[8] *Parl.* 306 is an aa/ax line if *als* is stressed, an aa/xx line if *als* is not stressed; *Parl.* 423 is an ab/ab line if *as* is stressed, an xa/xa line if *as* is not stressed.

## Introduction

*WW*. 47 (? on *was*), 85 (on *with*), 221 (on *sayde*), and 427 (on *sythen*); there are no examples in *WW*. of *qu* < OE. *cw*, OF. *qu*, alliterating with *wh* < OE. *hw* (OF. *qu* alliterates with [k] in 77 and 340); and *v* alliterates with *f* in 334.[1] But whether these points indicate different authorship or merely a change in habits (perhaps after a lapse of years), it is hard to say.

Work such as Oakden's on the phraseology of alliterative verse makes the verbal parallels between the two poems seem much less striking than they must have appeared to earlier scholars. Some of the closest of the parallels appear in other poems also: as *Parl*. 14, *WW*. 37, *Morte A*. 930; and *Parl*. 19–20, *WW*. 14, a line evidently well enough known to be parodied in a later poem.[2] Even a strikingly similar turn of phrase, as in *Parl*. 184, *WW*. 5, has a close parallel in other poems.[3] Some of the parallels, however, are not found outside the two poems, and do suggest a special connexion between them. Thus if *WW. sowrede* 215 is read as *sowede* (cf. *Parl*. 286), both poems have this rare verb in the same unusual context. Moreover, the phrase *by-fore-with his eghne* in *Parl*. 549 (see note) recalls *to-fore-with myn eghne* in *WW*. 434. It is certainly notable that the two poems use a similar form of this very rare compound preposition. Other lines in *Parl*. which are reminiscent of *WW*., though not always in verbal detail, are 189 (cf. *WW*. 240), 190–3 (cf. *WW*. 288–93), and 257–60 (cf. *WW*. 440–4). Gollancz compares also the 'description of Waster generally' with Youth in *Parl*., and Winner with Middle Age.

It may be noted on the other hand that the two poems differ considerably in their use of conventional line-filling devices, or 'tags'. *WW*. has comparatively few of these, in striking contrast with *Parl*., where line-fillers like '... in armes', 'als ferly were ellis', are freely used and often repeated. Similar differences are the use of 'full' to pad out lines, a device much overworked in *Parl*. (it occurs over a hundred times), but less noticeable in *WW*. (about twenty-one times); and the tendency in *Parl*. to begin a

---

[1] On this point, see K. Schumacher, 'Studien über den Stabreim', 62 ff. (see Bibliography, III). Occasional alliteration of *f* and *v* occurs in most of the alliterative poems, including some of undoubtedly N. origin such as *Morte A*., so it probably was a metrical licence and not dialectal.

[2] See note on *Parl*. 19–20.

[3] See note on *Parl*. 184.

*Introduction*

series of lines with 'And' or 'Of' and to end a line with 'thereaftir'. The reason for these differences may well be, of course, that the author of *WW.* was deliberately pruning his style for his satirical attack upon abuses in Edward III's reign.

But in the absence of any striking features of language and style such as those which distinguish the *Gawain* group of poems, one cannot feel certain that *Parl.* and *WW.* are by one author; the most that can be said is that if *Parl.* was not composed by the author of *WW.* it was surely the work of one who spoke approximately the same dialect and who knew this poem well enough to imitate even its use of somewhat rare words. It seems more likely that *Parl.* is the imitator, although there is nothing to prove this. The rather delicately satirical touches in the descriptions of Youth and Middle Age are more likely to be echoes of the strongly satirical accounts of Winner and Waster than to have inspired these: *WW.* was obviously inspired by contemporary events and written in the heat of the moment, whereas in *Parl.* the tone is reminiscent and contemplative. But here again there can be no certainty; and even if it is agreed that *WW.* was probably the earlier poem, there is no evidence to show how many years separate the two. The fairly close similarities of dialect and metre suggest that the interval of years may not have been very great; but it could have been thirty or forty. Thus, accepting Gollancz's date 1352–3[1] for *WW.*, we may assume that *Parl.* could have been written at any time between this date and about 1390, but a date before 1370 seems more probable.

The connexion of *Parl.* with other alliterative poems may be considered more briefly. With *GGK.* there are obvious parallels,[2] but no more than one would expect from two alliterative poems which have a deer-hunt in common, and descriptions of courtly

---

[1] This date has been confirmed by J. M. Steadman, Jr., in *Mod. Phil.* xix (1921), 211–19. Steadman argues from references in the poem to contemporary persons and events, such as the part played by William de Shareshull in settling certain disturbances of the peace. (*WW.* 317–18.) Jessie May Anderson in *MLN.* xliii (1928), 47–49, shows from a reference to an uprising in Chester that the poem is unlikely to have been composed earlier than 1353.

[2] The closest are: *Parl.* 7, *GGK.* 2172; *Parl.* 24, *GGK.* 2146; *Parl.* 122, *GGK.* 179; *Parl.* 254, *GGK.* 1655; *Parl.* 646, *GGK.* 1880; see notes on these lines in *Parl.*, and also notes on ll. 80, 109 ff., 179 ff., and 453.

## Introduction

life; there seems no 'clear evidence of borrowing', as J. P. Oakden[1] would have it.

With *PP.* the connexion of *Parl.* does not seem to extend beyond their common use of the vision form and of certain alliterative phrases, such as 'somer seson . . . soft'. The author of *PP.* probably knew—Gollancz suggests that he may have been inspired by—*WW.*;[2] he may have known *Parl.* too, but one cannot be more definite than that. The poem *DL.*, however, does seem to have a close connexion with both *Parl.* and *WW.* Its indebtedness to the B or C text of *PP.* shows that it cannot be earlier than the end of the fourteenth century,[3] so its author may well have known the other two poems. There are strong likenesses (not to be explained entirely by the use of a common tradition) in the setting of all three poems, there are obvious similarities in the theme, and 'Dame Death's' enumeration of the famous people she has struck down is strongly reminiscent of Elde's reflections upon mortality.

The only other poems that seem to have a fairly close connexion with *Parl.* are *Siege Jer.* and *Morte A.* In *Parl.* and *Siege Jer.* there are some striking verbal parallels[4] which may be the result of imitation. *Siege Jer.* has been shown to be later than 1385,[5] so its author may have known and occasionally borrowed from *Parl.* The date of *Morte A.* is too uncertain to justify any assumption about the order of borrowing, if this was direct, but several close parallels,[6] and the fact that it introduces the Nine Worthies, suggest some connexion with *Parl.*: not identical authorship—language, and habits of metre and style, are not close enough to raise any question of this—but possibly imitation.[7] Other poems have lines or whole passages reminiscent in tone or verbal detail of *Parl.*: detailed comparisons have been drawn between Paris's

---

[1] *A Survey of the Traditions*, p. 96.

[2] Preface to *WW.*, last paragraph.

[3] See the edition of *Death and Liffe* by Sir I. Gollancz, xii ff., and that by J. H. Hanford and J. M. Steadman, 246 ff. Hanford and Steadman date the poem *c.* 1450, but rather before than after.

[4] See notes on *Parl.* 178, 199, 398.

[5] See M. Day, *Siege Jer.* xxix.

[6] See notes on *Parl.* 14, 444–5, 459, 468, 611.

[7] In neither *Parl.*, *Siege Jer.*, nor *Morte A.* is the parallel line in question so peculiarly appropriate to its context as to suggest that other uses of it may be derivative.

## Introduction

vision in *Destr. Troy* and that of the poet in *Parl.*, but there is no real evidence of borrowing in either passage. The same may be said of occasional similar lines in the two poems, and of those in other alliterative poems mentioned in the Notes: they suggest the use of a common alliterative store which may sometimes have included whole sentences, rather than direct imitation.

Of the author of the *Parlement* nothing more than a vague impression can be formed. The poaching exploit—which even if it is not a record of personal experience[1] shows at least that he was familiar with such activities—gives no evidence as to his social status. During the fourteenth century, when game in the King's forests was plentiful but strictly preserved, and deer-hunting such a favourite sport, poaching must have been a frequent temptation. As G. M. Trevelyan says in his *English Social History* (chap. i), 'Poaching was not only the livelihood of outlaws, but the passion of men of all classes—gentry, clerks of Holy Church, besides farmers and workmen seeking a pheasant or hare for the pot'.[2] It is evident from his poem that the author had a countryman's knowledge of outdoor life; but he had also a knowledge of the technical terms used in venery and falconry which one would not expect from a man of humble rank. His joyous account of Youth's activities—jousting, hawking, love-making, dancing, romance-reading, merry-making with 'coundythes and carolles', chess—suggests that he himself was familiar with courtly life. At least one may conclude from his poem that he was a man who had read widely and stored up for himself a wealth of poetry and legend. Indeed, his many allusions to names which must once have moved and thrilled the hearer make him a kind of Widsiþ of the fourteenth century; but less remote and puzzling than the ancient Widsiþ, for his names still carry something of their old associations.

[1] H. L. Savage in *JEGP*. xxix (1930), 75–76, discusses the question how far we are to take the deer-stealing episode as autobiographical.

[2] Savage, loc. cit., 76, quotes a passage which points out that the annals of the forest of Pickering show that many of those who killed deer 'withoute warrante' were 'people of distinction' whom it would have been awkward to punish.

# Introduction

## SOURCES AND ANALOGUES

### 1. *The Dream Setting and the Debate*

The *Parlement* had probably no immediate literary source: it is a poetic homily, inspired by the poet's religious beliefs and his interest in medieval literature, and embroidered with his own experiences of hunting and hawking and courtly life. In making the framework of his poem a dream the author is, of course, using a popular convention, inherited from the *Roman de la Rose* and other allegorical love-visions. But the *Parlement* stands out among poems with this dream setting in its fresh and vivid description of the May morning scene in the woods; conventional touches there are, but observation has also played a part.

In using a debate to present his theme, the author is following another well-worn convention. His 'parlement' is not a debate, however, in the sense of a lively give-and-take of argument: the discussion between Youth and Middle Age contains some lively repartee, but the argument dies with the intervention of Old Age, who overrides the other two speakers ('sottes bene 3e bothe') and effectively carries out his threat to 'stynte 3our stryffe' and 'stillen 3our threpe'. (From this point Elde's attitude is that of the preacher addressing his flock, arousing not argument but awareness of folly and of the need to repent.) The 'debate' between types of the three ages of man has no exact analogue, but the theme of the melancholy contrast between age and youth is, of course, universal; it appealed particularly to medieval writers, with their strong feeling of the transience of this life. The contrast between the joys of youth and the miseries of old age is poignantly described in some of the Middle English lyrics.[1] But Elde is not only expressing a personal grief for the loss of his youth, nor is he merely preaching *vanitas vanitatum*: he is acting as Death's messenger, reminding his hearers that Death may strike at any time.[2] The idea of a 'debate' which becomes in effect an admonition by Death's messenger to Middle Age and Youth may have some

---

[1] See, for instance, Carleton Brown's *English Lyrics of the XIIIth Century*, no. 51; *Religious Lyrics of the XIVth Century*, no. 6; and *Religious Lyrics of the XVth Century*, no. 147.

[2] This conception of Elde may be compared with that of the mysterious

*Introduction*

affinities with the dialogue of the Three Dead Men and the Three Living Men: a theme which was widely known, particularly in French literature during the second half of the thirteenth century, and in medieval art (notably in manuscript illustrations and in wall-painting) from the fourteenth to the sixteenth centuries.[1] The usual form of the legend is that three young noblemen encounter three corpses (or sometimes skeletons). The three men express in turn their horrified reactions at this sight; then the corpses speak in turn, saying that they too were once young and rich, but 'Vous serez ce que nous sommes!' In the poems the Living Men are nearly always young, but in other representations the tradition varies a little: a German wall-painting at Badenweiler shows three kings at different ages of life.[2] This legend, then, is a warning to all mankind of Death's inevitability, but it is addressed above all to the worldly and the prosperous; and the author of the *Parlement* may well have been influenced by it when he made Age deliver his sermon to Middle Age and Youth.

2. *The Nine Worthies*

In recalling the Nine Worthies and their deeds, Old Age is fortifying his argument that the worldly joys praised by Youth and Middle Age are but vanity, since Death overtakes all men, however powerful in their day; but the long and detailed accounts given of some of the Worthies suggest that the subject had a special interest for the poet and his audience. How popular a *motif* it was is evident from the numerous references to the Worthies in early literature. It is closely linked with another common medieval *motif*, the *Ubi sunt*,[3] where famous names are recalled to suggest the transitoriness of worldly life and the ruthlessness of Death. Such names as Hector, Alexander, Caesar, are mentioned, among others like Samson and Solomon, or famous

old man in Chaucer's *Pardoner's Tale*, who proved to be a messenger of Death to the three rioters.

[1] See Hanford and Steadman, *DL.* 237 ff.; and Stefan Glixelli's account, in his edition of *Les Cinq Poèmes des trois morts et des trois vifs* (Paris, 1914).

[2] Glixelli, op. cit. 42.

[3] For discussions of the *Ubi sunt* theme, see *MLN.* viii. 65, 94, 253-4; xxiv. 257; xxviii. 106-7, 197-8.

## Introduction

lovers such as Helen and Paris. The idea of grouping nine famous names may, as has been suggested,[1] have originated in the Welsh Triads, a form of medieval Welsh verse 'originally perhaps of a mnemonic character, in which heroes (*inter alia*) are grouped together in threes on account of some distinction or peculiarity which they were believed to have in common'.[2] In Longuyon's *Vœux du Paon* and in most subsequent accounts, the Worthies are named in three groups: three pagans, Alexander, Hector, and Julius Caesar; three Jews, Joshua, David, and Judas Maccabeus; and three Christians, Arthur, Charlemagne, and Godfrey of Bouillon. Occasionally there is some concession to national or local tradition, as when Robert the Bruce[3] or Bertrand du Guesclin[4] are added as tenth Worthies, or when Guy of Warwick replaces Godfrey of Bouillon as the ninth Worthy;[5] but on the whole the traditional names remain constant.[6]

The earliest known treatment of the Worthies as a group is in Jacques de Longuyon's *Vœux du Paon*, written about 1312 and translated about 1438 as *The Avowis of Alexander* by an unknown Scottish poet. It is possible that the author of the *Parlement* knew the *Vœux*, or some English version, but if so he has not followed it closely. Some of his information about Alexander's adventures in the East may have come from the *Vœux*, but in the accounts of Hector, Caesar, Arthur, and Charlemagne the poet has obviously not followed any one source; they suggest rather that he has crammed into them all that he could remember, from reading or hearsay. The sketches of Joshua and David are briefer, but contain some information which is not found in the *Vœux*;[7] the only sketches which correspond fairly closely with the *Vœux* are those

---

[1] By J. C. Dunlop, *History of Fiction*, vol. i; quoted by Archibald Sparke in *Notes and Queries* clx (1931), 287.

[2] Chadwick, *Growth of Literature*, i. 46. Some of the Triads may be consulted in *The Myvyrian Archaiology of Wales*, vols. ii and iii (various editors, London, 1801).

[3] See the list of 'Verses on the Nine Worthies' given by R. S. Loomis in *Mod. Phil.* xv. 19–27.

[4] Ibid. 22.

[5] See Gerard Leigh's *Accedence of Armorie* (first printed in 1562).

[6] There is a humorous reference to the Worthies in *Love's Labour's Lost*, V. i. H. C. Hart in his edition (Arden, note on V. i. 110) gives other references to untraditional groupings of the Worthies.

[7] See notes on 426 ff., 451.

## Introduction

of Judas Maccabeus and Godfrey of Bouillon, but even here there are no striking verbal parallels. The author of the *Parlement* was clearly interested enough in the subject of the Nine Worthies to compose his own account of them. The only other notable treatment of the Nine Worthies theme in Middle English is that in *Morte A.* 3406–45. Here the Worthies are introduced briefly but more artistically than in the *Parlement* and are closely linked with the argument, the interpretation of Arthur's dream.[1]

### The Style of the Poem

Strong individuality of style is not often found among the Middle English alliterative poets, and the author of the *Parlement* is no more distinguished than the majority of his fellow-craftsmen in this respect. But although he does not rise to the heights of *Pearl* or *Piers Plowman*, he does not descend to the crudeness and monotony of some of the poems, and the *Parlement* shows him to have had a good command of alliterative technique. His phrases, however conventional, are always suited to his context, and he does not rely upon well-worn tags to fill out his lines to such an extent as the authors of, for example, *William of Palerne*, the *Destruction of Troy*, and *Morte Arthure*. Sometimes, however, he does repeat his tags,[2] and indeed occasionally whole lines.[3] Another weakness is the excessive use of 'full' to qualify adjectives or adverbs; this 'padding' device is found to some extent in all the alliterative poems, but the *Parlement* is one of the worst offenders. Some of the stylistic devices are happier: in ll. 141–8 the poet makes an effective use of *repetitio* and balance, with the whole neatly summed up in l. 149. This may be compared with ll. 631 ff., where l. 637 (the burden of Elde's message) comes as the climax of a series of parallel clauses.

In criticizing the style of alliterative verse we are often apt to

---

[1] There are numerous other allusions to the Nine Worthies in fifteenth and sixteenth-century literature, and representations of them in mumming plays and pageants and in wall-paintings, wood-cuts, and tapestries. See Bibliography, IV. 3.

[2] As in 25, 118; 106, 267; 400, 452; 530, 630.

[3] As 310, 566; 398, 575; 406, 465; 611, 632; in only the last instance is the repetition at all artistic.

## Introduction

forget that poems such as the *Parlement* were composed primarily to be heard[1] for entertainment. There is much in the style of these poems that would delight a receptive audience, for whom the repetition of familiar phrases would be expected and welcome. Moreover, many of the descriptive touches in the *Parlement* are not conventional, but have the freshness of actual observation and experience. The poet did not learn from books or hearsay that a deer-stalker had to watch for a breeze 'by waggynge of leues', and that he would be plagued by gnats; he had noticed that birches have 'bewes full smale' and 'leues þat lighte were and grene'; that spaniels, muddy from the chase, looked as if their coats were 'dagged'. Of sustained description too he shows himself to be a master. The portraits of Youth, Middle Age, and Old Age are skilfully contrasted:[2] for Youth the emphasis is on dress and trappings, with their joyful riot of colours and precious stones; Middle Age has only two lines on his appearance, in a drab gown of russet, and the rest is concentrated on his obsession with gain; while for Old Age the emphasis is on the repulsiveness and pathos of his appearance. Their conversation too is appropriately contrasted: the gay talkativeness of Youth with the brief impatient replies of Middle Age, and these two with the dignified sermonizing of Old Age, whose last line, with the grim pictorial image which it evokes, makes such an impressive close: 'Dethe dynges one my dore, I dare no lengare byde.' So, with this fearful reminder, the poet wakes from his dream, and fittingly the poem closes in a mood of quiet devotion.

[1] See *Parl.* 106, *WW.* 217.
[2] John Speirs (*Scrutiny* xvii. 225, 244) suggests that the poet may have had in mind the costumed actors in a pageant.

# SELECT BIBLIOGRAPHY

## I. *Editions*

By Sir Israel Gollancz: both texts printed, with *Wynnere and Wastoure*, for the Roxburghe Club in 1897; the Thornton text printed, with a list of some variant readings from Ware, for the series *Select Early English Poems* (London, 1915).

## II. *Modern Renderings*

(i) Of ll. 1-101, by H. S. Bennett in *England from Chaucer to Caxton* (London, 1928), 92-97. (The same author's *Life on the English Manor* (C.U.P., 1937), 270-3, contains another version of ll. 1-61.)

(ii) The poem is printed in *The Age of Chaucer* (Pelican Books, 1954), with a modern rendering of ll. 1-14 and footnotes by Francis Berry glossing words and phrases.

## III. *Notes on the Text or Language or General Discussions of the Poem*

E. Kölbing, 'The Parlement of the Thre Ages', *Eng. Studien* xxv (1898), 273-89. (This contains comments on Gollancz's edition of 1897, and notes on the text. Most of Kölbing's suggestions were adopted by Gollancz in his edition of 1915.)

K. Schumacher, *Studien über den Stabreim in der mittelenglischen Alliterationsdichtung* (Bonn, 1914), 170-4, 'Textcritische Bemerkungen' on *Parl.*

M. S. Serjeantson, 'The Dialects of the West Midlands in Middle English', *RES.* iii (1927), 331.

J. P. Oakden, *Alliterative Poetry in Middle English. The Dialectal and Metrical Survey* (1930), 51-54, 153 ff., and *A Survey of the Traditions* (1935), 53 ff., 93 ff.

H. L. Savage, 'A Note on *The Parlement of the Thre Ages* 38', *MLN.* xliii (1928), 177-9; 'Notes on the Prologue of *The Parlement of the Thre Ages*', *JEGP.* xxix (1930), 74-82; 'A Note on *The Parlement of the Thre Ages*, 220', *MLN.* xlv (1930), 169-70.

John Speirs, '*Wynnere and Wastoure* and *The Parlement of the Thre Ages*', *Scrutiny* xvii (1950), 221-52; and *Medieval English Poetry* (Faber and Faber, 1957), 263 ff.

# Select Bibliography

## IV. Analogues and Sources

1. *Hunting* (ll. 17–99):

William Twiti, *Le Art de Venerie*, ed. Gunnar Tilander, Uppsala, 1956. See also the edition by Sir H. Dryden, 1844, revised by A. Dryden, 1908.

*The Master of Game*, ed. Wm. A. and F. Baillie-Grohman, 1904 and (with modernized spelling and some abridgement) 1909. References in the Notes are to the 1904 edition (the punctuation of which has been slightly modified in the present edition).

*The Boke of Saint Albans*: facsimile of the 1486 version with Introduction by William Blades, 1899; edition of Wynkyn de Worde's version (1496) by Joseph Haslewood, 1810.

George Turbervile's *Booke of Hunting*, 1576 and 1611; the 1576 edition, from which quotations in the Notes are taken, was reprinted in the Tudor and Stuart Library, Oxford, 1908.

J. D. Bruce, 'The Breaking of the Deer in *Sir Gawain and the Green Knight*', *Eng. Studien* xxxii (1903), 23–36.

2. *Hawking* (ll. 208–45):

*The Booke of Hawkyng after Prince Edwarde Kyng of Englande*, ed. T. Wright and J. O. Halliwell in *Reliquiae Antiquae*, i (1841), 293 ff.

*The Boke of Saint Albans* (see above).

George Turbervile, *The Booke of Faulconrie or Hauking* (1575, 1611). Quotations in the Notes are from the 1575 edition.

Simon Latham, *New and Second Booke of Falconrie* (1618).

Nicholas Cox, *The Gentleman's Recreation* (1674, &c.).

3. *The Nine Worthies*

R. S. Loomis, 'Verses on the Nine Worthies', *Mod. Phil.* xv (1917), 19–27.

J. H. Roberts, 'The Nine Worthies', *Mod. Phil.* xix (1922), 297–305.

G. Cary, *The Medieval Alexander* (C.U.P., 1956), 246–8, 343–4.

## V. Editions of other Alliterative Poems

Editions used have generally been those of the E.E.T.S. or the S.T.S. In addition the following have been used:

*Death and Liffe*, ed. J. H. Hanford and J. M. Steadman, *Studies in Philology* xv, no. 3 (North Carolina, 1918); and ed. Sir I. Gollancz and M. Day, *Select Early English Poems* (London, 1930).

*Gests of King Alexander of Macedon*, ed. F. P. Magoun (Harvard University Press, 1929).

# Select Bibliography

*Morte Arthure*, ed. E. Björkman, *Alt- und Mittelenglische Texte* 9 (Heidelberg, 1915).
*Patience*, ed. H. Bateson (Manchester University Press, 1918).
*Purity*, ed. R. J. Menner, *Yale Studies in English*, lxi (1920).
*Cleanness*, ed. Sir I. Gollancz, *Select Early English Poems* (London, 1921); Glossary, revised by M. Day, 1933.
*St. Erkenwald*, ed. H. L. Savage, *Yale Studies in English*, lxxii (1926).
*Scotish Feilde*, ed. J. P. Oakden, *Chetham Miscellanies*, N.S. vi (Manchester, 1935).
*Sir Gawain and the Green Knight*, ed. J. R. R. Tolkien and E. V. Gordon (Oxford, 1936).
*Somer Soneday*, ed. Carleton Brown in *Studies in English Philology: a Miscellany in Honor of Frederick Klaeber* (Minneapolis, 1929), 362–74.
*Wynnere and Wastoure*, ed. Sir I. Gollancz, *Select Early English Poems* (London, 1920); revised by M. Day, 1931.

*Note.* References to works cited only incidentally will be found in the footnotes to the Introduction and in the Notes.

# THE TEXTS IN THIS EDITION

THE Thornton text has been transcribed from rotographs supplied by the British Museum. Doubtful readings were later checked from the manuscript. The Ware text has been transcribed from the manuscript. Wherever the present transcription differs from that of Gollancz in his editions it has been further collated with the manuscript.[1]

Since it was desired in this edition to present the Thornton text above all as a poem, punctuation has been supplied and capitals used as in modern English.[2] Abbreviations about which there is no doubt have been expanded. The stroke over words containing -*n*-, -*m*-, the curled stroke of *n*, *m*, the stroke through *ll*, and that through *h*, have been ignored.[3] Additions and emendations to words are enclosed in square brackets, and the manuscript reading is given in the footnotes. A † indicates the omission of one or more letters or a word.

The Ware fragment has been printed as a diplomatic version, since nothing would have been gained by emending a text so corrupt. The punctuation of the manuscript[4] and its capitals have been retained. Abbreviations about which there is no doubt have, however, been expanded,[5] and the writing of superior *e* and *i* in the words *þe* and *þi* has been ignored.

[1] See Introduction, p. xvii.
[2] Ibid., p. xii.
[3] Ibid., p. xiii.
[4] Ibid., pp. xiv-xv and footnote 1.
[5] Ibid., p. xv.

# THE PARLEMENT OF THE THRE AGES

THORNTON    (B.M. Additional MS. 31042)

In the monethe† of Maye when mirthes bene fele,   f. 169ʳ
And the sesone of somere when softe bene the wedres,
Als I went to the wodde my werdes to dreghe,
In-to þe schawes my-selfe a schotte me to gete
At ane hert or ane hynde, happen as it myghte;   5
And as Dryghtyn the day droue frome þe heuen,
Als I habade one a banke be a bryme syde,
There the gryse was grene, growen with floures—
The primrose, the pervynke, and piliole þe riche—
The dewe appon dayses donkede full faire,   10
Burgons & blossoms & braunches full swete,
And the mery mystes full myldely gane falle;
The cukkowe, the cowschote, kene were þay bothen,
And the throstills full throly threpen in the bankes,
And iche foule in that frythe faynere þan oþer   15
That the derke was done & the daye lightenede.
Hertys and hyndes one hillys þay gouen,
The foxe and the filmarte þay flede to þe erthe;
The hare hurkles by hawes & harde thedir dryves,
And ferkes faste to hir fourme & fatills hir to sitt.   20
Als I stode in that stede one stalkynge I thoghte:
Bothe my body and my bowe I buskede with leues,
And turnede to-wardes a tree & tariede there a while;
And als I lokede to a launde a littill me be-syde,
I seghe ane hert with ane hede, ane heghe for the nones:   25
Alle vnburneschede was þe beme, full borely þe mydle,
With iche feetur as thi fote, for-frayed in the greues,
With auntlers one aythere syde egheliche longe.
The ryalls full richely raughten frome the myddes,
With surryals full semely appon sydes twayne;   30
And he assommet and sett of vi and of †fyve,

1 *MS.* monethes    31 *MS.* of v fyve

And þer-to borely and brode and of body grete,
And a coloppe for a kynge, cache hym who myghte.
Bot there sewet hym a sowre þat seruet hym full ʒerne,
That woke & warned hym when the wynde faylede,      35
That none so sleghe in his slepe with sleghte scholde hym dere,
And went the wayes hym by-fore when any wothe tyde.
My lyame than full lightly lete I doun falle,

f. 169ᵛ And to the bole of a birche my berselett I cowchide;
I waitted wiesly the wynde by waggynge of leues,     40
Stalkede full stilly no stikkes to breke,
And crepite to a crabtre and couerede me ther-vndere;
Then I bende vp my bowe and bownede me to schote,
Tighte vp my tylere and taysede at the hert.
Bot the sowre þat hym sewet sett vp the nese,        45
And wayttede wittyly abowte & wyndide full ʒerne.
Then I moste stonde als I stode and stirre no fote ferrere,
For had I my[n]tid or mouede or made any synys,
Alle my layke hade bene loste þat I hade longe wayttede.
Bot gnattes gretely me greuede and gnewen myn eghne;  50
And he stotayde and stelkett and starede full brode,
Bot at the laste he loutted doun & laughte till his mete;
And I hallede to the hokes and the hert smote,
And happenyd that I hitt hym by-hynde þe lefte scholdire,
Þat þe blode braste owte appon bothe the sydes;      55
And he balkede and brayed and bruschede thurgh þe greues,
As alle had hurlede one ane hepe þat in the holte longede;
And sone the sowre þat hym sewet resorte to his feris,
And þay, forfrayede of his fare, to þe fellys þay hyen;
And I hyede to my hounde and hent hym vp sone,       60
And louset my lyame and lete hym vmbycaste.
The breris and the brakans were blody by-ronnen;
And he assentis to þat sewte and seches hym aftire,
There he was crepyde in-to a krage and crouschede to þe erthe.
Dede als a dore-nayle doun was he fallen;            65
And I hym hent by þe hede and heryett hym vttire,

48 *MS.* mytid     56 leues *crossed out before* greues

## The Parlement of the Thre Ages

Turned his troches & tachede thaym in-to the erthe,
Kest vp that keuduart and kutt of his tonge,
Brayde [owte] his bewells my bereselet to fede;
And I s[lit]te hym at þe assaye to see how me semyde,        70
And he was floreschede full faire of two fyngere brede.
I chese to the chawylls chefe to be-gynn,
And ritte doun at a rase reghte to the tayle,
And þan þe herbere anone aftir I makede;
I raughte the righte legge by-fore, ritt it þer-aftir,        75
And so fro legge to legge I lepe thaym aboute;
And þe felle fro þe fete fayre I departede,
And flewe it doun with my fiste faste to the rigge.
I tighte owte my trenchore and toke of the scholdirs,
Cuttede corbyns bone and keste it a-waye.                    80 f. 170
I slitte hym full sleghely and slyppede in my fyngere,
Lesse the poynte scholde perche the pawnche or the guttys;
I soughte owte my sewet and semblete it to-gedire,
And pullede oute the paw[n]che and putt it in an hole.
I grippede owte the guttes and graythede thaym be-syde,      85
And than the nombles anone name I there-aftire;
Rent vp fro the rygge reghte to the myddis,
And then the fourches full fayre I fonge fro þe sydes,
And chynede hym chefely and choppede of the nekke,
And þe hede and the haulse homelyde in sondree.              90
Þe fete of the fourche I feste thurgh the sydis,
And heuede alle in-to ane hole and hidde it with ferne,
With hethe and with horemosse hilde it about,
Þat no fostere of the fee scholde fynde it ther-aftir;
Hid the hornes and the hede in ane hologhe oke,              95
Þat no hunte scholde it hent ne haue it in sighte.
I foundede faste there-fro for ferde to be wryghede,
And sett me oute one a syde to see how it cheuede,
To wayte it frome wylde swyne that wyse bene of nesse.
And als I satte in my sette the sone was so warme,          100
And I for slepeles was slome, and slomerde a while;
And there me dremed, in that dowte, a full dreghe sweuynn,
And whate I seghe in my saule the sothe I schall telle.

    69 *MS. omits* owte    70 *MS.* sisilte    84 *MS.* pawche

# T  *The Parlement of the Thre Ages*

I seghe thre thro men threpden full ȝerne,
And mote[d] of myche-whate and maden thaym full tale.   105
And ȝe will, ledys, me listen ane hande-while,
I schall reken thaire araye redely for-sothe,
And to ȝowe neuen thaire names naytly there-aftire.
The firste was a ferse freke, fayrere than thies othire,
A bolde beryn one a blonke bownne for to ryde,   110
A hathelle on ane heghe horse with hauke appon hande.
He was balghe in the breste and brode in the scholdirs,
His axles and his armes were i-liche longe,
And in the medill als a mayden menskfully schapen;
Longe legges and large, and lele for to schewe.   115
He streghte hym in his sterapis and stode vp-rightes;
He ne hade no hode ne no hatte bot his here one—
A chaplet one his chefe-lere, chosen for the nones,
Raylede alle with rede rose, richeste of floures,
With trayfoyles and trewloues of full triede perles,   120
With a chefe charebocle chosen in the myddes.
f. 170ᵛ He was gerede alle in grene, alle with golde by-weuede,
Embroddirde alle with besanttes and beralles full riche;
His colere with calsydoynnes clustrede full thikke,
With many dyamandes full dere dighte one his sleues.   125
Þe semys with saphirs sett were full many,
With emeraudes and amatistes appon iche syde,
With full riche rubyes raylede by the hemmes;
Þe price of that perry were worthe powndes full many.
His sadill was of sykamoure that he satt inn,   130
His bridell alle of brente golde with silke brayden raynes,
His cropoure was of tartaryne, þat traylede to þe erthe;
And he throly was threuen of thritty ȝere of elde,
And ther-to ȝonge and ȝape, and Ȝouthe was his name;
And the semely[este] segge that I seghe euer.   135

The seconde segge in his sete satte at his ese,
A renke alle in rosette þat rowmly was schapyn,
In a golyone of graye girde in the myddes,
And iche bagge in his bosome bettir than othere.
One his golde and his gude gretly he mousede,   140

 105 *MS.* moten     135 *MS.* semely

## The Parlement of the Thre Ages

His renttes and his reches rekened he full ofte—
Of mukkyng, of marlelyng, and mendynge of howses,
Of benes of his bondemen, of benefetis many,
Of presanttes of polayle, of pufilis als;
Of purches of ploughe-londes, of parkes full faire, 145
Of profettis of his pasturs, that his purse mendis;
Of stiewarde[s], of storrours, stirkes to bye,
Of clerkes, of countours, his courtes to holde;
And alle his witt in this werlde was one his wele one.
Hym semyde for to see to of sexty ȝere elde, 150
And þer-fore men in his marche Medill Elde hym callede.

The thirde was a laythe lede lenyde one his syde,
A beryne bownn alle in blake, with bedis in his hande;
Croked and courbede, encrampeschett for elde;
Alle disfygured was his face, and fadit his hewe, 155
His berde and browes were blanchede full whitte,
And the hare one his hede hewede of the same.
He was ballede and blynde, and alle babirlippede,
Totheles and tenefull, I tell ȝowe for sothe;
And euer he momelide and ment and mercy he askede, 160
And cried kenely one Criste and his crede sayde,
With sawtries full sere tymes, to sayntes in heuen;
Envyous and angrye, and Elde was his name. f. 171
I helde hym be my hopynge a hundrethe ȝeris of age,
And bot his cruche and his couche he carede for no more. 165
Now hafe [I] rekkende ȝow theire araye, redely the sothe,
And also namede ȝow thaire names naytly there-aftire,
And now thaire carpynge I sall kythe, knowe it if ȝowe liste.

Now this gome alle in grene so gayly attyrede,
This hathelle one this heghe horse with hauke one his fiste, 170
He was ȝonge and ȝape and ȝernynge to armes,
And pleynede hym one paramours and peteuosely syghede.
He sett hym vp in his sadill and seyde† theis wordes:
'My lady, my leman, þat I hafe luffede euer,
My wele and my wirchip, in werlde where þou duellys, 175

---

147 *MS.* stiewarde    157 *MS. caret marks, and* his *supplied at the beginning of the line.*    166 *MS. omits* I    168 *MS. caret marks, and* kythe *supplied at the end of the line.*    173 *MS.* seyden

My playstere of paramours, my lady with pappis full swete,
Alle my hope and my hele, myn herte es thyn ownn!
I by-hete the a heste and heghely I a-vowe,
There schall no hode ne no hatt one my hede sitt,
Till þat I ioyntly with a gesserante iustede hafe [with] onere,   180
And done dedis for thi loue, doghety in armes.'

Bot then this gome alle in graye greued with this wordes,
And sayde, 'Felowe, be my faythe þou fonnes full ȝerne,
For alle [es] fantome and foly that thou with faris.
Where es þe londe and the lythe þat þou arte lorde ouer?   185
For alle thy ryalle araye renttis hase þou none,
Ne for thi pompe and thi pride, penyes bot fewe;
For alle thi golde and thi gude gloes one thi clothes,
And þou hafe caughte thi kaple þou cares for no fothire.
Bye the stirkes with thi stede and stalles thaym make:   190
Thi brydell of brent golde wolde bullokes the gete;
The pryce of thi perrye wolde purches the londes;
And wonne, wy, in thi witt, for wele-neghe þou spilles.'

Than the gome alle in grene greued full sore,
And sayd, 'Sir, be my soule, thi consell es feble.   195
Bot thi golde and thi gude thou hase no god ells;
For, be þe lorde and the laye þat I leue inne,
And by the Gode that me gaffe goste and soule,
Me were leuere one this launde lengen a while,
Stoken in my stele-wede one my stede balkke,   200
Harde haspede in my helme and in my here-wedys,
With a grym grownden glayfe graythely in myn honde,
And see a kene knyghte come and cowpe with my-seluen,
Þat I myghte halde þat I hafe highte and heghely avowede,
And parfourme my profers and prouen my strengthes:   205
Than alle the golde and the gude that thoue gatt euer,
Than alle the londe and the lythe that thoue arte lorde ouer;
And ryde to a reuere redily there-aftir,
With haukes full hawtayne that heghe willen flye;
And when þe fewlis bene founden, fawkoneres hyenn   210

180 *MS. omits second* with   184 *MS. omits* es   204 *MS. caret*
*marks, and* halde *supplied at the beginning of the line.*   208 *MS. caret*
*mark, and* a *supplied above the line.*

## The Parlement of the Thre Ages     T

To lache oute thaire lessches and lowsen thaym sone,
And keppyn of thaire caprons, and casten fro honde;
And than the hawteste in haste hyghes to the towre,
With theire bellys so brighte blethely thay ryngen,
And there they houen appon heghte as it were heuen angelles.   215
Then the fawkoners full fersely to floodes þay hyen,
To the reuere with thaire roddes to rere vp the fewles:
Sowssches thaym full serely, to seruen thaire hawkes.
Than tercelettes full tayttely telys doun stryken;
Laners and lanerettis lightten to thes endes,   220
Metyn with the maulerdes and many doun striken;
Fawkons þay founden freely to lighte,
With hoo and howghe to the heron þay hitten hym full ofte,
Buffetyn hym, betyn hym, and brynges hym to sege,
And saylen hym full serely, and sesyn hym there-aftire.   225

[T *text continued on the
following verso pages with
the parallel Ware version
on recto pages.*]

Then fawkoners full fersely founden þam aftire,
To helpen thaire hawkes thay hyen thaym full ȝerne,
For the bitt of his bill bitterly he strikes.
They knelyn doun one theire knees and krepyn full lowe,
Wynnen to his wynges and wrythen thaym to-gedire,     230
Brosten the bones and brekyn thaym in sondire,
Puttis owte with a penn þe maryo one his gloue,
And quo[p]es thaym to the querrye that quelled hym to þe dethe.
He quyrres thaym and quotes thaym, quyppeys full lowde,
Cheres [tha]ym full chefely ecchekkes to leue,     235
Than henttis thaym one honde and hodes thaym ther-aftire,
Cowples vp theire cowers thaire caprons to holde,
Lowppes in thaire lesses thorowe vertwells of siluere.
Þan he laches to his luyre, and lokes to his horse,
And lepis vpe one the lefte syde als þe laghe askes.     240
Portours full pristly putten vpe the fowlis,
And taryen for theire tercelettis þat tenyn thaym full ofte,
For some chosen to þe echecheke, þoghe some chefe bettire.
Spanyells full spedily þay spryngen abowte,
Be-dagged for dowkynge when digges bene enewede;     245
And than kayre to the courte that I come fro,
With ladys full louely to lappyn in myn armes,
f. 172 And clyp thaym and kysse thaym and comforthe myn hert;
And than with damesels dere to daunsen in thaire chambirs;
Riche Romance to rede and rekken the sothe     250
Of kempes and of conquerours, of kynges full noblee,
How tha[y] wirchipe and welthe wanne in thaire lyues;
With renkes in ryotte to reuelle in haulle,
With coundythes and carolles and compaynyes sere,
And chese me to the chesse that chefe es of gamnes;     255
And this es life for to lede while I schalle lyfe here;
And thou with wandrynge and woo schalte wake for thi gudes—
And be thou doluen and dede thi dole schall be schorte—
And he that thou leste luffes schall layke hym there-with,
And spend that thou haste longe sparede, the deuyll spede hym ells!'

    227 aftire *crossed out after* thaym    232 *A four-letter word* (? pene)
*crossed out before* penn    233 *MS.* quotes    235 *MS.* Cheresthe (*or*
Cheresche) hym    252 *MS.* how thaire

## The Parlement of the Thre Ages

WARE         (B.M. Additional MS. 33994)

Than fauconers ful frely foundyn hem aftur.       f. 19ʳ
To helpyn þer hawkes þay hyen hem yern.
For with þe butte of his bylle bytturly he strikes.
Thay knele down on þer kne & crepyn ful lowe.
Wynnen to þe wyngges & wrien þem to gidre.       230
Thay bristyn þe bones & brekyn þem yn sondre.
And puttes out with a penne þe marow on his glove,
And whopis hem to whirry þat whellid hem to deth.
He wharris & whotes hem & whopes ful lowde,
He cheris þem ful chefly othir chekes to leve,       235
Þey hentes þam on hand & haldes þem þer aftur,
And cowples vp þer cours hir caprons to hold,
Lappis vp ther leches & þurgh verteuels of siluer,
Þan he lachis to his lowre & lokes to his hors,
And laupis vp on þe lefte side as þe Lawe askes.       240
Porters full prestly putten vp þe fowles,
And taryn for the tarselettes þat tene hem ful ofte.
For sum chese to þe echecheke þough sum chese to þe be
Spaynelles ful spedely þay spryngyn a bout,
All dragild for dowkyng where dikes bene enewe,       245
And þan þay care to þe court þat þey come froo,
With ladis full lufly lapped yn armes,
And clap þem & kisse þem þat comforte my hert.
And with damsels full dere to daunce yn þer chaumbre.
Right romayns to rede & rekyn þe sothe       250
Of kempes of conquerours of kynges ful noble
How þey worship & weele wan yn þere lyves,
With cownduyttes & caralles & companys seere,
And with renkes & ryot to revell wele yn halle,       f. 19ᵛ
And chese me to þe chese þat chefe arn of þe game,       255
And thus my lyf lede whileme I am here,
And þow with wanryng & wo shall wake for þi gode
And be þou dolvyn & dede þi dole shall be shorte,
And he þat þou lest lovis shall leyke hym þer with.
And spende þat þou sparid þe devill spede hym elles.       260

      243 be: *the rest of the word has been cut off in the binding.*

Than this renke alle in rosett rothelede thies wordes:
He sayde, 'Thryfte and thou haue threpid this thirtene wynter;
I seghe wele samples bene sothe that sayde bene [full] ȝore:
Fole es that with foles delys; flyte we no lengare!'
Than this beryn alle in blake bownnes hym to speke, 265
And sayde, 'Sirres, by my soule, sottes bene ȝe bothe.
Bot will ȝe hendely me herken ane hande-while,
And I schalle stynte ȝour stryffe and stillen ȝour threpe.
I sett ensample bi my-selfe and sekis it no forthire:
While I was ȝonge in my ȝouthe and ȝape of my dedys, 270
I was als euerrous in armes as ouþer of ȝoure-seluen,
And as styffe in a stourre one my stede bake,
And as gaye in my gere als any gome ells,
And as lelly by-luffede with ladyse and maydens.
My likame was louely es lothe nowe to schewe, 275
And as myche wirchip I wane, i-wis, as ȝe bothen.
And aftir irkede me with this, and ese was me leuere,
Als man in his medill elde his makande wolde haue.
Than I mukkede and marlede and made vp my howses,
And purcheste me ploughe-londes and pastures full noble, 280
Gatte gude and golde full gaynly to honde,
Reches and renttes were ryfe to my-seluen.
Bot Elde vndire-ȝode me are I laste wiste,
And alle disfegurede my face and fadide my hewe,
Bothe my browes and my berde blawnchede full whitte— 285
And when he sotted my syghte, than sowed myn hert—
Croked me, cowrbed me, encrampeschet myn hondes,
Þat I ne may hefe þam to my hede ne noghte helpe my-seluen,
Ne stale stonden one my fete bot I my staffe haue.
Makes ȝoure mirrours bi me, men bi ȝoure trouthe— 290
This schadowe in my schewere schunte ȝe no while.
f. 172ᵛ And now es dethe at my dore that I drede moste;
I ne wot wiche daye ne when ne whate tyme he comes,
Ne whedir-wardes, ne whare, ne whatte to do aftire;
Bot many modyere than I, men one this molde, 295

261 *MS. does not indicate a new section here.* 262 ȝere *crossed out before* wynter 263 *MS. omits* full

## The Parlement of the Thre Ages

Then þis renke all yn russet ratild þise wordes,
He said rest & þou haue Iapid þis xiij wyntur,
I se sawmples bene sothe þat said bene ful yore.
Fole is with fole delis flite we no more,
Then þis berne all yn blak bownes hym to speke. 265
And said ye by my faith sottes bene ye boþe.
But ye hendly me herkyn on hand while.
I shal stint youre strif & still youre threpe,
I set Insaumple to my self and seche it no farþer.
Whils I was yong yn my youthe & yep of my dedes 270
I was als amerous yn armes as any of youre selvyn.
And as stif yn a stoure on my stede bak.
And als gay yn my gere as any gome els.
And as lowly bylovid with ladys & maydyns,
Mi lere was lovely þat is lathe now to shewe, 275
As moch worship I wan I wis as ye bothe.
And þat aftur þat irkid me with þis & ease was me leuer,
As man yn his mydell eld þat his make wold haue,
Þan I mutherd & murled & made up my hows
And purchest me plowlandes & pasturis full noble. 280
I gate good & gold gaynly to my horde, f. 20
Riches & rent was ryve to my hond.
But yeld vndur yede me or I lest wist,
And all disvigured my face & fadid my hue.
Bothe my browis & my berde blaunchid ful white, 285
Whan I sesid my sight þan sighed my hert.
Crokid combrid me encrapid my handes.
Þat I ne may heve them to my hed ne help my selvyn.
Ne stille stand on my fete but I my staf haue,
Makes youre myrrours by me by me by youre trouth. 290
This shadow yn my shewer shunt you wyll,
And now is deth at my dore þat I drede most.
And I ne wot what day ne whan ne what tyme he comes.
Ne whither ward ne where ne what to do þer aftur.
But many moo oþer þan I men of þis molde, 295

261 *In r.-h. margin*, Mideleld (*see Introduction, p.* xiv).   265 *In r.-h. margin*, Age   279 mutherd: *the third letter could be* c *or* t. *See note on this line.*

## The Parlement of the Thre Ages

Hafe passed the pase þat I schall passe sone;
And I schall neuen ȝow the names of nyne of the beste
Þat euer wy in this werlde wiste appon erthe,
Þat were conquerours full kene and kiddeste of oþer.
The firste was Sir Ector, and aldeste of tyme,    300
When Troygens of Troye were tried to fighte
With Menylawse þe mody kynge and men out of Grece,
Þat þaire cite assegede and sayled it full ȝerne,
For Elayne his ownn quene that there-inn was halden,
Þat Paresche the proude knyghte paramours louede.    305
Sir Ectore was euerous als the storye telles,
And als clerkes in the cronycle cownten þe sothe:
Nowmbron thaym to [nynety] and ix mo by tale
Of kynges with crounes he killede with his handes,
And full fele oþer folke, als ferly were ellis.    310
Then Achilles his adversarye vndide with his werkes,
With wyles and no wirchipe woundede hym to dethe,
Als he tentid to a tulke þat he tuke of were.
And he was slayne for that slaughte sleghely þer-aftir,
With the wyles of a woman as he had wroghte by-fore.    315
Than Menylawse þe mody kynge hade myrthe at his hert,
Þat Ectore hys enymy siche auntoure hade fallen;
And with the Gregeis of Grece he girde ouer the walles,
Þe prowde paleys dide he pulle doun to þe erthe,
Þat was rialeste of araye and rycheste vndır the heuen.    320
And þen þe Trogens of Troye teneden full sore,
And semblen þaym full serely, and sadly þay foughten;
Bot the lure at the laste lighte appon Troye,
For there Sir Priamus the prynce put was to dethe,
And Pantasilia þe quene paste hym by-fore.    325
Sir Troylus, a trewe knyghte þat tristyly hade foghten,
Neptolemus, a noble knyghte at nede þat wolde noghte fayle,
Palamedes, a prise knyghte, and preued in armes,
Vlixes and Ercules þat full euerrous were bothe,
And oþer fele of þat ferde fared of the same,    330
As Dittes and Dares † demed[e]n to-gedir.

   297 *MS.* ix *crossed out before* nyne    308 *MS.* xix    327 *MS.* anoble
331 *MS.* and demedon

## The Parlement of the Thre Ages

Han passed þe pase þat I shal passe sone.
I shall nevyn you þe names of ix of þe best.
That euer was yn þis world witest on erth.
Thay were conquerours full kene & kiddest of oþer,
The first was Ectoure and aldist of tyme, 300
The trochis of troy were tryed to fight,
With menelone þe mody king & oute of grece,
That oure Cite haue segid & salid it full yerne,
For Elan his owen quene þat þer yn was kepid,
That parych þat proud knyght þat paramour lovid. 305
Sir Ectoure was Emerus as þe story telles.
And as clerkes & cronycles conteyn þe sothe.
Numbyr them to nynety & ix may be take,
Of kynges with crownes he kylled with his hondes. f. 20ᵛ
And fellid fele of þe folk as ferly were ellis. 310
Than Achilles his aduersary vndid with his werkes,
With wiles & no worship woundid hym to dede,
As he tendid to a toure þat he toke of were,
And he was slayn for þat slight slyly þer aftur,
With wiles of a woman as he wrought before, 315
Þan Menelaws þe mody king had myrth at his hart.
That Ectoure his Enmy such awnters had fallen
And with þe grekes of grece he gird over þe walles.
The prowd palace he pulled down to þe Erth,
That was ryallest of aray & richest vndur hevyn. 320
And to the troge of Troy he tendith for socour.
And semblid þem full surely & sadly þay foughten,
But þe lere of þat þe last light upon troy.
For þere Sir piramus þer prynce put was to were,
And pantezelia the quene passid before hym. 325
Sir Trolus A tru knyght þat throly had foughten
Septelamus a noble knyght and proued yn armes.

Vlixes & arculus that Everus were bothe.
And other fele of þat feerd faren on þe same. (330)
As dites and darres demyn to gidre.

297 *MS. repeats and crosses out second of*   298 *witest: sic MS.*   300 *In r.-h. margin,* Ecto... de tro... (*part of the words cut off*).   317 fallen: *the* n *is partly defaced.*   328 *The line is missing; there is no gap in the MS.*

## The Parlement of the Thre Ages

Aftir this Sir Alysaunder alle þe worlde wanne,
Bothe the see and the sonde and the sadde erthe,
Þe iles of the Oryent to Ercules boundes—
f. 173 Ther Ely and Ennoke euer hafe bene sythen, 335
And to the come of Antecriste vnclosede be þay neuer;
And conquered Calcas knyghtly ther-aftire,
Ther ientille Iazon þe [Gr]ewe wane þe flese of golde.
Then grathede he hym to Gadres the gates full righte,
And there Sir G[adyfer]e þe gude the G[a]derayns assemblet, 340
And rode oute full ryally to rescowe the praye;
And þan Emenyduse hym mete, and made hym full tame,
And girdes Gadyfere to the grounde, gronande full sore;
And there that doughty was dede, and mekill dole makede.
Then Alixander the Emperour, þat athell kyng hym-seluen, 345
Arayed hym for to ryde with the renkes þat he hade:
Ther was the mody Meneduse, a mane of Artage—
He was Duke of þat douth and a dussypere;
Sir Filot and Sir Florydase, full ferse men of armes,
Sir Clyton and Sir Caulus, knyghtis full noble, 350
And Sir Garsyene the gaye, a gude man of armes;
And Sir Lyncamoure thaym ledys with a lighte will.
And than Sir Cassamus thaym kepide, and the kyng prayede
To fare in-to Fesome his frendis to helpe:
For one Carrus the kynge was comen owte of Inde, 355
And hade Fozome affrayede and Fozayne asegede
For Dame Fozonase the faire that he of lufe by-soughte.
The kynge agreed hym to goo and graythed hym sone,
In mendys of Amenyduse þat he hade mys-done.
Then ferde he to-warde Facron and by the flode abydes, 360
And there he tighte vp his tentis and taried there a while.
There knyghtis full kenely caughten theire leue
To fare in-to Fozayne Dame Fozonase to see,
And Idores and Edease, alle by-dene;
And there Sir Porus and his prynces to the poo avowede. 365
Was neuer speche by-fore spoken sped bettir aftir,

336 *MS. caret mark, and of supplied above the line.* 338 *MS.* Iewe
340 *MS.* godfraye; goderayns

## The Parlement of the Thre Ages

Aftur þis Sir Alexandre all þe world wan,
Bothe þe see & þe sand & þe said Erth,
And the yles of þe oryent to arcules Landis,
There Ely & Ennok evir hath bene sithen, (335)
And to the come of crist vnclosid be þei nevir,
And conquerid Clakas knyghtly þer aftur
There Ientill Iosue þe Iewe wan þe slevis of gold.
Þan grathid he hym to gedwyn gates ful right.
And Sir Godfray þe good his gedring assemblid. (340)
And rode out full ryally to rescewe þe pray.
And þan Amenowdows hym met & made hym ful tame.
And girdes Godyfere to ground gronand ful sore.
And þere þat dowty was dede & mykil dole makid.
Than Alexaunder þe Emperoure þat athil king hym selvyn. (345)
Arayed hym for to ride with rewkes þat he had.
There was þe mody Menodous a man of heritage.
A duke of þat duche and a duke pere,
Sir Fylet & sir Folidas knyghtes ful noble.
Sir Cliton & Cawlus ful ferse of Armes. (350)
And sir Garsayn þe gay a gode man of were.
And sir Lyncamoure hym led with a light wille.
And þan Sir Casamus hym kepid & þe kyng prayed.
To fare yn to feysoun his frende for to helpe.
For Icarras þat was comyn out of ynde, (355)
He had his fomen afrayed & fighon asegid.
For dame Fezonas þe faire þat he of love besought,
In mendis of Emeneduce þat he has mysdone,
Þen faren toward facron & both þe feld abidis.
The king ayrathid hym to goo & grathid hym sone, (360)
Tolid vp his tentes & tarid þer a while.
Ther knyghtes full kenely caghten þere leve.
To faire to feane dame Fesonas to see,
And ydoes & Odias all þes by dene.
And ther Sir Pyrres & his peris to þe pode avowid. (365)
Was neuer speche bifore spokyn bettur sped aftur,

332 *In r.-h. margin*, Alexander    360 *Probably misplaced: cf.* 358 *in* T.
363 feane: *perhaps* feeane; *the first* e *partly covers another letter which may be* e, *but is not clear.*    365 Fol. 21ᵛ *is headed (in the same hand but a different ink)*: And ther Sir Pyrr . . . *(end very faded).*

For als þay demden to doo thay deden full euen.
For there Sir Porus the prynce in-to the prese thrynges,
And bare the batelle one bake and abaschede thaym swythe;
And than the bolde Bawderayne bowes to the kyng,    370
And brayde owte the brighte brande owt of the kynges hande,
And Florydase full freschely foundes hym aftir,
And hent the helme of his hede and the halse crakede.
Than Sir Gadefere the gude gripis his axe,
And in-to the Indyans ofte auntirs hym sone,    375
And thaire stiffe standerte to stikkes he hewes.
And than Sir Cassamus the kene, Carrus releues:
When he was fallen appon fote he fet hym his stede.
And aftyr that Sir Cassamus Sir Carus he drepitt,
And for þat poynte Sir Porus perset hym to dethe.    380
And than the Indyans ofte vttire þam droghen,
And fledden faste of the felde and Alexandere suede.
When þay were skaterede and skayled and skyftede in sondere,
Alyxandere, oure athell kyng, ames hym to lenge,
And fares in-to Fozayne, festes to make,    385
And weddis wy vn-to wy that wilnede to-gedire.
Sir Porus the pryce knyghte, moste praysed of othere,
Fonge Fozonase to fere, and fayne were thay bothe;
The bolde Bawderayne of Bade-rose, Sir Cassayle hym-seluen,
Bele Edyas the faire birde, bade he no noþer;    390
And Sir Betys, the beryne the beste of his tyme,
Idores his awnn lufe aughte he hym-seluen;
Then iche lede hade the loue that he hade longe ʒernede.
Sir Alixander oure Emperour ames hym to ryde,
And bewes to-wardes Babyloyne with the beryns þat were leuede,    395
By-cause of Dame Cand[ac]e that comforthed hym moste;
And that cite he by-segede, and assayllede it aftire,
While hym the ʒatis were ʒete, and ʒolden the keyes;
And there that pereles prynce was puysonede to dede;
Þare he was dede of a drynke, as dole es to here,    400
That the curssede Cassander in a cowpe hym broghte.
He conquered with conqueste kyngdomes twelue,

396 *MS.* Candore      401 cr *crossed out before* curssede

## The Parlement of the Thre Ages

For as þay demyd to dye þay dyen all aftur.
For Sir perse þe proude yn to the preese thrynges.
And bare þe penand abak & basshed hem swithe.
And þan the bold baudren bowis to þe kyng. (370)
And bradid out þe bright brand out of þe kinges hond.
And floridyse ful fersely foundid hym aftur.
And hent the helme of his hed þat þe halse crakid.
Þan Sir Godfray the gode gripes his ax.
In to the Indayn oft he awnturs hym sone. (375)
And there stif stenderdes to stikkes he hewes.
And þan Sir Dasamus þe kynges caris relevis.
Whan he was fallen upon fote he fet hym his stede.
And aftur þat sir Casamus Carrace he drepis.
And for þat poynt Sir Corrus receyvid hym to deth. (380)
And þan Indaynce eft vttir þem dryven.
And fleyn fast yn þe feld & Alexaundir swid.
Whan þey scatird & shiverd all yn sondre.
Alexaunder a thik kyng ames to lyng.
And fared in fesane festis to make. (385)
And wendes swithe vnto vage þat wil not to gidre.
Sir peerse þe price knyght & praysid of other.
Fong fezonas to feere & frendes were þay bothe.
The bold baron of betrise & Sir Casabull his felaw.
Bolde Edcas þe burde bede home othere. (390)
And Sir Bothos þe beern þe best of his tyme.
Edores his owen love aght he hym selvyn.
Þan ich lord had þe love þat he had langid aftur.
Sir Alexaundre oure Emperoure armes hym to ride, f. 22
And caris toward babilon with bernes þat were levid. (395)
Bi cause of dame Cadace þat comforth hym most.
And þat Cite asegid & saylid full oft.
Whill the yates were yolden & yoven þe keyes.
And þurgh þat the pereles prynce was poysened to deth.
And there he was deed with a drynk as dole was to here. (400)
That þe cursid Cassaunder in a Coupe hym brought.
He conquerid with his conquest kyngdoms xij.

384 ames: *MS*. a mes

## The Parlement of the Thre Ages

And dalte thaym to his dussypers when he the dethe tholede;
And thus the worthieste of this werlde went to his ende.
Thane Sir Sezere hym-seluen, that Iulyus was hatten, 405
Alle Inglande he aughte at his awnn will,
When the Bruyte in his booke Bretayne it callede.
The trewe toure of Londone in his tyme he makede,
And craftely the condithe he compaste there-aftire,
And then he droghe hym to Dovire, and duellyde there a while, 410
And closede ther a castelle with cornells full heghe;
Warnestorede it full wiesely, als witnesses the sothe,
For there es hony in that holde holden sythen his tyme.
Than rode he in-to Romayne, and rawnsede it sone,
And Cassabalount þe kynge conquerede there-aftire; 415
Then graythed he hym in-to Grece and gete [it] be-lyue;
The semely cite Alexaunder seside he ther-aftire,
Affrike and Arraby and Egipt the noble;
Surry and Sessoyne sessede he to-gedir,
With alle the iles of the see appon iche a syde. 420
Thies thre were paynymes full priste, and passed alle othire.

f. 174 Of thre Iewes full gentill iugge we aftir,
In the Olde Testament as the storye tellis,
In a booke of the Bible that breues of kynges,
And renkes þat rede kane Regum it callen. 425
The firste was gentill Iosue þat was a Iewe noble,
Was heryet for his holynes in-to heuen-riche.
When Pharaoo had flayede the folkes of Israelle,
Thay ranne in-to the Rede See for radde of hym-seluen;
And than Iosue the Iewe, Ihesu he prayed 430
That the peple myghte passe vnpereschede that tyme;
And than the see sett vp appon sydes twayne,
In manere of a mode walle that made were with hondes;
And thay soughten ouer the see, sownnde alle to-gedir,
And Pharaoo full fersely folowede thaym aftire; 435
And efte Iosue þe Iewe Ihesus he prayede,
And the see sattillede agayne and sanke thaym there-inn—
A soppe for the Sathanas, vnsele haue theire bones!

416 MS. gete hym

## The Parlement of the Thre Ages

And dalt þem to his duche peris whan þe deth tholid.
And with worship yn þis world he went to his ende.

Then sir Sesar hym self þat Iulyus hight. (405)
All ynglond he aught at his owen wille.
Whan þe brute yn his boke bretayn yt called.
The true toure of londone yn his tyme he made.
Trirtely þe colonduyte he compast þer aftur,
Than he drowe hym to dovir & dwellid þer a while. (410)
And closid þer a castill with cornelles full highe.
Warme storid it a while & witnes þe sothe.
For þere is hony yn þat hald halden siþen his tyme.
Þan rode he yn to Romayn & raunsomed it sone.
And Cassabolaunt þe kyng conquerid þer aftur, (415)
He grathed þen yn to grece & gat them by lyve.
The semely Cite of Alexaunder sesid he þer aftur,
Affrik & arabs & Egipt þe noble,
Surry & sesoun sesid he to gidre.
With all the Iles of the se vpon ich side. (420)
Thise iij were paynyms ful prest & passid all oþer.

Of iij Iewis Ientill Iugges were aftur. f. 22ᵛ
In þe old testament as þe story tellis.
In a boke of þe bybull þat tretes of kynges.
And rekyn þat rode comon regum it calles. (425)
The first was gentill Iosue þat was a Iew noble.
Was harid for his nobylnes yn to hevyn riche.
Whan pharao had affligid þe folk of Israell.
Þat ran yn to þe red see for feerde of hym selvyn.
And Iosue þe Iew to Iesu he prayed. (430)
That the pepull myght passe vnperisshed þat tyme.
And than the see set vp his sidis twayn.
In maner of a mudde walle þat made was with hondes
And þai sought on ovir þe se sond all to gidre.
And pharao full fersly folowd þem aftur. (435)
And oft Iosue the Iue Ihesu he prayed,
And the se satild ayayn & sank þem þerynne.
A sope for Sathanas vncele haue þer bones.

405 *In r.-h. margin,* Iulius Cesar      409 Trirtely: *this might be* Trutely
422 *In r.-h. margin,* Iosue Iud . . . (*the ending cut off*).

And aftire Iosue þe Iewe full gentilly hym bere,
And conquerede kynges and kyngdomes twelue,  440
And was a conqueroure full kene and moste kyd in his tyme.

Than Dauid the doughty, thurghe Drightyn[es] sonde,
Was caughte from kepyng of schepe & a kyng made.
The grete grym Golyas he to grounde broghte,
And sloughe hym with his slynge & with no sleghte ells.  445
The stone thurghe his stele helme stong† in-to his brayne,
And he was dede of that dynt: the deuyll hafe that reche!
And than was Dauid full dere to Drightyn hym-seluen,
And was a prophete of pryse, and praysed full ofte;
Bot ȝit greued he his God gretely ther-aftire,  450
For Vrye his awnn knyghte in aventure he wysede;
There he was dede at that dede, as dole es to here;
For Bersabee his awnn birde was alle þat bale rerede.

The gentill Iudas Machabee was a Iewe kene,
And there-to worthy in were, and wyse of his dedis:  455
Antiochus and Appolyne aythere he drepide,
And Nychanore, anoþer kynge, full naytly there-aftire;
And was a conquerour kydde, and knawen with the beste.
Thies thre were Iewes full ioly and iusters full noble,
That full loughe haue bene layde sythen gane full longe tyme:  460
Of siche doughety doers looke what es worthen.

Of the thre Cristen to carpe couthely there-aftir,
þat were conquerours full kene and kyngdomes wonnen:
Areste was Sir Arthure, and eldeste of tyme,
For alle Inglande he aughte at his awnn will,  465
And was kynge of this kythe and the crowne hade.
His courte was at Carlele comonly holden,
With renkes full ryalle of his rownnde table,
þat Merlyn with his maystries made in his tyme,
And sett the sege perilous so semely one highte;  470
There no segge scholde sitt bot hym scholde schame tyde,
Owthir dethe with-inn the thirde daye demed to hym-seluen,
Bot Sir Galade the gude that the gree wanne.
There was Sir Launcelot de Lake full lusty in armes,

442 *MS.* drightyn   446 *MS.* stongen

## The Parlement of the Thre Ages W

And aftur Iosue the Iewe gentill hym bare.
And conquerid kinges & kyngdoms xij. (440)
And was A conqueroure kene kid yn his tyme.
Then David the dowty th..gh drighten found,
Was caught fro keping of shepe & a king makid.
That gret grymme golias he to þe ground brought.
And slowgh hym with his slyng & no sleight elles. (445)
The stones þurgh his stele helme stang yn to þe braynes.
And he was deed of þat dynt þe devill haue þat rech.
And þan was David ful dere to drightyn hym selvyn.
And provid of price & prophecied ofte.
But yit grevid he his god gretly þer aftur (450) f. 23
For vry his awn knyght yn awntur he vised.
Þere he was ded yn þat dede as dole is to here.
For Bersabye his own byrd was þat bayl reryd.
The Ientill Iudas Machabe was a Iue kene.
And þerto worþi & ware & wise of dedis. (455)
Antiochus & Appolyn ayther he drepid.
And Nycanor an oþer knyght nathly þer aftur.
And was A Conqueroure kid & know of þe best.
Thise iij were Iues & Iusters noble.
That ful low han be laid of ful long tyme. (460)

Of iij Cristen to carpe courtly þer aftur,
That were Conquerours kene & kyngdoms wan.
Eldist was Sir Arthur & best yn his tyme.
And ynglond he aught at his own wille. (465)
And was kyng of kith & þe Crown hadde.
His court was at Carlile comly holdyn.
With renkes ful ryall of þe round table.
That Marlyn with his maistris made yn his tyme.
And set þe sege perilous semely on hight. (470)
That no segge shuld sit þerynne but hym shame tyde.
Or deth withynne þe threde demyd to hym selvyn
But Sir Galaad þe gode þat the gree wan.
Þer was Sir launcelat de lake ful lusty yn ermes.

442 th..gh: *two letters defaced. In r.-h. margin,* David ... *(rest cut off)* Rex
454 *In r.-h. margin,* Iudas, mac ... *(rest cut off)* Dux    461 *is missing; there is no gap in the MS.*    462 *In r.-h. margin.* Arthurus

And Sir Gawayne the gude, that neuer gome harmede, 475
Sir Askanore, Sir Ewayne, Sir Errake fytz Lake,
And Sir Kay the kene and kyd of his dedis,
Sir Perceualle de Galeys þat preued had bene ofte,
Mordrede and Bedwere, men of mekyll myghte,
And othere fele of that ferde, folke of the beste. 480
Then [R]oystone þe riche kyng, full rakill of his werkes,
He made a blyot to his bride of the berdes of kynges,
And aughtilde Sir Arthures berde one scholde be;
Bot Arthure oure athell kynge anoþer he thynkes,
And faughte with hym in the felde till he was fey worthen. 485
And þan Sir Arthure oure kyng ames hym to ryde;
Vppon Sayn Michaells Mounte meruaylles he wroghte,
There a dragone he dreped, þat drede was full sore.
And than he sayled ouer the see in-to sere londes,
Whils alle the beryns of Bretayne bewede hym to fote. 490
Gascoyne and Gyane gatt he there-aftir,
And conquered kyngdomes and contrees full fele.
Than ames he in-to Inglonde in-to his awnn kythe:
The gates to-wardes Glassthenbery full graythely he rydes;
And ther Sir Mordrede hym mett by a more syde, 495
And faughte with hym in the felde to alle were fey worthen,
Bot Arthur oure athell kyng, and Wawayne his knyghte.
And when the felde was flowen & fey bot thaym-seluen,
Than Arthure Sir Wawayne athes by his trouthe
That he swiftely his swerde scholde swynge in the mere, 500
And whatt selcouthes he see the sothe scholde he telle.
And Sir Wawayne [start] swith to the swerde and swange it in the mere,
And ane hande by the hiltys hastely it grippes,

f. 175 And brawndeschet that brighte swerde and bere it a-waye;
And Wawayne wondres of this werke, and wendes by-lyue 505
To his lorde, there he hym lefte, and lokes abowte,
And he ne wiste in alle this werlde where he was by-comen.
And then he hyghes hym in haste, and hedis to the mere,
And seghe a bote from the banke and beryns there-inn.

481 *MS.* Boystone  482 *MS.* ablyot  502 *MS. omits* start

And Sir Gawayn þe gode þat nevir grome harmed. (475)
Sir Escamour & Sir Evayn sir Errak fight lake.
And Sir kay þe kene & kidde of his dedis.
Sir Persevall de Galays þat provid had bene ofte,
Modrede & bodward men of mykyll myght.
And felle of þat ferde folk of þe best, (480)
Than of Rusten the best ful rekill of warkes.
He made a billet to his bride of byrdes of kynges.
And Athild that Arthure berde shuld be.
But Arthoure oure Athil kyng an oþer he thinkes
And faught with hym yn þe feld with feres whil he was for-
  ward (485)
And arthure oure kyng armes hym to ride.
Vpon Michelmount meruels he wrought.
There A Dragon he drepid was drede wondure sore.
And he sailed þan ovir the see yn to sere landes.
Whil all þe bernes of Bretayn bowid to his fote. (490)
Gascon & guyon gate he þer aftur
And conquerid kyngdoms & Cuntrees sere
Than highes yn to ynglond yn to his owen kith.
The gate toward Glastonbery grathly he ride.
And þere Sir Modred hym met by the more side. (495)
And faught with hym yn þe feld whil all was forworþed.
But Arthure oure Athill kyng & Ewan his knyght.
And whan þe folk was floyn & fewe but þem selvyn
Than Sir Ewan hym hentes by his trowth
Þat he swithely his swerd shuld swyng yn þe more. (500)
And what selcouth he se þe soth he shuld telle.
And Ewan start swith to þe swerd & bare it away.

And Ewan wondirs of þis werk & wendes belyve. (505)
To hys lord þer he hym left & lokes aboute.
And he ne wist yn all þis world where he was becomyn.
And he hyes hym yn hast & hedes toward þe more.
And he se a bote fro þe bank & bernes þer ynne.

---

485 *Punctuation at the end of the line has been cut off.*  503, 504 *are missing; there is no gap in the MS.*

## The Parlement of the Thre Ages

There-inn was Sir Arthure and othire of his ferys, 510
And also Morgn la Faye that myche couthe of sleghte.
And there ayther segge seghe othir laste, for sawe he hym no more.
Sir Godfraye de Bolenn siche grace of God hade,
Þat alle Romanye he rode and rawnnsunte it sone;
Þe Amorelle of Antyoche aftire he drepit, 515
Þat was called Corborant, kiluarde of dedis;
And aftir he was callede kynge, and the crownn hade
Of Ier[u]salem and of the Iewes gentill to-gedir;
And with the wirchipe of this werlde he went to his ende.
Than was Sir Cherlemayne chosen chefe kynge of Fraunce, 520
With his doghty doussypers, to do als hym lykede;
Sir Rowlande the riche and Duke Raynere of Iene,
Olyuer and Aubrye and Ogere Deauneys,
And Sir Naymes at the nede that neuer wolde fayle,
Turpyn and Terry, two full tryed lordes, 525
And Sir Sampsone hym-selfe of the Mounte Ryalle,
Sir Berarde de Moundres, a bolde beryn in armes,
And gud Sir Gy de Burgoyne, full gracyous of dedis;
The katur fitz Emowntez were kydde k[nyght]es alle,
And oþer moo than I may myne or any man elles. 530
And then Sir Cherlles þe chefe ches for to ryde,
And paste to-wardes Polborne to prouen his strenghte:
Salamadyne the Sowdane he sloghe with his handis,
And þat [cite] he by-segede and saylede it full ofte,
While hym his ȝernynge was ȝett and the ȝates opynede; 535
And Witthyne thaire waryed kynge wolde nott abyde,
Bot soghte in-to Sessoyne socoure hym to gete;
And Cherlemayne, oure chefe kynge, cheses in-to the burgh,
And Dame Nioles anone he name to hym-seluen,
And maried hir to Maundevyle þat scho hade myche louede; 540
And spedd hym in-to hethyn Spayne spedely there-aftire,
And fittilled hym by Flagott faire for to loge.
There Olyuer the euerous aunterde hym-seluen,
And faughte with Sir Ferambrace & fonge hym one were;

511 *MS.* lafaye     518 *MS.* Ierasalem     529 *MS.* kynges
534 *MS. omits* cite

## The Parlement of the Thre Ages

Ther yn was Sir Arthure & oþer of his feris. (510)
& also morgon of Layfay þat moch coude of sight.
That segge se he last þer for sye he hym no more.
Sir Godfray de Boleyn such grace of god he had.
Þat all romayn he rayed & raunsomed it ful sone.
The Amerall of Antioch aftur he drepid. (515)
That was called Corboraunt kilward of dedes.
And aftur he was called king & Crown had.
Of Ierusalem & Iury gentilly to gidre.
And with worship of þis world he went to his ende.
Then sir Charlemayn was chosyn kyng of Fraunce. (520)
With his doughti ducheperis to do as hym likith.
Sir Rowland þe rich Duke & Sir Raner þe sayn.
Olyvere & Awbrey & oggerd the denys.
And Sir Names attned þat nevir wold fayll.
Turpyn & terry two ful tried knyghtes. (525)
And Sir Samson hym selvyn of þe mownt Royall.
Sir Berard de Mundres a bold berne yn armes.
And gode Sir Guy of Burgon full gracious of dedes.
And katurfiz Emountez were kid knyghtes all.
And other mo þan I may meene or any man elles. (530)
And kyng Charles þe chef chese for to Ride.
And passe toward puerne to prove his strenth.
Salomoydym þe Sawdon he slough with his hondes. f. 24ᵛ
And þat Cite he segid & sailed full ofte.
Whils hym his yernyng was het & þe yates opynd. (535)
And Wyghtelyne hir Warrid þe kyng wold not abide.
But sought yn to Seloun socoure hym to gete.
And charles oure chef kyng chese yn to þe burgh.
And dame Milos on he chese to hym selvyn.
And maried hir to Mawndevill þat sho had moch Lovid. (540)
And sped hym yn to hethyn Spayn spedely þer aftur.
And fetuld hym by Vagot fayre for to ligge.
There Olyuere þe Emerous aunturd hym selvyn.
And faught with Sir Feumbrace & fong hym yn were.

513 *In r.-h. margin,* Godfra ... (*rest cut off*) boleyn   520 *In r.-h. margin,*
Charl ... (*rest cut off*).   522 *In l.-h. margin,* A. (*in a different ink*).

# T      *The Parlement of the Thre Ages*

And than they fologhed hym in a fonte, and Florence hym
   callede.      545
And than moued he hym to Mawltryple Sir Balame to seche,
f. 175ᵛ And that Emperour at Egremorte aftir he takes,
And wolde hafe made Sir Balame a man of oure faythe;
And garte feche forthe a founte by-fore-with his eghne,
And he dispysede it and spitte and spournede it to the erthe,    550
And one swyftely with a swerde swapped of his hede;
And Dame Floripe þe faire was cristened there-aftire,
And kende thaym to the Corownne þat Criste had one hede,
And the nayles, anone, nayttly there-aftire,
When he with passyoun and pyne was naylede one the rode.    555
And than those Relikes so riche redely he takes,
And at Sayne Denys he thaym dide, and duellyd there for euer.
And than bodworde vn-to Merchill full boldly he sendys,
And bade hym Cristyne by-come and one Criste leue,
Or he scholde bette doun his borowes and brenn hym there-inn;    560
And garte Genyone goo that erande that greuede thaym alle.
Thane rode he to Rowncyuale, þat rewed hym aftire,
There Sir Rowlande the ryche Duke refte was his lyfe;
And Olyuer, his awnn fere that ay had bene trewe,
And Sir Turpyn the trewe, that full triste was at nede,    565
And full fele othir folke, als ferly were elles.
Then suede he the Sarazenes seuen ȝere and more,
And the Sowdane at Saragose full sothely he fyndis;
And there he bett downn þe burghe and Sir Merchill he tuke,
And that daye he dide [hym] to the dethe als he had wele
   seruede.      570
Bot by than his wyes were wery, and woundede full many,
And he fared in-to France to fongen thaire riste,
And neghede to-warde Nerbone that noyede thaym full sore;
And þat cite he asseggede appone sere halfues,
While hym the ȝates were ȝette & ȝolden the keyes,    575
And Emorye made Emperour, euen at that tyme,
To [haue]† and to holde it to hym and to his ayers.
And then thay ferden in-to Fraunce to fongen thaire ese,

548 *MS.* aman     558 Merchill: *could be* Merthill, *but cf.* schall, scholde *in MS., where* c *equally resembles* t.     570 *MS. omits* hym     577 *MS.* kepe it

## The Parlement of the Thre Ages

Þan þay halowd hym yn fount & florance hym called. (545)
Than mevid he to mowtrible Sir Marchel to seche.
The Emperoure at Egremourt aftur he takes.
And wold haue had marcel A man of oure faith.
And garte feche forth a fount by fore his Eyen.
And he dispisid & spit yn it & spronyd to þe Erth. (550)
And on swithely with a swerd swappid of his hed.
And dame Florissh þe faire was halowd þer aftur.
And kend þem to þe Crown þat Crist had on hed.
And to þe naylis anon natly ther aftur
Whan he with passion & pyne was on þe rode naylid. (555)
And than the relikes so riche rathely he takith.
At Saynt Denys he dud þem & dwellid þere for dowt.
Than Bodword to Balaam boldly he sendith.
And bad hym cristen be come & on crist leve.
Or he shuld bete down his burgh & bryng hym þer yn (560)
And gat Golyan to god þat grevid þem sore.
Than raied he to renovaill þat he rewid aftur, f. 25
There Rowland þe riche duke reft was his lif.
And Olyvere his owen fere þat hay had bene true.
And sir Turpyn þe true þat trusty was at nede, (565)
And full feell othir folk as ferly were ellis.
Þan swide he þe Sarsyng sevyn yere & more.
The Sawdon of Saragos sothely he fyndes
And þere he betes down þe burgh & balam he takes
That day he dud hym to deed as he had wel seruyd. (570)
Þan he weys wery & woundid full many.
And he farid yn to fraunce to fongyn rest.
And nyghed toward Norburgh þat nyghed hym sore.
And þat Cite he assegid vpon þe sere halfes.
Whill hym þe ȝates were yolden & yeve hym þe keyes. (575)
And Emer made Emperoure evyn at þat tyme.
To haue & hald it to hym & his heyris.
Than þei faren yn to fraunce to fongen þer ease

And at Sayn Denys he dyede at his dayes tyme.
Now hafe I neuened ȝow the names of † nyne of þe beste  580
Þat euer were in this werlde wiste appon erthe,
And the doghtyeste of dedis in thaire dayes tyme;
Bot doghetynes when dede comes ne dare noghte habyde.
O f wyghes þat were wyseste will ȝe now here,
And I schall schortly ȝow schewe and schutt me ful sone.  585
Arestotle he was arste in Alexander tyme,
And was a fyne philozophire and a fynour noble,
The grete Alexander to graythe and gete golde when hym liste;
And multiplye metalles with mercurye watirs,
And with his ewe ardaunt and arsneke pouders,  590
With salpetir and sal-ieme and siche many othire,
And menge his metalles and make fyne siluere,
f. 176  And was a [b]launchere of the beste thurgh blaste of his fyre.
Then Virgill thurgh his vertus ver[r]ayle he maket
Bodyes of brighte brasse full boldely to speke,  595
To telle whate be-tydde had and whate be-tyde scholde,
When Dioclesyane was dighte to be dere Emperour;
Of Rome and of Romanye the rygalte he hade.
T han Sir Salomon hym-selfe sett hym by hym one;
His Bookes in the Bible bothe bene to-gedirs:  600
That one of wisdome and of witt wondirfully teches,
His sampills and his sawes bene sett in the toþer;
And he was the wyseste in witt that euer wonnede in erthe,
And his techynges will bene trowede whills þe werlde standes,
Bothe with kynges and knyghtis and kaysers ther-inn.  605
M erlyn was a meruayllous man and made many thynges,
And naymely nygromancye nayttede he ofte,
And graythe[d] Galyan a boure to [gete] hyr þer-in,
That no wy scholde hir wielde ne wynne from hym-seluen.
Theis were the wyseste in the worlde of witt þat euer ȝitt were,  610
Bot dethe wondes for no witt to wende were hym lykes.

580 *MS.* ix nyne    593 *MS.* plaunchere    594 *MS.* veruayle (*or* vernayle)    608 *MS.* Graythen; kepe

## The Parlement of the Thre Ages

And at Saynt Denys he dyed at his deed tyme.
Now haue I nevid you þe names of ix of þe best. (580)
Þat evir were yn þe world wist upon erth.
And the doughtiest of dede yn there dayes tyme.
But doughtynes whan deth comys dare not abide.

Of wightes þat were wisist will ye now here.
& I shall shortly shew & shift me ful sone. (585)
Aristotle he was eldist yn alexaundre tyme.
& was a fyne philosofre & a finor noble.
And gret Alexar to grath gold when he hym list
And multyply metelles with marmry waturs.
And with his hewe ardaunt & arsenek powdres. (590) f. 25ᵛ
With sal petur & sal geme & such many other.
And myngyng his materalse & make fyne siluer.
And was a blawchere of þe best þurgh blastyng of his fire.
Then Virgill þurgh his vertus veryall he makid.
Bodies of bright brasse boldly to speke. (595)
Telle what be tyd had & what betide shuld.
Whan Dioclisian was dight dere Emperoure.
Of Rome & Romans þe regalte he had.

Then Sir Salamon hym self set hym by his one.
His bokes yn þe bybyll bothe bene to gidre. (600)
That of wisdom and of wit wonderly teches.

He was þe wisest of wit þat yn Erth was.


Marlyn was meruelous & made many þinges.
Namely Nygramancy natid he most.
And grathid golyan a boure to gete her þer ynne.
Þat no wight shuld hir weld ne wynne fro hym self.
Thise were þe wisest of wit yn world þer euer were. (610)
But deth wondes for no wit to wende where hym likes.

579 *MS. caret marks, and* deed *supplied above the line (in a different ink).*
584 *In r.-h. margin,* Aristotul ... *(rest cut off).*   587 *First* a *supplied above the line.*   595 *In r.-h. margin,* Virgili ... *(rest cut off).*   599 *MS. caret marks, and* self set hym *added above the line; in r.-h. margin,* Salomon.   602, 604, *and* 605 *are missing; there are no gaps in the MS.* 606 *In r.-h. margin,* Marlinus.

Now of the prowdeste in presse þat paramoures loueden
I schalle titly 3ow telle, and tary 3ow no lengere.
Amadase and Edoyne, in erþe are thay bothe,
That in golde and in grene were gaye in thaire tyme; 615
And Sir Sampsone hym-selfe, full sauage of his dedys,
And Dalyda his derelynge, † now dethe has þam bo[th]e.
Sir Ypomadonn de Poele, full priste in hi[s] armes,
Þe faire Fere de Calabre, now faren are they bothe.
Generides þe gentill, full ioly in his tyme, 620
And Clarionas þat was so clere, are bothe nowe bot erthe.
Sir Eglamour of Artas, full euerous in armes,
And Cristabelle the clere maye es crept in hir graue;
And Sir Tristrem the trewe, full triste of hym-seluen,
And Ysoute his awnn lufe, in erthe are þay bothe. 625
Whare es now Dame Dido was qwene of Cartage?
Dame Cand[ac]e the comly was called quene of Babyloyne?
Penelopie that was price and pas[sed] alle othere,
And Dame Gaynore the gaye, nowe grauen are thay bothen;
And othere moo than I may mene, or any man elles. 630
Sythen doughtynes when dede comes ne dare noghte habyde,
Ne dethe wondes for no witt to wende where hym lykes,
And ther-to paramours and pride puttes he full lowe;
Ne there es reches ne rent may rawnsone 3our lyues,

f. 176ᵛ Ne noghte es sekire to 3oure-selfe in certayne bot dethe, 635
And he es so vncertayne that sodaynly he comes,
Me thynke þe wele of this werlde worthes to noghte.
Ecclesiastes the clerke declares in his booke
Vanitas vanitatum et omnia vanitas,
Þat alle [es] vayne and vanytes and vanyte es alle. 640
For-thi amendes 3oure mysse whills 3e are men here,
Quia in inferno nulla est redempcio—
For in helle es no helpe, I hete 3ow for sothe;
Als God in his gospelle graythely 3ow teches:
Ite ostendite vos sacerdotibus, 645
To schryue 3ow full schirle, and schewe 3ow to prestis.

612 *Two letters have been deleted after* þat    617 *MS.* & now; boghte
618 *MS.* hir    627 *MS.* Candore    628 *MS.* pasten    640 *MS.*
*omits the first* es

## The Parlement of the Thre Ages

Now of prudist yn preste þat paramours lovedyn.
I shall tytly yow telle & tary you no while.
Amadas & ydonye yn erth ar þey bothe.
That yn gold & yn grene wer gay yn þer tyme.  (615)
And Sir Sampson hym self ful savage of his dedes.
And Daliday his derlyng now deth hath þem bothe.                  f. 26
Sir ypomodon de pole ful prest yn his armes.
And his faire fere of Calabre now faren ar þei bothe.
Genarid þe gentill & ful Ioly yn his tyme.  (620)
& clarionas þat was so clere ar bothe now but erth.
Sir Eglamour of artes ful emerus yn ermes.
And cristabell þat clere may is cropyn yn her grave.
And trystram ful true & trusty yn hym self.
And Isode his lovely love yn erth ar þey bothe.  (625)

Dame Candore þe comly was called quene of babilon.
Penelop þat was of pryce & passid all oþer.
And dame Gaynor þe gay now graued ar þei all.
& oþer many mo þan I may mynne or any man elles.  (630)
Then doughtynes whan deth comes dare not abide.
Ne deth wondes for no wite to wende where hym likes
And þerto paramours & pride put he full lowe.
Now þer is no Riches ne rent may raunsom your lyves.
Ne naught is sikir to your self ne certayn but deth.  (635)
And he is seyn certayn þat sodenly comes.
Me þink þe welle of þis world worthes to nought,

Vanitas vanitatum & omnia vanitas.
That all vayn & vanytes & vanyte is.  (640)
Therfore amend youre mysse whill ye be men here.
Quia In inferno nulla est redempcio,
For In helle is no help I hit yow for sothe.
And god yn his gospell grathly yow techis.
Ite ostendite vos sacerdotibus.  (645)
Go shryve you full stilly & shew yow to prestes.

626 *is missing; there is no gap in the MS.*   631 *MS. does not indicate a new section here.*   638 *is missing; there is no gap in the MS.*
646 *MS. caret mark, and* you *added above the line.*

Et ecce omnia munda sunt vobis,
And ȝe þat wronge wroghte schall worthen full clene.
Thou man in thi medill elde, hafe mynde whate I saye!
I am thi sire and thou my sone, the sothe for to telle,   650
And he the sone of thi-selfe, þat sittis one the stede,
For Elde es sire of Midill Elde and Midill Elde of Ȝouthe;
And haues gud daye, for now I go; to graue moste me wende;
Dethe dynges one my dore, I dare no lengare byde.'
When I had lenged and layne a full longe while,   655
I herde a bogle one a bonke be blowen full lowde,
And I wakkened ther-with, and waytted me vmbe;
Than the sone was sett and syled full loughe;
And I founded appon fote and ferkede to-warde townn.
And in the monethe of Maye thies mirthes me tydde,   660
Als I schurtted me in a schelfe in þe schawes faire,
And belde me in the birches with bewes full smale,
And lugede me in the leues þat lighte were & grene.
There dere Drightyne this daye dele vs of thi blysse,
And Marie, þat es mylde qwene, amende vs of synn. Amen. Amen.

    Thus Endes the Thre Ages.

652 *A letter (? d) has been deleted after the first* Midill

## The Parlement of the Thre Ages

Et ecce omnia sunt vobis munda.
& þat ye haue wrong wroght shall worth ful clene.
Than man yn mydileld haue mynd what I say.
I am þi sire & þow my son þe sothe for to telle. (650)
And he the son of þe þat sittes on þe stede.
For eld sir & mydel eld & myddilleld of yowthe.
And haues gode Day for to my grave must I wend.
Deth dynges on my dore I dare no lenger abide.
Whan he langid and lane a ful lang while. (655)
He hard a bugull on a bank blawn ful lowde.

And þan þe sonne was set & salid full lowe.
And I foundid vpon fote & went toward þe town.
And yn A moneth of May whan myrthes me bytide. (660)
As I serchid me a shote yn A shawe faire.
And beldid me yn the byrches with bowes ful faire.
And logid me yn the levis þat light were yn greue.
The dere dryghten the day dele vs of þi blisse.
And Mary þat is myld quene amend vs of oure mysse. (665)

### Explicit

657 *is missing; there is no gap in the MS.*
663 greue: *might be* grene

# ABBREVIATIONS OF TITLES

T: the Thornton text of *Parl.* (in B.M. Additional MS. 31042).
W: the Ware text of *Parl.* (in B.M. Additional MS. 33994).
*Avowis*: *Avowis of Alexander*.
*Awntyrs*: *Awntyrs off Arthure*.
*Boke St. A.*: *Boke of Saint Albans*.
*Buik*: *Buik of Alexander*.
*Buke H.*: *Buke of the Howlat*.
*Destr. Troy*: *Destruction of Troy*.
*DL.*: *Death and Liffe*.
*GGK.*: *Sir Gawain and the Green Knight*.
*Gol. & Gaw.*: *Golagros and Gawane*.
*MG.*: *The Master of Game*.
*Morte A.*: *Morte Arthure*.
*Mum & S.*: *Mum and the Sothsegger*.
*ON.*: *The Owl and the Nightingale*.
*Parl.*: *The Parlement of the Thre Ages*.
*PP.*: *Piers Plowman*.
*Pur.*: *Purity*.
*Qu. Love*: *Quatrefoil of Love*.
*Sc. F.*: *Scotish Feilde*.
*Siege Jer.*: *Siege of Jerusalem*.
*Sowdone*: *Sowdone of Babylone*.
Turb., *Hunting*: George Turbervile's *Booke of Hunting*.
Turb., *Hauking*: George Turbervile's *Booke of Faulconrie or Hauking*.
Twiti: William Twiti, *Le Art de Venerie*.
*Vœux*: *Les Vœux du Paon*.
*Wars Alex.*: *The Wars of Alexander*.
*Wm. P.*: *William of Palerne*.
*WW.*: *Wynnere and Wastoure*.

A list of abbreviated linguistic terms will be found preceding the Glossary, p. 71.

# NOTES

**1.** Cf. *Destr. Troy* 12969, 'Hit was the moneth of May when mirthes begyn'.

**1 ff.** Other passages in ME. alliterative verse comparable with this description of a May morning in the woods are: *Somer Soneday* 1–32, *PP.*, Prologue 1–10, Passus viii. 62–69 (B text), *Qu. Love*, st. I, *WW*. 31–44, *DL*. 22–38, and (with considerable differences) *Mum & S.* 876 ff., especially 923–43. A ME. version of what was probably the prototype of all these passages except the last is contained in the Chaucerian *Romaunt of the Rose*, 49 ff.

**2.** Cf. the opening line of *PP.*, 'In a somer seson whan soft was the sonne'.

**4–5.** This was obviously a poaching expedition, but not necessarily out of season. The translator of *MG.* does not say when the season began; but as he speaks of how to judge a hart from its fumes in April and May, and says that harts run best from the 'entry of May into St. John's tide', it seems likely that they were hunted from May on in England as they were in France, where the season began on 3 May. (See *MG.*, Appendix, 'Seasons of Hunting', and A. Dryden's edition of Twiti (1908), 31–32.)

**7. a banke be a bryme syde:** cf. *GGK.* 2172, 'a bonke þe brymme by-syde'.

**8.** See Language, 'Vowels', 4, pp. xvii–xviii, and *OED.* s.v. Grass, for examples of *grise, grissis. Grysse* rhymes with *blisse* in *Qu. Love* 66, 68. This *i(y)* form in ME. seems to be confined to the N. and Sc. dialects; the metathesized form *girs(e)* occurs also, as in *Morte A.* 3944, *girse*; and cf. *Awntyrs* 366, *Buke H.* 28.

**10. The dewe ... donkede:** a fairly common formula. Cf. *Sc. F.* 310, *Destr. Troy* 7997, *Siege Jer.* 624, *Morte A.* 3248, *GGK.* 519, Dunbar, *The Twa Maryit Wemen and the Wedo* 10512.

**11.** Cf. *Destr. Troy* 2736, *DL.* 71.

**14. threpen:** this might be emended to *threp[d]en* (see 104); but pt. and pr. tenses alternate fairly often in the poem. The meaning is perhaps 'are vying with one another to see who can sing best (or loudest)'. Cf. *Morte A.* 929–30:

> Of þe nyghtgale notez þe noisez was swette,
> They threpide wyth the throstills, thre hundreth at ones,

and *WW.* 37, 'The throstills full throly they threpen to-gedire'. Or *threpen* may have its primary sense of 'chide, scold', and refer to the bird's loud, scolding notes when it is alarmed. In early English, the term 'throstle' was used of the blackbird as well as of the song-thrush: see Toller's *A.-S. Dictionary*, Supplement, *þrostle*, and cf. Robert Mannyng of Brunne's *Handlyng Synne* 7480 (*Manuel des Pechiez*

## Notes

5943); *Promptorium Parvulorum* glosses 'Thrustyl, bryd' as *merula*. On the other hand, there are many instances where it obviously means what we understand by 'song-thrush' or 'mavis' (see *OED*. s.v. Throstle), so 'compete in song' is perhaps more likely, especially in view of the *Morte A*. passage. (See H. L. Savage, *JEGP*. xxix. 77–78. Savage thinks that if the poet used *threpen* with its meaning of 'chide, scold', he could also have meant the missel-thrush, which like the blackbird has a harsh cry when it is disturbed.)

15–16. Cf. *Wars Alex.* 2264; *Siege Jer.* 853, 1009; *Destr. Troy* 1079, 6061, 7554, 12531.

17. **one hillys**: 'The hertes þat bene in greet hilles, whane it commeþ to Rut, some tyme þei come adoun in to grete forestis and in þe hethes and into þe laundes and þer þei abide alle þe wyntere in to þe entryngis of Auerille, and þan þei take hure hauntz for to lat her heuedes wexe, nye þe townes and þe villages in the playn contre þeras þei fynde good fedyng in þe newe growyng lond. And whan þe gras is hie and wel wexen þei drawe hem into þe grettest hilles þat þei may fynde for þe faire pastures and fedynges and faire herbes þat bene þer vpon' (*MG.* 21, edition of 1904).

**gouen**: the form with *o* [ɔ:] is probably from ON. *gófom* (earlier *gáfum*) rather than from a WS. pl. *geáfon* with shift of stress from the first to the second element of the diphthong. The use of this verb here is unusual; Gollancz glosses 'betook themselves', but gives no explanation of the word, and *OED*. has no example of 'give' used in this sense. It may, however, have arisen from the sense 'to give up, devote oneself to' (an action, pursuit, &c.): see *OED*. s.v. Give, v., 12 and 13. A sense of *gefa* in ON. is 'to give fodder, to feed' (*gefa nautum, kúm, hestum*, &c.), but there appears to be no other example of this use in ME. In either case one would expect the refl. *paym* rather than *þay*, and it is possible that the copyist, not understanding this use of *gouen* (perhaps confusing it with a form of 'go'), has omitted the *-m* of *þaym*. Another possibility is that *gouen* is not a form of 'give' but of 'gaw', ON. *gá* 'to heed'. *OED*. gives examples of *gaw, gou*, &c., meaning 'to gape, stare; to look intently'. One would expect a verb of motion here, but the sense 'stare about' would be possible: cf. 51, 'starede full brode'.

18. Cf. *Pur.* 534.

19–20. Cf. *WW*. 14: 'And hares appon herthe-stones schall hurcle in hire fourme'; and the alliterative fragment from a fifteenth-century manuscript (ed. T. Wright and J. O. Halliwell, *Reliquiae Antiquae*, i. 84), where this type of line is parodied: 'The hare and harthestone hurtuld to-geydur'.

20. **fatills hir to sitt**: cf. *DL*. 30, 'I [f]ettled me to sitt'. The form with *a* is exceptional and may be a scribal corruption from *e*. The *i* forms, which are common, probably show the raising of *e* to *i* before a dental cons. *Fittle* occurs in mod. Yorks. dialect.

## Notes

**21–99.** This description of a deer-hunt may be compared with the hunting scenes in *GGK*. (especially 1319 ff.), and in *Awntyrs* 33–65, *Sir Tristrem* 441–528, *Ipomedon*, Kölbing's edition, 1st version 587–680, 2nd version 365–416.

**24.** Cf. *GGK*. 2146, 'Þenne loke a littel on þe launde . . .'.

**26. beme:** the beam is the main horn, from which the antlers spring. **vnburneschede:** 'Deer are said to burnish their heads, when rubbing off a white downy skin from their horns against a tree' (*Dictionary of Sports*, 1835). When the newly-grown horns had been 'burnished', they would be at their final stage of perfection.

**27. feetur:** see *OED*. s.v. Feature, sb. †2, a and b. As Savage (loc. cit.) points out, OF. *faiture*, from which it is derived, is glossed by Godefroy as 'action de faire, de produire, de créer, et le résultat de cette action, production, créature, personne'. Here the word is applied to the newly-growing antlers and tines. Cf. *(af)feted*, *MG*. 17: '. . . whan þe tyndis bene wel growe in þe beem by good mesure, that oon nye þat oþer, þan is it cleped wel affeted . . .' and 'wel feted wiþ smale tyndes'.

**as thi fote:** a curious comparison. The horns branching off the beam suggested from a distance the outline of a foot?

**for-frayed:** 'fraying' was an earlier stage in the process than 'burnishing'; cf. *MG*. 16: '. . . her hornes bene rekeuered with a soft here . . . and vndir that skynn and þat here, þe hornes wexen hard and sharpe; and aboute Marie Magdalenes day, þei fray here hornes to þe trees and haven away þat skynn frome here hornys, and þan wexe þei hard and stronge, and þan þei go to burnyssh and make hem sharpe into colers places [charcoal pits] þat men make somtyme in þe greet graues. And ȝif þei mowe non fynde, þei goo aȝeinst corners of Rokkes, or to crabtre or hawthorne or oþer trees.'

**28–30.** Cf. *MG*. 17: 'And þe first tynde [tine] þat is next þe hede is cleped Aunteler, and þe secound Riall, and the thred [third] above Susreal.' These are now called the brow tine, the bay, and the tray.

**31. assommet:** a hart was said to be 'summed' when its horns were fully formed (though not necessarily completed in growth). Cf. *MG*. 16: 'Thei rekeuere heere hornes and someth here tyndes as mony as þei shal haue þorgh alle the yere, from March that þei han mwed hem in to the myddel of June . . .'; and Turb., *Hunting*, 47: 'and by the middest of Iune, their heades will be somed of as much as they will beare all that yeare'.

**of vi and of †fyve,** i.e. with six 'troches' on one horn, and five on the other.

**34. a sowre:** the term 'soar' was used of a fourth-year male, whether of the fallow or of the red deer species. See G. Tilander's edition of Twiti, 86 (s.v. *sour*), and cf. Turb., *Hunting*, 238: 'A Bucke is called the first yeare a Fawne, the second a Pricket, the third a Sorell, the fourth a Sore, the fifth a Bucke of the first head, and the

## Notes

sixth a Bucke.' 'Soar' is derived from OF. *sor*, 'reddish-brown', which would be the colour of the hide at this stage in both the fallow and the red deer.

It is common for an old stag to train a younger male deer to act as a kind of squire, watching out for danger and providing a decoy when the chase is on. Cf. *MG.* 16: 'And somtyme a greet hert hath a noþer felawe that is called his squiere, for he is withe hym which done as he wil, and þere þei wil abyde al that sesoun so that þei be notte lette, into þe laste eende of August.' Savage, loc. cit. 81, quotes C. P. Collyns in *The Chase of the Wild Red Deer* (London, 1862, ed. L. J. Bathhurst, London, 1902), who gives a lively account of the tricks and dodges of an old stag (see chap. i, 49–53, in the edition of 1902).

35. Gollancz's note here ['*when the wynde faylede*, refers to the deer getting to windward of the hunter, and smelling him; when there was no wind, the stag had to watch all round'] is confusing. As Savage (loc. cit. 81) points out, if the hart and soar were to windward of the hunter, his scent would be carried away from them. But if the hunter were to windward of the deer, his scent would be carried to them as long as there was a wind blowing. Savage suggests that the poet is referring to 'the fact that the "sowre" lies or feeds to windward of the hart', and gives an illustration from Sir John Fortescue's *The Story of a Red Deer* (New York, 1908), where an old stag tells a younger one: 'Now I am quite comfortable. Do you go on and lie down by yourself; but don't go too far, and keep to windward of me, so that I can find you if I want you.' When the wind dropped, the old stag would have to be on the alert again, and probably the 'squire' would rejoin his master.

**woke**: 'kept watch'; or possibly trans., 'woke': the soar woke his master up when danger threatened.

38. i.e. 'I dropped my leash gently.'

**lyame**: this was the 'rope made of silk or leather by which hounds were led. . . . This strap was fastened to the collar by a swivel, and both collar and liam were often very gorgeous' (*MG.*, Appendix). H. L. Savage (*MLN.* xliii. 178) quotes from *MG.* 152–3, a passage which suggests that the hound accompanying the quester is secured in some way, not free; and so he argues that *lyame* here must mean not 'leash' but 'lyam-hound', a sense attested by a phrase in *Boke St. A.*, 'A Sute of a lyam', and by Edgar's use of it in *King Lear*, III. vi. 72, '. . . Hound or Spaniell, Brache or Lym'. It seems unlikely, however, that 'lete . . . falle' would have been used of a dog; surely it suggests an inanimate object. Moreover, the poet is definite about the kind of dog he is using: it is a 'berselett', a dog used specially for hunting with the bow; 'lym' or 'limer' was a more general term, 'leash-hound' or 'bloodhound'.

39. **berselett** (see note above): a corruption of OF. *berseret*, a

## Notes

hunting dog; OF. *bercer, berser*, meant 'to hunt', especially with the bow. Cf. *Awntyrs* 38 (Thornton MS.), 'With bowe and with Barcelett', and see *MG.*, Appendix, s.v. *bercelet*.

**44. Tighte vp my tylere:** i.e. set up the stock of my cross-bow into position. The *tylere* or stock was the main beam of the cross-bow; it had a groove to guide the arrow, and a mechanism for holding and releasing the cord.

51. Cf. *Wars Alex.* 4754, *Pistill of Susan* 285, and *Awntyrs* 109. *Stotais, stotays* also occurs in *Morte A.*

**stelkett,** cf. *stalkede* 41. *Stelkett* is presumably from an OE. form *stéalcode* with the stress on the first element of the diphthong, and *-d* of the ending unvoiced to *-t*; and *stalkede* from an OE. form *steálcode* with the stress shifted to the second element of the diphthong.

51-52. Cf. Nicholas Cox, *The Gentleman's Recreation* (1677), p. 52, on 'The Nature of a Hart': 'The Hart is strangely amazed when he hears any one call, or whistle in his Fist ... He heareth very perfectly when his Head and Ears are erected; but heareth imperfectly when he holdeth them down. When he is on foot, and not afraid, he wonders at every thing he seeth, and taketh pleasure to gaze at them.'

**53. I hallede to the hokes:** i.e. drew back the catches (in such a way as to release the cord). For an interesting account of the types of cross-bow used in the chase, see *MG.*, Appendix, under 'Arms of the Chase'.

**56. balkede:** an alternative meaning to that given in the Glossary would be 'bellowed, roared'; cf. OE. *bælcan* 'to cry out', cognate with Du. *balken* 'to bray' (of an ass). *OED.* has only one quotation, dated 1603, for this sense of 'balk'. If *balkede* means 'bellowed', *brayed* in this line is perhaps not from OF. *braire*, but an alternative form of *brayde* from OE. *bregdan*. The meaning then would be 'made a sudden jerky movement', 'started'. Cf. *St. Erkenwald* 190, where *brayed* appears to mean 'moved slightly'.

**57. hurlede one ane hepe:** this is a common formula.

**longede:** 'lived', 'dwelt'; for this sense, cf. *DL.* 60.

**61. vmbycaste:** cf. *MG.* 86, 'And þan he shuld fetch his lymer and vmbicast ...'.

**62. blody by-ronnen:** cf. the OE. *Crist* 1174-5: 'beam ... blodgum tearum birunnen'. The expression 'blody byronnen' seems to have attracted the later alliterative poets. It occurs frequently in *Destr. Troy* (1328, 7033, &c.); and in several other poems.

**64. crouschede:** this may mean 'crouched', but its derivation is obscure; see *OED.* s.v. Crouch. *Crouschede* may be a form of 'crush' (see *OED.* s.v. Crush, †Croose), derived from OF. *cruis(s)ir, croussir* 'to make a crashing or cracking noise'. In early English the idea of noise is sometimes present, but 'crush' in the sense of 'compress', 'push

## Notes

down', &c., is found quite early too. Thus *crouschede* here may mean 'pressed down'. For the sound represented by *sch* and its connexion with the OF. form, see under Language, 'Consonants', 6, p. xxi.

65. **Dede als a dore-nayle**: this was a favourite simile in the alliterative poems; cf. *Wm. P.* 628.

66-99. With this account of the brittling of the deer, cf. especially *GGK*. 1323-64 and *Sir Tristrem* 452-515. Detailed instructions for the brittling are to be found in all the authorities on hunting, from the fourteenth to the seventeenth centuries: see especially *MG*. 98 ff.; *La Chace dou Cerf* 346 ff. (ed. G. Tilander, *Studier i Modern Språkvetenskap*, xiv, Uppsala, 1940; translated in A. Dryden's edition of Twiti, 119 ff.); *Boke St. A.*, sig. f ii<sup>v</sup> ff. (edition of 1486); Turb., *Hunting*, 127 ff.; and Nicholas Cox, *The Gentleman's Recreation*, 72-73. The author of *Parl*. knew his rules well, but he was anxious to dispose of the hart as quickly as possible (before the forester caught him), so he wasted no time on the finer points; unlike the huntsmen in *GGK.*, where the description of the 'undoing' and 'breaking up' is deliberately detailed.

67. **troches**: these are the 'clustered short projections near the tip' of a stag's antlers (Gollancz, in his note on *GGK*. 795). The adj. *troched* from this term came to be used figuratively in architecture, meaning 'adorned with small pointed pinnacles', as in *GGK*. 795, *Pur.* 1383. Cf. *MG*. 99: '. . . oon of þe beerners shuld . . . turne his hornes to þe erþward and þe þrote vpward and slitte þe skynne of þe þrote alenonlong the neke . . .'.

68. **Kest**: ON. *kasta*; cf. *keste* 80. The *e* of the stem vowel may be due to analogy with strong vbs. of Cl. VII, such as *late* pt. *lete*, *wax* pt. *wex*. (See J. K. Wallenberg, *The Vocabulary of Dan Michel's Ayenbite of Inwyt*, 135.)

**keuduart**: there appears to be no other instance of this word in ME. The term 'rascal' was used, strictly speaking, of a young or lean deer, unfit for hunting or for eating. But see *Boke St. A.*, 'Bestys of the Chace' (sig. e i, edition of 1486):

> Where so ye hem fynde Rascall ye shall hem call
> In fryth or in fell: or in forest I yow tell.

**kutt of his tonge**: 'Firste he shall take out the tongue . . .'. At a great chase, the tongue was the delicacy reserved for 'the Prince or . . . the chiefe personage' (Turb., *Hunting*, 128).

69. The entrails were given to the hounds, as their 'reward'. Cf. Twiti (Tilander) 49, ll. 160-1, 'the houndes shal be rewardid with . . . þe bewellis'. The addition of *owte* (Gollancz adds *out*) is probably justified: cf. *GGK*. 1609-10, 'Brayde3 out þe boweles, . . . his braches rewarde3'.

70. **I s[lit]te hym at þe assaye**: MS. *sisilte*. Gollancz emends to *s[clis]te* 'sliced', but *slitte* gives a better sense here. The 'assay' was

40

## Notes

the part of the breast where the deer's flesh was tested. Cf. *Boke St. A.*, f ii$^v$:

> At thessay cut hym that lordys may see:
> A noon fat or leen wheder that he bee.

Turb., *Hunting*, 133-4, gives the clearest account of this process.

71. **And he was floreschede full faire**: cf. *Destr. Troy* 2737, 'florisshet full faire'.

**of two fyngere brede**: i.e. he had fat on him of the breadth of two fingers. This was a standard way of measuring the fat: cf. *GGK*. 1329.

72. Cf. *Boke St. A.*, f ii$^v$–f iii:

> ... and then shall ye goo
> At chaulis: to begynne assone as ye may
> And slyttith hym downe euen to thassay.

**chefe**: probably adverbial (see Glossary), giving emphasis to the decision to start at the 'chawylls'; but Gollancz's gloss [(?) first, (?) = *at the c.*, at the top] is unsatisfactory. E. Kölbing, op. cit. 279, compares *Awntyrs* 114, 'One þe chefe of þe cholle', where F. J. Amours glosses *chefe* as 'upper part, top'. But *chawylls chefe* = 'jowls' top' is very unlikely.

74. 'Making the arber' was the process of removing the first stomach of the animal, opening it and emptying it of its contents, and filling it with blood and fat from the paunch. The final injunction, according to *Boke St. A.*, is to take needle and thread and sew the arber up again; it could also, according to *La Chace dou Cerf*, be tied up.

Gollancz in his notes on *GGK*. 1323-64, quotes J. D. Bruce, *Eng. Studien*, xxxii. 23-36. Bruce notes that only in *Parl.* and *GGK*. 'the first step in the process of disembowelling—the making of the erber—is taken before the animal is skinned'.

75-78. See H. Dryden, *Twiti*, 36: 'The larger beasts of Venary were skinned as a sheep or other large animals. The hide is slit from the place where the throat is cut downwards towards the tail; from the breast up the inside of the forelegs, and from the vent up the inside of the thighs. The hide is then flayed by degrees.'

79. See Turb., *Hunting*, 134-5, for a detailed account of the cutting out of the shoulder.

80. **corbyns bone**: cf. *GGK*. 1355, *Sir Tristrem* 502-3. There was a small piece of gristle at the end of the sternum which was thrown up into a tree to crows or ravens, as a kind of luck-offering. Cf. *Boke St. A.*, f iii:

> Than take owt the shulderis . and slyttith a noon
> The baly to the syde from the corbyn bone
> That is corbyns fee: at the deeth he will be.

Turbervile's account is the most explicit: see *Hunting*, 135.

## Notes

**81. I slitte hym full sleghely**: cf. *Destr. Troy* 5939, 'Slit hym down sleghly'; and *Morte A.* 2975.

**83. sewet**: 'suet' was the technical term for the fat of red and fallow deer.

**86.** Cf. *La Chace dou Cerf* 379–80, 'Puis en dois le[s] nomble[s] lever, Les cuisses n'i dois oublier'. The numbles are the 'parts of a deer between the thighs, that is to say, the liver and kidneys and entrails' (*MG.*, Appendix, 178).

**87–90.** Cf. *Boke St. A.*, f iii$^v$–f iiii:

> And after the Ragge boon cuttis euen also
> The forchis: and the sydes euen betwene . . .
> Than shall ye cut the nek the sydes euen fro
> And the hede fro the nek cuttyth also.

**91.** *Fourche* here, and *fourches* in 88, means 'fork of the body', i.e. 'haunch', or 'legs'. Thus: 'I fastened the feet of the haunch through the sides.' Cf. *GGK*. 1356–7, and Turb., *Hunting*, 134: 'It must be remembered . . . that the feete be all foure left on. The hynder feete must be to fasten . . . the hanches to the sydes, and the two forefeete are left to hang vp the shoulders by.'

**94.** A 'foster of the fee' was a forester who held his office 'in fee', i.e. by legal inheritance. 'All the ordinary work of the forests, such as watching for trespassers, pursuing them, attaching or arresting them—in short, all the work of a modern gamekeeper—was performed by a group of officers called foresters. . . . In most of the larger forests there were, in addition to the wardens, verderers and ordinary foresters, certain other officers, who were styled foresters in fee. . . . All that the words "forester in fee" necessarily connoted was a forester holding his office hereditarily.' (G. J. Turner, *Select Pleas of the Forest*, Selden Society, xiii, from pp. xx and xxiii.) See H. Dryden, *Twiti*, 94–97.

**97. for ferde**: see note on 101.

**99.** Cf. *MG.* 28, 'Of the Wilde Boor and of His Nature': 'They eten al maner of fruytes and alle maner Corn. And whan al þat failleþ hem þe[i] wroot in the grounde with þe rowel of her snowte, þe which is ryght hard; þei wroot so depe in þe grounde til þei fynde þe Rootes of þe feerme [fern] and of þe spryng [spurge] and of oþer rootes of þe whiche þei han þe sauoure in þe erthe. And þerfore haue I saide þat þei wynde wondirly ferre and mervelously.'

**101. for slepeles**: ? = 'because of sleeplessness'. *Slepeles* may derive from the OE. n. *slǣplēast*, perhaps influenced in form by the adj. *slǣplēas*; or it may be the adj. used as a n., as in *for radde* 429. This construction is common in fourteenth-century English: cf. Chaucer's *Knight's Tale* 2142–4, *for old* and *for blak*, and *Qu. Love* 137, *chosen for chaste*. In some instances of this idiom in ME., as in *for old* and *for blak, for* may be an intensive prefix = 'very, extremely', but in the

## Notes

examples from *Parl*. it is probably a prep. This type of phrase occurs also with what looks like a pp. (as in *Troilus and Criseyde*, ii. 656, *for pure ashamed*), and *for ferde* in *Parl*. 97 could be explained in this way, with *ferde* as pp. of OE. *fǣran, fēran* 'to frighten': thus, 'because of being afraid'. Or *for ferde* may derive from OE. *\*forfēred*, pp. 'terrified', with the original sense of *for* as an intensive prefix lost and a false division made into prep. and n. In *for ferde to be wryghede* 97 the poet apparently thought of *ferde* as a n. Cf. *for feerde* W 429, where T has *for radde*; *radde* (< ON. *hrædd-r* adj. 'afraid') was probably thought of as a noun. (For a discussion of this type of phrase, see M. L. Samuels in *English Studies*, xxxvi (1955), 310–13.)

101–2. Cf. *Destr. Troy* 2378–9. The whole account of Paris's vision (2340–448) may be compared with that of the poet in *Parl*.

104. Cf. *Destr. Troy* 5246, 'þat were þro men in threpe, & thretyms mo'.

105. MS. *moten*. Probably a scribal error for a pt. here: perhaps *mote*[*d*] or, as Gollancz emends, *mot*[*ed*]*en*. Cf. *GGK*. 1280, '... meled of much-quat'.

**and maden thaym full tale**: a difficult line. If *tale* derives from OE. *ge-tal, ge-tæl*, 'lively, quick (of speech)', the sense may be: 'and made themselves full lively in speech', ? 'became heated in argument'. However, I have found no other instance in ME. of *tale* as an adj. with this meaning, and the use of *maden* is odd. If *tale* = 'speech, statement' (OE. *talu*), the sense would be 'and made (for themselves) a full statement', i.e. spoke at great length. On the other hand, *full* occurs nowhere else in the poem as an adj.; it occurs over 100 times as an adv.

106. **ane hande-while**: a favourite second half-line. There is no need to emend: see Introduction, 'Alliteration', 4, p. xxxi.

107. Cf. *Wm. P.* 1602, 'for to reken al þe arai ...'.

109 ff. The description of the Green Knight in *GGK*. 136 ff. may be compared with this passage.

110. Cf. *Siege Jer.* 271, 'A bold burne on a blonke ...'.

112. Cf. *Wars Alex*. 4923, 'Balgh brade in þe brest ...'. For the meaning of *balghe*, see instances cited in *OED*. s.v. †Balgh, a., 1 and 2, especially *GGK*. 2032, 2172, where the word is used of a round, swelling surface; there may be some connexion with OE. *bælg* 'bag, bulge', Goth. *balgs* 'leather bag, wineskin'. Gollancz in his note on *GGK*. 2172 comments that in all the instances the underlying idea seems to be 'smooth', and compares ON. *bali* 'a soft grassy bank'. But Youth in *Parl*. would surely have a full, rounded chest rather than merely a smooth one.

113. **i-liche**, MS. *I liche*: possibly a corruption of *egheliche* (cf. 28), but it is not necessary to emend. Cf. *WW*. 48, 'One a loueliche lande þat was ylike grene', *Wars Alex*. 1422, '... þe baistell & þe burȝe ware bathe elike hiȝe', and *Patience* 161. Line 113 could be rendered 'His shoulders were broad, and his arms, too, were long'.

## Notes

114. Men of fashion in the fourteenth century affected an elegant waist-line: cf. *GGK.* 144, *Wars Alex.* 4923.

119. The combination of red, rose, and richness occurs in several of the alliterative poems: e.g. *Destr. Troy* 624, *DL.* 24, *Sc. F.* 26.

120. Cf. *Awntyrs* 510, 'Trayfolede with trayfoles, and trewluffes by-twene'. J. Robson in *Three Metrical Romances*, 95, quotes from Planché's *History of British Costume*, 104, a description of the stole of white tissue in which Edward I was buried. It was 'studded with gilt quatrefoils in philagree work, and embroidered with pearls in the shape of what are called true-lovers' knots'. The true-love knot seems to have been a favourite form of ornamentation on dress or armour: Sir Gawain had 'trulofeȝ' and turtle-doves embroidered on the covering of his helmet, and cf. *Sir Degrevant* 471, 1048, 1055, 1500.

120 ff. R. J. Menner in his note on *Pur.* 1464 ff. remarks that 'all the poets of the alliterative school delight in ornamenting their descriptions with lists of precious stones', and cites a number of parallel passages.

122. Cf. *GGK.* 179, *DL.* 83–84.

126. Cf. *Siege Jer.* 760, '& so with saphyres sett :' þe sydes a-boute'.

128. Cf. *Wars Alex.* 1538.

130. Cf. *Eger and Grime* 971 (Percy Folio MS.): 'His sadle with selcamoure [? = sekamoure] was sett.' Medieval saddles were generally made of wood, which was often richly painted.

132. **His cropoure:** Gollancz's emendation to '[t]r[a]poure' is unnecessary: there are other examples in the poem of xa/ax alliteration; see Introduction, 'Alliteration', 7, p. xxxii. A 'saddle-cloth', if it 'trailed to the earth', would impede the horse's movements; and Youth is 'bownne for to ryde', perhaps on one of his hawking expeditions. A fine crupper is a more likely piece of equipment: it would be fastened to the back of the saddle, and would hang down low under the horse's tail. The workaday crupper would be a leather strap, but with a gold saddle and silk reins it would certainly be of silk. Kölbing (op. cit.) compares *Richard Coer de Lion* (Weber, vol. ii) 388, 'His cropere was of sylke'.

133–4. Thirty in medieval tradition was more often regarded as the approach to middle age; and forty to sixty, according to J. L. Lowes, 'represented a well established literary convention for old age'. (Quoted by G. R. Coffmann, in 'Old Age in Chaucer's Day', *MLN.* lii (1937), 25–26.) Brother C. Philip, in 'A Further Note on Old Age in Chaucer's Day' (*MLN.* liii (1938), 181–2), mentions some 'further violations of the accepted medieval tradition regarding old age': the fourteenth-century *Stanzaic Life of Christ*, where the age from twenty-eight to fifty is called youth, fifty to seventy the 'time of soburnesse', seventy until death the time of senility; and the York play, *Abraham's Sacrifice of Isaac*, where Isaac, who describes himself as 'wighte and

## Notes

wilde of thoght', is thirty years old, and Abraham, who is 'alde and alle vnwelde', is 100 years old.

137. Middle Age was wearing homely, workaday clothes. 'Russet' was a reddish-brown woollen cloth, coarse in texture and hardwearing. Cf. *PP*. B viii. 1, &c., and Skeat's note, p. 132.

138. Cf. *WW*. 95, '... girde in the myddis'.

141. Cf. *Morte A*. 3571, 'With renttes and reches ...'.

144. **pufilis**: Gollancz emends to *pu[r]filis*, i.e. 'borders for robes', but there seems to be a case for retaining the manuscript reading. Place-name evidence points to the existence of an OE. word \**pofel*, which may be connected with *poffle* mentioned in *OED*. and in *EDD*. Instances cited are from the eighteenth and nineteenth centuries, meaning 'a small parcel of land', but *OED*. cites also the place-name *Max poffil*, now Maxpoffle in Scotland, mentioned in 1317. A. H. Smith in *English Place-Name Elements* (Cambridge, 1956) notes also the forms *Pouelingtun* (Domesday Book) and OE. *on pofle* (now Pool), from the Yorkshire West Riding, and *Prestpofle* (1391), from Northumberland. The meaning and origin of \**pofel* are unknown, and its connexion with *poffle* is not certain, but the sense 'small pieces of land' fits the context here better than does the sense of *pu[r]filis*.

146. **mendis**: For the sense 'increase', cf. the York play *The Harrowing of Hell* 79, 'my mirthe to mende'.

147. A steward was the representative of the lord of the manor; he would supervise the bailiff and other officers, and act as a general overseer for the domestic and business affairs of an estate. **Storrours**: 'store-keepers', or perhaps more specifically, 'stock-men', 'herdsmen'; see *OED*. s.v. Storer.

148. Gollancz reads 'clerkes of countours', presumably 'treasurers' clerks'; but the courts would be held by the 'countours', not by their clerks. *Countours* surely has its legal significance here: see Glossary, and *OED*. s.v. † Countour, 2.

152. **lenyde**: probably pt. 3 s. '(who) leant (over)', with suppression of the rel. pron., rather than an adjectival pp., as Gollancz glosses it. J. M. Steadman, Jr. (*Mod. Phil.* xxi. 10), notes the omission of the rel. pron. as a characteristic of the style of this poem; other examples are in ll. 104, 275, 427, 626.

158. Cf. the description of Avarice in *PP*. B v. 190: 'He was bitelbrowed and baberlipped also.'

164. The manuscript has clearly *hopynge*, not *hapynge*. For *hoping* = 'belief', cf. *Wars Alex*. 4518, 'ȝe haue na hoping in þat hathill at on hiȝe sittis'. This sense of *hope* seems to be confined to the N. dialects of ME.: see *OED*. s.v. Hope, v. † 4.

175. **wele ... wirchip**: one of the commonest alliterative phrases.

176. **My playstere of paramours**: for the idea of the lady as a physician, cf. Chaucer's *Book of the Duchess* 39-40.

**my lady with pappis full swete**: Gollancz omits *my lady*. But the

## Notes

long first dip is possible; or there may be three full stresses, as in a few other possible instances in the second half-line: see Introduction, 'Metre', p. xxx.

178. **and heghely I a-vowe**: cf. *Siege Jer*. 199, '& heyly y a-fowe'. 179–81 may be compared with *GGK*. 91 ff.

180. **gesserante**. The jesserant was a light coat of mail, 'composed of splints or small plates of metal riveted to each other, or to a lining of some stout material' (Fairholt's *Costume in England*, ed. H. A. Dillon, ii. 260).

**[with] onere**: manuscript *onere*. To omit *with* is perhaps a more likely scribal error than to write *onere* for *ones* (as Gollancz emends). *OED*. notes several examples of the spelling *onnere*.

184. There may be an echo of this line in *Mum & S*. i. 61: 'For all was felawis and felawschepe þat ӡe with ferde.' There is a similar turn of phrase in *WW*. 5, 'For nowe alle es witt and wyl[l]e that we with delyn'. The idea of worldly activities being but 'fantome' was frequently expressed in the Middle Ages: cf. the lyric beginning 'Al it is fantam þat we mid fare', No. 43 in *Religious Lyrics of the XIVth Century*, ed. Carleton Brown.

189. That is, he uses his horse only for pleasure, not for work on the land or for carrying merchandise: cf. *WW*. 240, 'Bot a cuttede capill to cayre with to his frendes'.

190 ff. Cf. the injunctions of Winner to Waster in *WW*. 288–93.

193. **wonne, wy, in thi witt**: i.e. 'keep your wits about you!'

199. **one this launde lengen**: a variant of the very common *lengen in londe*: cf. *Destr. Troy* 7617, &c. With this line, and 206, cf. *Siege Jer*. 83–84:

> Me wer leuer, at þat londe ; le[ngede] þat y wer,
> Þan alle þe gold oþer good ; þat euer god made.

200. **stele-wede**: a rare word, belonging to the poetic vocabulary. Apparently the only other examples of it are in *Destr. Troy* 9634, *Sc. F*. 363.

201. **here-wedys** also is rare; cf. *Beowulf* 1897, and *Wars Alex*. 1010.

202. Cf. *Destr. Troy* 13824, *Morte A*. 3761.

204. Cf. *Rauf Coilӡear* 780, 'For to hald that I haue hecht ...'.

208 ff. Cf. *Siege Jer*. 887–9, especially 887: 'Ride to þe reuer ; & rer vp þe foules'. *Reuere* here and in 217 probably has the sense 'riverbank', 'banks of a stream', rather than 'river': see *OED*. s.v. River † 2, and quotations; and Manly's note, Chaucer, *Canterbury Tales*, pp. 630–1.

209. For the epithet *hawtayne*, cf. Chaucer's *L.G.W*. 1120.

209–45. This is the fullest and liveliest account we have of a hawking scene in the fourteenth century, the heyday of falconry. There was a fully-developed 'science' of falconry, just as there was

## Notes

of hunting, with a separate word for every possible act done to or by the hawk and for every incident in its flight or chase; and so there arose 'an endless array of appropriate verbs, nouns, and adjectives, the misapplication of any one of which stamped the offender as no gentleman' (D. H. Madden, *The Diary of Master William Silence* (1897), note ii, p. 363). Most of the details and technical terms used in 209-45 can be explained or paralleled from the various treatises on falconry which exist; for a select list of these, see Bibliography, IV. 2.

211. 'Lease, or Leash, is a small [i.e. narrow] long thong of Leather by which the Faulconer holdeth his Hawk fast, folding it many times about his Finger' (Nicholas Cox, edition of 1677, p. 159).

212. **keppyn**. This verb is used here in what was probably its original sense, 'to lay hold' with the hands (and hence, later, 'to watch, guard'). *Keppyn*, with (presumably) short *e*, may be a N. form: see *OED*. s.v. Kep, v.

Hawks in captivity were always hooded when they were not in flight: this kept them tranquil, and so by preventing too much movement or fluttering it helped to avoid injury to the feathers. The hood was a little cap of soft leather, carefully made to fit close to the hawk's head and keep out any ray of light; there was, of course, a slit for the beak and nostrils. To make it more comfortable, the parts over the eyes were often filled out with soft green velvet. The hoods were usually fine pieces of workmanship: those used at Court would be specially magnificent, embroidered perhaps with gold and pearls and surmounted with feathers of birds of paradise.

213. **towre**: a technical term for the soaring flight of the hawk. Cf. Turb., *Hauking*, 53, '... hye fleeing and towre hawkes, as the Falcon, the Laner, and the Sacre be', and Skelton's phrase 'hawke of the towre' (*Magnyfycence, Garlande of Laurell*). *Towre* is from OF. *tour*, a turn, flight, wheel; it was probably confused in popular etymology with the word 'tower', late OE. and early ME. *tūr*: cf. *Macbeth*, II. iv. 12, 'A falcon towering in her pride of place'.

214. **bellys**: 'She must haue twoo good belles, to the ende she may the better be founde and hearde, when she stirreth or scratteth' (Turb., *Hauking*, 100). The bells were attached low down, one at the back of each leg. As one bell was a tone higher than the other, they did not sound in unison; so the noise they made was very distinct, and they could often be heard even when the hawk was too high in the air to be seen. These little bells were very carefully made, and often had the owner's crest on them. They generally came from Italy; Milan was noted for them.

**blethely**: probably from OE. *blīðe* 'glad' rather than OE. *blēað* 'weak, gentle, timid', with which its meanings do not appear to be associated. J. K. Wallenberg, 35-36 (op. cit. in note on *Kest* 68), suggests that the *e* in the adv. forms may possibly be explained as 'a shortening of the originally long vowel'. The occurrence of *blethely*

## Notes

in a N. Midl. dialect of ME. is not exceptional: *OED.* notes examples from *Cursor Mundi* and Richard Rolle.

217. Cf. 208, and note.

218. **Sowssches** = *sowsses* or *sowses*. (Cf. *lessches* < OF. *lesse*, 211; *Paresche* 305.) A phrase *at (the) souce, source, souse, sowrce*, &c., meaning 'in the act of rising from the ground', is fairly common in the treatises on falconry. See *OED.* s.v. Source, sb. † 2a, † Souse sb.³ *Souce, souse*, &c., seem to be variants of *source*, from the pp. of F. *sourdre*, 'to rise or spring'. Their use in E. as a verb is not so well attested, but see *OED.* s.v. †Source, v.¹ and a quotation from Gavin Douglas's *Aeneid*, where *soursand*, used of an eagle, means 'soaring up'. *Sowssches* might possibly, therefore, be a form of this verb, used transitively, meaning '(they) make them spring up, rise'; but this is a very doubtful use of it. It is more likely to be a form of the word *souse* = 'heavy blow'; 'to strike, beat severely'. (See *OED.* s.v. Souse, sb.² and Souse, v.²) The meaning 'to strike, beat' is common until the eighteenth century, and is recorded in dialect glosses in the nineteenth century. *Sowssches*, then, may be a form of *souse* v.² and mean 'beat up'; *OED.* compares MHG., MLG. *sûs*, 'noise, din'.

**to seruen thaire hawkes**: to 'serve' a hawk was a technical term in falconry: see Glossary.

219. **tercelettes**: tercelet is a general term for the male of any kind of hawk, but in the language of falconry it seems to have been used more specifically for the male of the peregrine falcon or the goshawk. For a note on its possible etymology, see *OED.* s.v. Tercelet.

220. **Laners and lanerettis.** These were regarded as rather quiet, gentle hawks. OF. *lanier* is evidently a substantival use of the adj. *lanier* 'cowardly'; Godefroy (*Dictionnaire*) quotes 'le lannier . . . est mol et sans courage', and Turb. speaks of the 'gentle Lanner'. The section on Hawking in *Boke St. A.* ends with a list, probably traditional, of the different kinds of hawks and the people to whom they 'belong'; 'a Lanare and a Lanrell' 'belong to a Squyer'.

**lightten to thes endes**: Gollancz glosses *lightten* as 'alight', *endes* as 'regions, parts'. But *ende* in this context is more likely to be derived from OE. *ened* 'duck'. (Cf. *Havelok* 1241, 'Ne þe ende, ne þe drake'.) *Lightten* (OE. *līhtan*) then may be glossed as 'descend, swoop down (upon)'. It was characteristic of the male peregrine and the lanner to make a sudden pounce down, from some height, on to their prey.

223. **With hoo and howghe**: these were the falconer's traditional cries when the game was being roused from cover. Cf. *Boke St. A.*, sig. d iv, 'then smyte youre tabur. and cry huff. huff. huff and make the fowle to spryng. and with that noyse the fowle wil rise and the hàwke wyll nym it', and Simon Latham's *Second Booke of Faulconrie*, 47: '. . . he shall secretly let the Partridge spring, with such iudgement in the deliuery, that the Hawke may discerne and see it, and crying with a lowd voyce Howe, howe, howe, that shee

## Notes

may haue vnderstanding, and learne to know the word of aduertisement or warning'. E. B. Michell in *The Art and Practice of Hawking* (1900) remarks that 'Hoo, ha, ha!' is 'an old-fashioned cry for encouraging a falcon to stoop from her pitch' (p. 122), and 'The orthodox cry for encouraging the hawk when the game is . . . routed out is "Howit! howit!"' (p. 125). So probably 'hoo' was the cry that warned the falcon when to swoop, 'howghe' the cry of encouragement when she was attacking her prey.

The flight of the heron, according to Turb., is 'the most noblest and stately flight that is, and pleasant to behold' (p. 160).

**224. brynges hym to sege,** i.e. drive him into the open, to a defensive position by the water-side. The heron is said to be 'at siege' when he takes his stand by the water-side patiently watching his prey, just as an army might settle down to besiege a castle; the word was also used collectively for a company of herons (as in *Boke St. A.*, 'A Sege of heronnys'). The phrase 'at siege' lingered on into the eighteenth century: cf. William Somerville, *Field Sports*, 1742, p. 14:

> Lo! at his Siege the Hern,
> Upon the bank of some small purling Brook,
> Observant stands to take his scaly prize;
> Himself another's Game.

**228. his,** i.e. the heron's. The heron with its long sharp bill could be a fierce and determined opponent, often more than a match for the hawk.

**230–1.** The heron's wings were twisted or crossed to prevent them from injuring the hawk. Cf. Turb., *Hauking*, 154, '. . . runne in apace to help hir, and crossing the fowles wings, let your Hawke take hir pleasure on it', and James Campbell, *A Treatise of Modern Falconry* (1773), 234, '. . . you must always cross their wings as soon as you can, least by their beating they hurt your hawk'.

**232.** Gollancz supplies *pyth* for *maryo*, but it is doubtful whether the poet would have used this term. The marrow out of the bones was the falcon's 'reward'. Cf. *The Booke of Hawkyng after Prince Edwarde Kyng of Englande*, 299 (see Bibliography, IV. 2), '. . . then kutte the grete bonys of the wynggis and with a penne draw oute the merowe', and cf. Turb., *Hauking*, 113, '. . . take y$^e$ marrow of the bone in the Hearons wing, and giue it your Hawke'. A large, thick glove (sometimes embroidered with gold, in royal establishments) was worn by the falconer on his left hand, to protect it from the hawks.

**233.** i.e. 'And "whoops" them in to the quarry—they crushed it to death'. *Thaym* refers to the hawks, *hym* to their prey, the heron. *Quotes* here is probably an error for *quopes*: cf. W *whopis*. The 'whoop' was a signal for the falcon to come in to her quarry; cf. Turb., *Hauking*, 156–7: 'If a Falcon use to rake out after checke or otherwise, and leane out so farre, as neyther for whouping, lewring, or for

## Notes

casting the Hawkes gloue about your head, she will come in againe to the flight . . . you muste followe after hir, lewring and whouping a good [sic], proffering hir to the lewre, to make hir put in hir head againe.' W has *to whirry*: 'to *the* whirry' was probably the correct phrase. The term 'quarry' is taken from the vocabulary of hunting: the hounds' reward was so called, because it was eaten on the hide, 'sur le quir'. In hawking the word came to mean 'the game at which a hawk was flown, whether it was taken or not' (H. Dryden, Twiti, 60).

234. **quyrres,** W **wharris.** Gollancz has *quysses* here, but the manuscript reading is clearly *quyrres*, i.e. 'quarries'. For the use of this verb, cf. Turb., *Hauking*, 121: 'But at the beginning rewarde hir and feede hir well vpon the quarrey . . . When she is well in bloude, and well quarried, then let her flee with other hawkes. . . .'

**quotes**: poss. 'gluts, satisfies their appetite': see *OED*. s.v. Quat, v.$^1$ 1 b, Quot.

**quyppeys**: 'whips', or 'slashes': presumably the falconer did this with his rod, perhaps 'to rere vp the fewles' (217). One would expect from the context that he did something to bring in his hawks, since 235 means 'encourages them especially to leave checks'. Some of the hawks have been quarried, but perhaps others are still on the wing, and the better to encourage these to leave their checks, he slashes loudly (with his rod) to make the game rise from cover; or perhaps as a peremptory sign for these hawks to come in. If they went after check and did not seize their legitimate prey, they were probably not quarried—'Than henttis thaym one honde and hodes thaym theraftire' 236. The poet wants to convey something of the excitement of the scene, and he moves from one action to another without always giving us the connecting links.

235. **ecchekkes**: 'checks', a technical term in falconry: '*Check*, or to kill *check* is when Crows, Rooks, Pies, or other Birds coming in the view of the Hawk, she forsaketh her natural flight to fly at them' (John Ray, *The Ornithology of Francis Willughby*, 1678, p. 397). Cf. Turb., *Hauking*, 110: 'If your Hawke go out to anye checke, and kill a Dooue or a Crow, or anye other checke and feede vpon it, . . . seeme not roughly to rebuke hir at first.'

237. **Cowples vp theire cowers**: at the back of the hood were fastened two leather braces (*cowers*, F. *cuir*). Each brace was passed through three slits cut in the leather at the back of the hood and crossed to the opposite side. Thus two ends of the braces, pulled from opposite sides, would draw the hood tight, while the other two would relax it. In the language of falconry, 'to couple up the cowers' is to draw up the braces to close the hood tight over the falcon's head.

238. There was a short leather strap (the 'jess'), fastened round each of the falcon's legs; at the free end each strap was attached to a 'varvel', and to this also the swivel of the leash was fastened. The

## Notes

varvels were little rings, generally of silver, and flattened so that the owner's name could be engraved on them: '... put on her Jesses made of soft Leather, at the end thereof fix two Varvels, the one may bear your Coat of Arms, the other your Name, that if she chance to be lost, they that take her up may know where to return her' (Nicholas Cox, *The Gentleman's Recreation*, 193).

239. The lure was a device made with bits of leather, cloth or wool, to which talons or wings were fixed, and baited with a piece of flesh. This was used to lure the hawk back when it seemed in danger of straying. J. C. Belany in his *Treatise upon Falconry* (1841), p. 207, remarks that 'The lure is a most essential instrument in the art of falconry. It may be said to be to the falconer what the helm of the ship is to the mariner, because it is by the signals made by it alone that the movements of the bird in the air are controlled.'

243. Cf. 235 and note.

245. **Be-dagged**: see *OED*. s.v. Dag v.¹, †1 and 2. *Be-dagged* may be used in the sense in which Caxton uses *dagged* (*Aesop*, III. xvii, 'Al to-fowled and dagged'), i.e. dirtied, muddied. Or the poet may possibly have had in mind the 'dagged' garments, with their edges slashed into long pointed pendants, which were fashionable in his time. The jags of mud, or the tufts of wet hair, along the sides of the spaniels' coats, made them look as if they were 'dagged'.

**enewede**: 'And if it happyn as it dooth oftimes the fowle for fere of yowre hawke woll spryng and fall ayen in to the Ryuer. or the hawke sees hir. and so lie styll and dare not arise . ye shall say then yowre hawke hath ennewed the fowle in to the Ryuer . and so shall ye say and ther be moo fowles in the Ryuer then thatt yowre hawke nymmyth if they darenot arise for fere of yowre hawke' (*Boke St. A.*, d ii).

247. Cf. *Morte A*. 3292, 'And ladys me louede, to lappe in theyre armes', and *Wm. P.* 1908, 2153.

248. **clyp ... kysse**: a very common formula. It occurs about ten times in *Wm. P.* alone.

250–2. Cf. 1516–19 in *GGK.*, where the poet dwells on the typical theme of chivalric romance. The author of *Parl.* is thinking perhaps of the 'epic' type of 'romance', such as *Morte A*. or poems dealing with Alexander the Great or the legends of Troy, rather than those in which the spirit of chivalry (and the 'love-element') was strong.

254. Cf. *GGK*. 1655, 'As coundutes of kryst-masse & carole3 newe', and *ON*. 482–3. The condut was a part-song, generally with three voices: a tenor leading, and two descants. In origin it was probably the liturgy sung in procession to the altar, but it came to be associated with singing, and often dancing too, on secular occasions. 'Carolles' were plainsong accompanied by dancing, usually ring-dances.

257. **wandrynge and woo**: one would expect *wandreth* rather than *wandrynge*. *Wandreth* is very common in early ME. (as in the

## Notes

'Katherine Group' and *Ancrene Wisse*), in alliterative combinations, usually with *wo*: e.g. 'for wa ne for wontreaðe', in *Seinte Iuliene* 132 (Bodl. 34). For later uses of this formula, cf. *Destr. Troy* 10097, 11191, 11514; *Wars Alex.* 528; *Qu. Love* 30; and *DL.* 250, 440, 451 (here it is 'wondering (once "wandering") and woe'). ON. *vandrǣði* meant 'difficulty, trouble, distress'; the phrase in *Parl.* and *DL.* may be a corruption, not necessarily scribal, of the early alliterative formula.

The general sense and tone of 257-60 are reminiscent of *WW*. 440-4.

258. **dole**: probably from OF. *doel* as in 344, &c. ME. *dol* < OE. (*ge-*)*dāl* appears to mean in ME. 'alms' or 'charitable gift' rather than 'wealth', i.e. what one owns. Thus *there-with* in 259 refers back to *gudes* in 257, not to *dole*.

260. Gollancz omits *haste longe*.

261. **rothelede.** This curious word occurs twice in *Pur.*: 59, 'Al is roþeled & rosted ryȝt to þe sete', and 890, '& vchon roþeled to þe rest þat he reche moȝt'. Both contexts are difficult; see Menner's note on 890. Gollancz in *Cleanness* p. 91 differentiates the form in 890 from that in 59 and connects it with 'rottle', 'rattle'. If *rothelede* in *Parl.* is connected with 'rattle' (cf. W *ratild*), the meaning could be 'croaked', or perhaps 'railed, scolded': see *OED.* s.v. Rattle, v.¹, 3. Another possible derivation is from ON. *ráða*, ME. *rothe*, 'to counsel, advise', and also, apparently, 'to rave, talk nonsense'; see *OED.* s.v. †Rothe, v.¹ and v.²

262. 'For a dozen or more years past, you and Thrift have been at loggerheads.' Gollancz compares *Morte A.* 2216 for a similar use of 'thirtene'. 'Rest . . . Iapid' in W can be made to give a feeble sense, but is obviously corrupt.

263. Probably [full] (cf. W) has dropped out before ȝore. Cf. *WW*. 321, 'For now I se it es full sothe þat sayde es full ȝore'.

269. Cf. *Wars Alex.* 3879, 'Seis ensampill at my-selfe & seke ȝe na ferre'. *Sekis* might be imper. pl.; but the 'and' suggests rather that it is 1 pr. s. and thus an example of the N. 1 s. ending (*i*)*s*. There is no need to emend, with Gollancz, to *seke*.

270. **ȝape of my dedys**: variations of this phrase are extremely common in the alliterative poems. A similar tag, very common, is (*ferse*, &c.) *men of armes*; cf. *Parl.* 349, 351.

271. **euerrous**: probably related to OE. *gīfre* 'greedy'. Cf. *Destr. Troy*, ȝener 3955, ȝenerus 3917, &c. (read ȝeuer, ȝeuerus). This word survives today in Sc. and Nth. dialects as *aiverie, every, yevery*, &c., meaning 'hungry, greedy, eager'; see *EDD.* s.v. Aiverie, adj. The scribe of W was unfamiliar with the word: he writes *emerus, amerous*, but once *everus*.

272. **styffe in a stourre**: a very common tag in the ME. rhyming romances, but rare in the poems of the alliterative revival. There

## Notes

seems to be only one other instance of it outside the rhyming romances, in *Wars Alex.* 1322.

275. Gollancz reads *as*, but the manuscript reads clearly *es*. See note on 152.

279. The earliest recorded instance in *OED.* of 'to muck' = 'lay manure' is from the fifteenth-century *Promptorium Parvulorum*. W has either *mucherd* or *mutherd*, it is hard to determine which. *Mucherd* could be connected with the v. 'to mucker', of which the earliest meaning, used transitively, seems to be 'to hoard', from 'muck' applied in a derogatory way to 'money' or 'riches'. *Mok(e)re* 'to hoard' occurs in Chaucer, e.g. *Troilus and Criseyde*, iii. 1375. It is recorded as an intr. v. 'to moil' under the year 1566, but this apparently is a rare use. (See also *EDD*. s.v. Mucker, v.) *Mutherd* might possibly be connected with the dialectal verb 'moider', 'moither', 'to labour hard, toil'; this fits the sense better than 'hoard, moil'. See *OED.* s.v. Moider, *EDD*. s.v. Moither.

280. **ploughe-londes**: strictly speaking, the plough-land was as much land as could be tilled every year by the plough drawn by eight oxen; its extent averaged roughly 120 acres. As a unit of assessment, this term seems to have been used mainly in the N. and E. counties in ME., corresponding to the *Hide* of the S. and W. See *OED.* s.v. Plough-land.

284. Cf. 155; and *Morte A.* 2769, 3304, *Wm. P.* 891.

286. **than sowed myn hert**: cf. *WW*. 215, 'it sowede [MS. sowrede] bothe myn eghne'. *Sow, sou*, &c. (see *OED.* s.v. Sow, v.²), seems to be a Sc. and N. word. Its usual meaning is 'smarted': according to Jamieson it is used of a tingling or stinging sensation. Cf. Minot, v, l. 12, where *sowed* is synonymous with *smerted*. Its origin is not certain, but it may derive from ON. *svíða* 'to smart' (of a wound), 'burn'. Cf. *Ancrene Riwle, suwinde* (Cott. MS. Nero, other manuscripts *suhinde, suinde*) 'biting, smarting', which may be an earlier form of this word. If so, it seems to be the only recorded instance outside the N. area.

290. i.e. 'Look on me as in a mirror, wherein you may see your own fate'. There may be an echo of this line in *Buke H.* 970, 'Now mark ȝour mirour be me, all maner of man'. Cf. also Henryson's poem *The Ressoning Betwixt Deth and Man*:

> Deth. O Mortall Man! behold, tak tent to me,
> Quhilk sowld thy mirrour be baith day and nicht;
> . . . . .
> Man. Now quhat art thow, that biddis me thus tak tent
> And mak ane mirrour day and nicht of the ?

(Elde in *Parl.* speaks as Death's messenger.) For other instances of this use of 'mirror', see the note by F. J. Amours on *Gol. & Gaw.* 1226–32, in *Scottish Alliterative Poems*, S.T.S. 27, 38 (1891–2, 1896–7).

## Notes

**295. men one this molde**: one of the ancient alliterative phrases, OE. *men ofer moldan*. It is very common in ME.

**296.** Cf. *Morte A.* 3496, 'Bot I will passe . . . þis pas', and *Somer Soneday* 26 and 27, 'So passede I þe pas'.

**300. firste**: possibly *areste* or *erste* in the original; cf. 464. The ultimate source of this account of Hector, as Gollancz notes, is probably Guido delle Colonne's *Hystoria Troiana*; see *Destr. Troy*, especially 3877 ff.

**308.** Manuscript *xix and ix mo* (W *nynety & ix*). Cf. *Destr. Troy* 14006-21, a list headed 'Thies Ector Slogh With Hond, Of Kynges', where only eighteen names are mentioned.

**310.** This line is repeated at 566.

**311 ff.** Cf. the account of Hector's death in *Destr. Troy* 8643 ff.

**313.** Hector had just encountered a king and taken him prisoner. With his shield temporarily shot behind him and his breast bare he was leading the prisoner off to his tent, when Achilles, seeing his advantage, gripped a spear and 'Woundit hym wickedly, as he away loked' (*Destr. Troy* 8658).

**of were**: i.e. 'in war'. For this unusual use of the prep., see *OED*. s.v. Of, 52, †55, †56.

**314-15.** Accounts of the death of Achilles differ very much; this tradition probably comes ultimately from Dictys Cretensis (iii. 29).

**315. With the wyles of a woman**: cf. *Destr. Troy* 668, 'Thurghe wyles of [a] woman'; *GGK*. 2415, 'þurʒ wyles of wymmen'.

**320. rialeste of araye**: cf. 186, and *Rauf Coilʒear* 478, '. . . the Ryallest of array'.

**322. semblen**: probably hist. pr., 'assemble (themselves)': there is no need to adopt Gollancz's emendation *semble[d]*.

**serely**: see Glossary. Gollancz emends to *s[ar]rely*.

**325.** Manuscript *Puntusiliu þe quene*. Gollancz supplies [*prowde*]; an adj. like *prowde* or *prise* may have dropped out, but it is not essential for the metre; cf. 486, and note. For other examples in ME. of the use of 'pass' in the sense 'die', see *OED*. s.v. Pass, v. A. IV, 11.

**329.** *Ercules*, 'Hercules': probably a mistake for 'Achilles'.

**full euerrous**: Gollancz omits *full* here.

**331. Dittes and Dares**: Dictys Cretensis and Dares Phrygius, who were alleged to have written eyewitness accounts of the fall of Troy, made known by Benoît de Sainte-Maure and Guido delle Colonne. These entirely fictitious works were much referred to by medieval writers on the story of Troy, who regarded them as the best authorities, and despised Homer. This curious attitude is well illustrated in the Prologue to *Destr. Troy* 27-77.

**332.** The account of Alexander in *Parl.* is mainly a résumé of some of his adventures in the East, of how he vanquished the Indian king Porus and then captured Babylon. The source may have been Jacques

## Notes

de Longuyon's *Vœux du Paon* (c. 1312), either directly or through an English version now lost. A fifteenth-century Scottish version of the poem, including the earlier portion, *Li Fuerres de Gadres*, was printed in or about 1580 by Alexander Arbuthnet; this was reprinted by the Bannatyne Club in 1831. It has since been edited (with the French text) for the Scottish Text Society by Dr. Graeme Ritchie (*The Buik of Alexander*, S.T.S., N.S., 12, 17, 21, and 25 (1921–9)).

334. **Ercules boundes**: probably a reference to two pillars or rocks thought to have been set up by Hercules at the end of his journey to the extreme west to obtain the cattle of Geryon. (See *Destr. Troy* 310–15, Lydgate's *Troy Book* 600–4, 610–13, *Kyng Alisaunder* 5583–4 (B) and the note by G. V. Smithers, E.E.T.S. 237 (1957), p. 131.)

335–6. These lines have no parallel in *Vœux*. There are many references in medieval literature to the idea of Enoch and Elias as the challengers of Antichrist, but the allusion in *Parl.* is noteworthy in that they are thought of as being confined in some way—*vnclosede be þay neuer*—until the coming of Antichrist. There is no need, however, to assume, with Gollancz, that the poet has confused Elias and Enoch with the Gog and Magog of the Alexander legends. M. Lascelles, in 'Alexander and the Earthly Paradise in Mediaeval English Writings' (*Medium Ævum*, v. 31 ff., 79 ff.), suggests that the poet may have known a version of the story of Alexander's voyage to the Earthly Paradise, where, it was believed, 'Enoch and Elias lived, rapt away from earth before death could reach them, ready to return when they should be needed and challenge Antichrist'. Miss Lascelles gives abundant evidence from medieval writings of the association of Enoch and Elias with the Earthly Paradise; see also G. Cary, *The Medieval Alexander*, 133, 150–1. In *Parl.* 335 it is possible that 'Ther' refers not to 'Ercules boundes' but to 'þe iles of the Oryent', i.e. the Earthly Paradise; and Miss Lascelles would read 332–5 as 'Alexander conquered all the world, from the eastern islands to the Pillars of Hercules—the eastern islands where Enoch and Elias await the coming of Antichrist'. 'Vnclosede' in 336 would then refer to Enoch and Elias, who will be released from the Earthly Paradise upon the coming of Antichrist.

338. Manuscript *Iazon þe Iewe* (W *Iosue þe Iewe ... slevis*). Perhaps the poet himself was inaccurate about the Jason story, and 'Iosue' in W was an attempt to make sense of 'Iewe'; but Gollancz's emendation of *Iewe* to [*Gr*]*ewe* is a tempting one.

339. The poet deals rather summarily with the story of 'The Forray of Gadderis'. See *Buik*, vol. i.

340. Manuscript *godfraye* is obviously an error for *gadyfere* (as in 343), who is referred to as 'Gadifer des Laris' or 'du Larris' in *Li Fuerres de Gadres* and *Vœux*.

344. **that doughty**: i.e. Gadifer, who was unhorsed and slain by

## Notes

Emenidus. *Makede* might be a pp., as Gollancz glosses it; if so, the construction would be unusual. It is more likely to be a pt. s.: the subject would be Emenidus, who as we are told in 'The Forray of Gadderis' made lamentation over Gadifer as the bravest of knights. (Cf. 359, note.) 'Doughty . . . dede' is very common.

**346. Arayed hym for to ryde:** cf. *Alexander A* 418, 'All redie araied to ryden hem till'.

**347. Meneduse ... of Artage:** i.e. Emenidus, who is described in the Sc. version as 'de Archade', and 'Constabill and ledere Of all the Kingis oist in were'. The French has 'd'Arcage', and 'celui d'Arcadïon'. *c* and *t* are very much alike in this manuscript, but the letter here is probably *t*. W has 'heritage', so *t* may have stood in the common original of the two manuscripts.

**353-9.** Cassamus was an old man, the brother of Gadifer the elder; he greatly desired vengeance on Emenidus. *Vœux* describes how Alexander met and reasoned with Cassamus, who at last agreed to forgo vengeance and to make his peace with Emenidus. Cassamus told the king that Gadifer had left two sons, young Gadifer and Betis, and a daughter Fesonas; and that Clarus, the wicked king of Ind, was seeking to dispossess the heirs and to wed Fesonas against her will. Alexander promised to set things right, as a token of his respect for Gadifer.

**354. Fesome, W feysoun:** *Vœux* has 'Phezon', *Avowis* 'Effesoun'. This may correspond with the *Fa(a)cen* mentioned several times in *Kyng Alisaunder*. Smithers in his gloss (p. 215) derives *Fa(a)cen* from the *Phasiacen* of the *Epistola Alexandri Macedonis ad Aristotelem* (ed. B. Kuebler, Leipzig, 1888). It is the 'country of the river Phasis or Rion, which flows into the Black Sea'.

**356. Fozome,** ? i.e. 'Fesonas', the daughter of Gadifer of Larris; **Fozayne,** a variant of *Fesome*, 'Epheson'. The similarity in sound between 'Epheson' and 'Fesonas', combined with the usual ME. tendency to vary spellings of proper names, has produced a confusing mixture of forms in this passage. Presumably the meaning is that Clarus had alarmed Fesonas (in trying to force her to wed him), and had besieged Epheson. The allusion to Fesonas here seems odd when she is mentioned again in 357, and it is just possible that *Fozome* is a variant of *Fozayne*—i.e. 'had alarmed (or attacked) Epheson (i.e. the district around?) and besieged Epheson (itself)'. **his fomen** in W avoids the confusion of names, but is obviously scribal.

**357. Dame Fozonase:** Fesonas; see above. K. Schumacher's suggestion, p. 173 (see Bibliography, III), 'that he fayne wold love' for the second half-line, is too far from the original. Examples of this type of line occur so frequently that there is no need to emend.

**358.** In W this line is misplaced (360). W **ayrathid** may be a form of *agrathid* (see *OED*. s.v. Agraith), but is probably a scribal error.

## Notes

**359. In mendys of Amenyduse þat he hade mys-done:** i.e. to make amends for what Emenidus had done amiss (in slaying such a valiant knight as Gadifer the elder). Gollancz's 'maltreated' for *mys-done* is not in accord with the story.

**360. Facron:** presumably, the river which flowed through Epheson. The F. text has 'Faron', the Sc. text 'Pharoune'. See note on 354.

**361. W Tolid vp his tentes.** Cf. *Wars Alex.* 3860, &c., 'He gert tild vp his tentis'; and *Destr. Troy* 1088, &c., *Sc. F.* 253.

**364.** 'Idores and Edease': see *Buik*, ii. 505-8.

**365-7.** The story of the vows is told at some length in the second part of *Vœux* (*Buik*, iii, especially 5171 ff.). During the siege of Epheson some of Clarus's men, including his son Porrus, were captured and taken prisoner, but were treated with courtesy. One day when Porrus was walking in a courtyard, he saw a peacock and slew it. The bird was roasted and borne into the hall for a feast. Cassamus proposed that, as was the custom, vows should be made to the peacock, and each man present made a vow. Porrus spoke out proudly that he would take Emenidus's horse from under him in battle. The rest of *Avowis* deals with the ensuing battle and the accomplishment of vows made at the feast.

**369.** Cf. *Destr. Troy* 1333, 'Bere the batell a-bake', and 5957, 'The batell on backe was borne to þe se'.

**370.** The 'bolde Bawderayne' was one of the men who had been taken captive with Porrus. In *Avowis* 1355-6 he is called 'Cassiell ... That lord of Bauderis was and Medy', but after that he is referred to as 'the Bauderane' ('li Baudrains'). His vow had been that he would wrest the sword from the hands of Alexander himself, amid all his men.

**371. kynges:** K. Schumacher (op. cit. 173) suggests *beryns* for *kynges*; but see Introduction, 'Alliteration', 4, p. xxxii.

**377 ff.** Cassamus had vowed that if he came upon Clarus dismounted in the field, he would relieve him and set him on his steed again, 'for Porrus saik'. This he did in the course of the battle; but in the end it was by Cassamus that Clarus was slain (*Buik*, iv. 9557-72).

**380.** Cassamus was in his turn slain by a great blow from Porrus, who at this point seemed near to fulfilling his vow. His prowess encouraged the Indians for a time, but it was their last success and they eventually withdrew before Alexander. Porrus himself was captured, and rebuked by Alexander for his outrageous vow; yet because of his valour he was shown every respect, and treated as the hero of the day.

**387-8.** Porrus for his heroism was given the fair Fesonas, who had vowed to wed none but the man whom Alexander should choose.

**389.** Literally, 'the bold ruler of Bauderis from Bauderis'.

## Notes

Evidently the origin of *Bawderayne* was forgotten. 'Sir Casabull his felaw' in W seems to be an invention on the part of the scribe.

390. **bade he no noþer**: cf. *WW*. 239, '. . . biddes he no noþer'.

391–2. **Betys**: one of the brothers of Fesonas. *Buik* also does not mention the other brother, Gadifer, at this point, but the French text says that he was given Lydoine, 'La plus bele qui fust desci en occident'.

394 ff. The story of *Avowis* ends with an account of the great marriage-feast, and a brief allusion to Alexander's journey on to Babylon.

395. Cf. *Pur*. 1373, 'Þer bowed toward Babiloyn burnes so mony'.

396. **Carid[ac]e**: manuscript *Candore*. W preserves the correct form of the name here: Cadace, i.e. Cādace, 'Candace'; but it is curious that in 627 W also has *Candore*. The poet may have confused it with the name of one of Candace's children, Candoile, but it is more likely that bad copying, at some earlier stage of transmission, was responsible for the error; *-ac-* might easily be misread as *-or-*. The fullest account in ME. of Alexander's brief romance with Queen Candace is in *Kyng Alisaunder*: see 6648 ff., 7616 ff. (B). See also *Wars Alex*. 5075 ff. The name *Candace* means 'Queen': it was the title of the queens of Ethiopia in the first century A.D., and was probably transferred to the Alexander legend from Biblical sources: see Acts viii. 27.

398. This line is repeated at 575. Cf. *Siege Jer*. 974, '[Tille] me þe ȝates ben ȝet ;' & ȝolden þe keyes', and 1237; and *Wars Alex*. 2147.

400. Cf. 452: and *Destr. Troy* 11946, *Siege Jer*. 1097.

405–20. The account of Caesar in *Voeux* and in *Avowis* has only a passing reference to the conquest of Britain. Here, the poet gives greater prominence to Caesar's connexions with Britain, and to local traditions concerning him.

407. The term 'Brut' (from 'Brutus', who according to medieval tradition was grandson of Aeneas and the founder of Britain) was originally used only of such works as the *Roman de Brut* of Wace or Laȝamon's *Brut*, but later it came to be applied to any Chronicle of early British history. The poet probably thought of 'the Bruyte' as an author.

408–9. For the tradition that Julius Caesar built the Tower of London, cf. *A Short English Metrical Chronicle* (quoted by Kölbing and Gollancz), ed. E. Zettl, E.E.T.S., O.S. 196 (1934), D. 945–62. This tradition held for a long time; cf. Shakespeare's *Richard III*, III. i. In the reign of Henry VIII, the Salt Tower (in the Inner Ward) was called Julius Caesar's Tower, though it apparently belongs to the reign of William Rufus. Archaeological research, however, has shown that there may have been a Roman fort on the site of the Tower of London: see the *Royal Commission on Historical Monuments*, London, iii. 69 ff. As for the 'condithe', a number of Roman conduits have been excavated in various parts of the City.

411. The 'castelle with cornells full heghe' is certainly not of

## Notes

Roman origin, though tradition has connected Dover Castle with Julius Caesar. See the *Victoria County History of Kent*, iii. 48–49.

413. I have found no other reference to this tradition about the honey. Gollancz quotes an interesting passage from Lambarde's *Perambulation of Kent* (1570) which is probably an echo of the same tradition: 'The castle of Dover (say Lydgate and Rosse) was first builded by Iulius Caesar the Romane Emperour, in memorie of whome, they of the Castell keepe till this day, certeine vessels of old wine and salts, which they affirme to be the remaine of such provision as he brought into it. As touching the which (if they be naturall, and not sophisticate), I suppose them more likelye to have beene of that store, which Hubert de Burgh laid in there. . . .'

414. **rawnsede**: a possible form of this verb in the fourteenth century (see *OED*. s.v. Ransom).

416–20. Cf. *Buik*, iv. 9931–6.

422. **iugge**: this is a correct form for the pl. opt. (cf. *flyte* 264).

424–5. Inaccurate as far as Joshua and Judas Maccabeus are concerned, but it is true of David: the two books of Samuel are in the Vulgate called *Primum Regum* and *Secundum Regum*. Cf. *PP*. C iv. 416–17.

426 ff. The poet has apparently confused the story of Joshua and the crossing of the Jordan with that of Moses leading the Israelites over the Red Sea. The reference to Joshua in *Vœux* and in the Sc. version is brief but accurate and does not mention Pharaoh or the Red Sea— 'The flum Iordane partit he euin in twa'. See Exodus xiv, Joshua iii.

427. **heryet**: see Glossary. Or *heryet* may possibly = 'praised' here (OE. *herian*). *In-to* would then = 'from here to', 'as far as' (cf. *GGK*. 2023).

429. **for radde**: see note on 101.

430. **Ihesu he prayed**: a similar anachronism occurs in the Towneley *Shepherds' Play* I, where the shepherds, on their way to Bethlehem, invoke 'Ihesus . . . Crucyefixus'.

432–7. Exodus xiv. 21–29; cf. Joshua iii. 14–17.

438. **Sathanas**, i.e. 'Satan'. This form has come into English by way of Vulgate Latin and, in some cases, Old French.

440. Cf. *Buik*, iv. 9954–8.

442. **Drightyn[es]**: Gollancz reads *deightyn* here, but the manuscript has clearly *drightyn*.

444–5. Cf. *Morte A*. 3418–19:

> For he slewe with a slynge þe sleyghte of his handis
> Golyas the grette gome, grymmeste in erthe,

and *Awntyrs* 616. The combination 'slogh . . . sleghly', &c., is common in *Destr. Troy*. 'Golias' was the usual spelling for 'Goliath' in med. L.; it occurs in Chaucer too, though the manuscripts of Wyclif's Bible have only 'Goliath' and 'Golie', and Coverdale has only 'Goliath'.

## Notes

446. T has *stone* ... *stongen*, W *stones* ... *stang*. Perhaps the original had *stone* ... *stong* (or *stang*, as Gollancz emends). See 1 Regum xvii. 49 in the Vulgate (1 Samuel xvii. 49).

447. **the deuyll hafe that reche**: cf. *Siege Jer.* 782, 'ȝif ȝe as dogges wol dey ⁖ þe deuel haue þat recche', and *PP.* B vi. 122, 'And though ȝe deye for dole, the deuel haue that reccheth!'

451. i.e. 'For he sent his own knight, Uriah, into peril'. See 2 Regum xi. 14–15. There is no reference in *Vœux* to the story of Bathsheba and Uriah; evidently the author of *Parl.* did not agree that David was 'ouer all sa wele doand' (*Buik*, iv. 9963). David and Uriah are imagined as medieval knights, and David's conduct is seen in the light of the medieval code of chivalry.

453. **Bersabee** is the usual form of the name in ME.; cf. *Barsabe* in *GGK.* 2419. It is derived ultimately from the Septuagint version of the Old Testament.

454–8. The poet's account of Judas Maccabeus agrees closely with that in *Vœux* (*Buik*, iv. 9967–78). See the Apocrypha, 1 and 2 Maccabees.

456–7. **Antiochus**: probably Antiochus Epiphanes, king of Syria in 175–164 B.C. His armies were defeated by Judas Maccabeus, but according to 2 Maccabees ix, he himself died of a disease. Chaucer in the *Monk's Tale* mentions Antiochus as an example of one who 'fil fro heigh prosperitee'. *Appolyne* is probably the Syrian general who was slain in battle by Judas Maccabeus (1 Maccabees iii. 10–12). *Nychanore*: this may be the Nicanor whose army was defeated by Judas Maccabeus and who was himself slain in the battle and later mutilated by his victors (1 Maccabees vii. 39–47); or it may refer to the Nicanor, governor of Judea, whose death and mutilation at the hands of Judas Maccabeus are described in 2 Maccabees xv.

459. **iusters full noble**: cf. *Morte A.* 3412, 'a justere full nobill'.

460. Gollancz substitutes [*of*] for *sythen gane*.

461. **looke**: Gollancz emends this to [*deme*].

464 ff. The account of Arthur in *Vœux* (*Buik*, iv. 9981–92) is brief and mentions only the encounters with various giants.

466. **kynge ... kythe**: one of the commonest alliterative phrases.

468. Cf. *Morte A.* 17, 'Off the ryeall renkys of the rownnde table'; and 719, 2919.

469. Cf. *GGK.* 2448, 'þe maystrés of Merlyn'.

475. **Sir Gawayne the gude**: this was the usual epithet for Sir Gawain: cf. *Awntyrs* 313, *Morte A.* 1368, 2218, &c.

476 ff. All the names in this list of knights were well known in Arthurian legend, but the three mentioned in 476 are less familiar in English versions.

**Sir Askanore**, W *Escamour*: a 'sir Ascamour(e)' ('Ascamore', 'Ascomore') is briefly mentioned five times in Malory: see E. Vinaver's edition (1947), 215, 221, 1048, 1148, 1164. He is called 'Askanere' in

## Notes

*Morte A.* 1739; and 'Achinour' in 1824 is probably the same knight. We hear so little about him that it is hard to say whether he corresponds to the 'Escanor' of French romance, but it is possible that he does. The *Escanor* of Gerard of Amiens (written about 1280) is a long prose romance in which the enmity of Escanor li Biauz and his uncle Escanor le Grant towards Gawain plays an important part. Most of the action takes place in Northumberland, in and around Bamborough; possibly the English poet knew it as a local tale.

**Ewayne** was well known: he appears in Malory as 'Ewayns' or 'Uwayne' 'le Blaunch Maynys', and as 'Yvain, le Chevalier au Lyon', in Chrétien de Troyes' romance. He is most memorable, perhaps, in Welsh legend, as 'Owain ap Urien' in *The Lady of the Fountain*, *The Dream of Rhonabwy*, and other tales in the *Mabinogion*.

**Errake fytz Lake:** *Errake* is the Celtic name 'Arrak': cf. 'Arrake' in *Awntyrs* 654. Erec, son of King Lac, is the hero of the romance *Eréc et Enide* by Chrétien de Troyes (ed. W. Foerster, Halle, 1896 and 1909). This romance corresponds to the Welsh tale of *Geraint the Son of Erbin* in Lady Charlotte Guest's *Mabinogion* (*Gereint and Enid* in the edition by Ellis and Lloyd).

481 ff. **[R]oystone**, MS. *Boystone*, W **Rusten**. In *Vœux* the name is 'Ruiston', in *Avowis* 'Rostrik'. See Geoffrey of Monmouth, *Historia Regum Britanniae*, x. iii (ed. A. Griscom, 1929). The giant is named 'Retho' in the Cambridge and Bern MSS. of the *Historia*, 'Rito' in the Harlech MS. In *Morte A*. the story of the beards is told of the giant on St. Michael's Mount, who is not named. In Malory it is told of a 'kyng Royens', 'Royns', 'Ryens', or 'Ryons', 'of North Walis'. According to one account in the prose *Merlin* (English version chap. xxxi), a king 'Rion' had flayed off the beards of nine kings, and he now wanted Arthur's beard for the tassels. The passage in *Parl.* is noteworthy in that the giant is mentioned as wanting the beards to make a mantle for his 'bride', not for himself.

482. W **Billet** makes sense (see Glossary), but **blyot** accords with other versions of the story.

486. *Athell* (which Gollancz supplies) may have dropped out before *kyng*, but the poet may well have intended this to be an ax/ax line, preferring not to repeat *athell* (484) so soon.

487–8. Geoffrey of Monmouth (x. iii) describes the fight with a giant (not a dragon) on St. Michael's Mount; cf. *Morte A*. 840 ff., and Malory, v. 5 (Vinaver, 202–4). There may have been a tradition about Arthur's having slain a dragon here too, but according to all the known sources the dragon appeared only in a vision. (Cf. Geoffrey of Monmouth, x. ii; *Morte A*. 760–73; Malory v. 4, Vinaver 196–7.)

490. **hym to fote:** a relic of an older construction, OE. *him to fōtum*. W has the Mod. E. construction but preserves the *o* of the old dat. pl.

497 ff. There is no need to emend *Wawayne* to *Ewan* or *Ewayne* on the grounds of alliteration. There are fairly numerous examples in the

## Notes

poem of aa/xx alliteration as in this line, and of ax/ax as in 499; see Introduction, 'Alliteration', 2, 4, p. xxxi. *Ewan* of W may be a scribal correction at a later stage of transmission; cf. note on 546. In the ME. stanzaic *Le Morte Arthur*, and in Malory, it is 'sir Bedwere' or 'Bedyvere' who is ordered to throw Arthur's sword Excalibur into the water (the sea, in *Le Morte Arthur*); in the F. *Mort Artu*, Arthur bids 'Lanselot Gyrfles' throw Excalibur into a lake. No other source mentions either Gawain or Ywain in this connexion, but the poet may have known some other version. However, this rather bald account of Arthur's passing does not suggest that he had any source in front of him. It is not intended to be more than a summary, and was probably drawn from memory. In the other versions, Bedivere or Lancelot Gyrfles tries to evade Arthur's command and to hide the sword; it is only when Arthur has made his request for the third time that the knight obeys. The coming of the boat, too, is treated much more dramatically in these versions.

503. **hiltys**: cf. Malory, 'And there he bounde the gyrdyll aboute the hyltis' (xxi. 5). This use of the pl. with s. meaning goes back to OE. verse, and there are sporadic instances of it down to Shakespeare's time; see *OED*. s.v. Hilt.

504. **brawndeschet**: this act is mentioned in all the versions.

505–6. According to the other English versions, Sir Bedivere goes back to tell the king what he has seen, and helps him to the water-side when the boat appears. In the *Mort Artu*, the king dismisses Lancelot Girfles, who does not see the boat until later, when he is on a hill-side sheltering from rain and looks down to the valley below.

507. Cf. *Wm. P.* 222, 'þat he ne wist in þis world were þei were bi-come'.

513 ff. The poet deals briefly with Godfrey; he was evidently much more interested in Charlemagne, to whom, disregarding chronology, he gives place of honour at the end. His account of Godfrey of Bouillon agrees closely with that in *Vœux*, adding nothing new. (See *Buik*, iv. 10003–9.) The source of information on the achievements of Godfrey of Bouillon was the Latin history composed in Palestine by William of Tyre, between 1163 and 1183. (For an account of this history, see the Introduction to Caxton's *Godeffroy of Boloyne*, ed. Mary N. Colvin, E.E.T.S., E.S. 64 (1893).)

514. **Romanye**: cf. *Avowis* 10004, 'the plane of Romany'. This evidently corresponds to William of Tyre's phrase 'interea de partibus Romaniae', by which he seems to have meant a region in Asia Minor, around and to the west of Antioch. Caxton has 'fro Rome': see *Godeffroy of Boloyne*, 47.

516. **Corborant**: similarly *Corborant* in *Vœux*. This or *Corboran*, *Corbaran*, was the usual French form of the name. Caxton spells it 'Corbagat'. These are versions of the original 'Kerbogha', Sultan of Aleppo at the time of the First Crusade, as Dr. Colvin notes on p. 333 of her edition of *Godeffroy of Boloyne*.

# Notes

**519. wirchipe . . . werlde:** a common alliterative formula.

**520 ff.** The poet has considerably expanded the nine lines on 'Charlemainne' in *Voeux* (7558-66). After naming the 'doussypers', he outlines Charlemagne's campaign against the Saxons, describes some incidents from the *Ferumbras* story, and mentions the treachery at Roncesvalles, the attack on Saragossa, the siege of Narbonne, and the death of Charlemagne at Saint-Denis.

**521. doussypers:** 'twelve peers': a term applied originally to the twelve peers or knights bound in special loyalty to Charlemagne. The derivation of the word (*douze pers*, 'twelve equals') was soon obscured, and there are many perversions of it in the romances: e.g. 'Dutchpeeres', in one manuscript of Barbour's *Bruce*, iii. 440; and the Ashmole MS. of *Sir Ferumbras* has 'doþþeperen'. Consequently the original meaning is often entirely lost: e.g. *Otuel and Roland* 2782 '. . . off the twelf dussypers', and *Sir Degrevant* 1869-70 'þer com in a daunse IX Doseperus of Fraunce'. It comes to be applied to other knights too, as in *Parl.* 348 where 'the mody Meneduse' is called 'a dussypere', and in *Morte A.* where Arthur's knights are often called 'dusperes'; or even to any illustrious personage: see quotations in *OED.* s.v. †Douzepers.

**522-9.** There seems to have been no constant tradition as to the names of the peers, and the list differs almost from text to text. See Gaston Paris, *Histoire poétique de Charlemagne* (Paris, 1905), ii, chap. xi. On p. 507, Gaston Paris gives lists of the names of the peers in seven OF. texts from different periods. The later OF. and the ME. Charlemagne texts in particular add several of the less familiar names to the list. Roland and Oliver appear to be the only constant names; next in order of frequency are Ogier the Dane, Naimes, Thierri, and Turpin. Of the names given in the *Chanson de Roland*, *Parl.* has only three: Roland, Oliver, and Samson. The list of peers in *Parl.* is not identical with that in any of the extant English or French romances, but it is closest to those in the *Firumbras* poems. In the OF. *Fierabras* and the ME. versions of *Firumbras* and *Sir Ferumbras*, eight of the names correspond: Roland, Olivier, Thierri, Naime, Ogier, Bérard, Aubri, and Gui de Bourgogne.

**522. Sir Rowlande the riche:** Roland, the nephew of Charlemagne and hero of the twelfth-century *Chanson de Roland*.

**Duke Raynere of Iene:** Reiner de Gennes, the father of Oliver. Reiner is mentioned only once, in retrospect, in the *Chanson de Roland*; he plays a more active part, though not as one of the peers, in *Ferumbras* and in *Otuel and Roland*—see the Ashmole MS. of *Sir Ferumbras*, ed. S. J. Herrtage, E.E.T.S., E.S. 34 (1879), and the Fillingham MS. of *Firumbras* and *Otuel and Roland*, ed. M. O'Sullivan, E.E.T.S., o.s. 198 (1934). *Sayn* in W appears to be an ingenious misreading of the name *Iene*, 'Gennes' or 'Genoa'.

**523. Olyuer:** son of Reiner, and Roland's comrade-in-arms.

# Notes

**Aubrye**: Aubrey of Burgogne, son of Basin le Borgoignon. Aubrey first appears as a douzeper in the OF. *Fierabras*, and in the ME. versions; also in the fragmentary *Song of Roland* (? 1400, ed. S. J. Herrtage, E.E.T.S., E.S. 35 (1880) ), although the OF. *Roland* does not mention him.

**Ogere Deauneys**: Ogier the Dane, a popular figure in the Charlemagne romances. Although he is not mentioned as a douzeper in the *Chanson de Roland*, he plays an important part in the poem as one of Charlemagne's fighting barons.

524. **Sir Naymes**: Duke Naimes of Bavaria, Charlemagne's friend and chief counsellor. He is mentioned fairly often as a douzeper in poems of the Charlemagne cycle, though not in the *Chanson de Roland*. There, however, he plays an important part as Charlemagne's friend and counsellor, and as a valiant fighter.

525. **Turpyn and Terry**: alliteration, not brotherhood-in-arms, has linked these two together here. Cf. 'tirry and turpyn', in the *Song of Roland*. Archbishop Turpin, who fights so valiantly for France in the *Chanson de Roland*, has a less warlike historical counterpart in Archbishop Turpin of Rheims, who according to the *Gallia Christiana* held the see of Rheims from A.D. 753–94. Turpin, though not one of the douzepers, fights heroically beside Oliver and Roland at Roncesvalles, where he is slain. 'Terry' is Tierri l'Angevin, the brother of Geoffrey of Anjou. Tierri is not a douzeper in the *Chanson de Roland*, as he is in most of the Charlemagne romances, but he plays an important part there as the champion of Charlemagne against Pinabel during the trial by combat of the traitor Ganelon.

526. **Sir Sampsone**: Samson was one of the douzepers in the *Chanson de Roland*, and his name occurs fairly often in subsequent lists; though not in poems of the *Ferumbras* cycle or in *Otuel and Roland* or *Sowdone*. He is the boon companion of Anseïs, with whom he is often coupled in the *Chanson de Roland*.

527. **Berarde de Moundres**: Berard de Mondisdier is one of the later names in the list. He appears as Bernard in the OF. *Voyage à Jérusalem*; as Bérard in the *Fierabras* and in the Ashmole MS. of *Sir Ferumbras*; as Gerard(e) de Mo(u)ntendre, Gerrard de Mountender, and Bernard de Mountendre in the Fillingham MS. of *Firumbras*; and as Bryer of Mountez in *Sowdone*. Berard was celebrated for his prowess in the art of love.

528. **Gy de Burgoyne**: Guy of Burgundy also is a late-comer among the douzepers. He appears in *Fierabras* and in the ME. versions, where he fights desperate battles against the Saracens and saves Floripas from an assault by a thief who had stolen her magic girdle. He later marries Floripas, and shares the kingdom of Spain with Ferumbras.

529. The 'katur fitz Emowntez, the Four Sons of Aymon, occur only here as douzepers. The poet may have intended them to count

## Notes

as one, but some lists do give as many as sixteen names—e.g. in *Sowdone* and in Caxton's *Charles the Grete*. The adventures of the Four Sons of Aymon are related at great length in the French prose romance *Les Quatre Fils Aymon*, translated by Caxton about 1489. (See the edition by Octavia Richardson, E.E.T.S., E.S. 44, 45 (1884-5).) The reading *knyghtes* of W is probably the true one here; the Four Sons had many adventures, but it is not recorded that they were ever kings.

531-40. The campaign against the Saxons.

532. **Polborne, W puerne**: evidently Paderborn in Saxony, where Charlemagne, attracted by the strategic advantages and by the beauty of the place, had built a palace for himself.

533. **Salamadyne the Sowdane**: the name is *Agoulant* in *Vœux*, *Agoment* in *Avowis*. Perhaps the poet was thinking of Soliman or Saladin, but neither of these had any connexion with Charlemagne.

536. **Witthyne, W Wyghtelyne**: the Westphalian chief Widukind or Witikind, who led the earlier Saxon revolts against Charlemagne, but was eventually baptized and became a subject of the Emperor. In Jean Bodel's *Chanson des Saxons*, this chief is named 'Guiteclins de Sessoigne'. There is apparently only one other record of his name in early English literature, in Caxton's version of *The Four Sonnes of Aymon*, chap. i: '. . . wherof the cheef of the sayde Sarasins was named Guithelym the sesne . . . ye paynym Guetelym.'

539-40. *Nioles* should perhaps be *Ni[lo]es*: cf. W *Milos*. The allusion to these lovers may have been understood by the poet's hearers (unless, as seems unlikely, he invented the names), but their story must have vanished without a trace. The characters who provide the 'love interest' in the *Chanson des Saxons* are Sebile, the young wife of Guiteclin, and the valiant Baudoin, Roland's brother; their marriage, after Charlemagne's victory over Guiteclin, ends the story of the *Chanson*.

541-57. Of all the Charlemagne romances, that of *Fierabras* or *Ferumbras* has been the most popular. The first romance to be printed was a prose version of *Fierabras*, and the poem was one of the first to be re-edited when the study of medieval metrical romance was revived in the nineteenth century. In this passage, the poet recalls rather than summarizes the story, touching upon some of the more dramatic incidents and leaving the rest to be inferred.

545. Cf. *Sir Ferumbras* 1086-7.

546, 548. The form *Marchel* in W may be a correction from *Balame* by someone (perhaps a minstrel reciting the poem) who preferred to be alliterative rather than accurate. This is perhaps more likely than that *Balame* in T is a later correction by someone who knew the story better. See note on 497, and cf. 558, 569, where W again has 'regular' alliteration, but the wrong name. Balan belongs to the *Ferumbras* cycle; Marsile, the Saracen king of Spain, to the Roland story.

**Mawltryple**: there was a bridge here across the river Flagot. In

## Notes

*Firumbras* 1259 it is referred to as 'þe Brygge of mautreble'. For a discussion of variant spellings of the name, see Herrtage, *Sir Ferumbras*, pp. 199–200.

**547. Emperour at Egremorte**, i.e. Balan, the 'heghe Amerel' (according to *Sir Ferumbras*) of Aigremore.

**549. by-fore-with his eghne**: cf. *WW*. 434, *to-fore-with myn eghne*. These phrases have hitherto been read as *by-fore with*, *to-fore with*, and the *with* has been assumed to be redundant. Professor A. McIntosh has pointed out to me that they should probably be read as compound words, *by-fore-with*, *to-fore-with*. These do not seem to be recorded elsewhere in ME., but they may be compared with *for(e)-with* 'before', adv. and prep. used of place, time, &c.: fairly common in *Cursor Mundi*, especially in the Cotton MS. (other manuscripts generally replace it by *before*). *For(e)-with* occurs several times also in *Wars Alex.*, e.g. 2242 (Ashmole MS.): 'Quare-to feynys þou þis fare for-with myne eȝen?' For the alternation of *before/fore*, &c., in 'compound prepositions', Professor McIntosh compares *before-outen* (from the *Prestwick Register*), beside common though mainly N. *for-(o)ut(en)*. Cf., also, *foranent*, *fornent*, 'opposite, facing', *fore-gain*, *fore-gainst*, 'directly opposite to'.

**552. cristened**: cf. 545. Here in both texts a scribe may have substituted a more familiar word, but see Introduction, 'Alliteration', 4, p. xxxi. The form *Florissh* 'Floripas' in W may be genuine: cf. *floyres* in the lyric *Annot and Johon* (no. 76, l. 46, in *English Lyrics of the XIIIth Century*, ed. Carleton Brown).

**553–5.** Cf. *Morte A*. 3426–8.

**557. and duellyd there for euer**: as Gollancz notes, presumably 'and [they] duellyd there', &c.

**558.** Cf. *Wars Alex*. 48, *Destr. Troy* 8315.

**558–70.** A summary account of the disaster at Roncesvalles. *Merchill*: see note on 546. His name is variously spelt: Marsil(l)e, Marsilies, Marsiliun(s) in the *Chanson de Roland*, Mansour(e), Mansure in *Otuel and Roland*.

**560.** Gollancz emends *borowes* to *b[urgh]*. But perhaps the pl. may be allowed as a 'poetic licence'.

**561. Genyone, W Golyan**: Ganelon the traitor, who is generally connected with the historical Wanilo, archbishop of Sens during the reign of Charles the Bald. His name shows a variety of forms. In the *Chanson de Roland* it occurs as *Guenes, Guenelun, Guenelon*, in the ME. *Roland* as *Gwynylon*; in ME. poems of the *Ferumbras* cycle it appears as *Gweneloun, Gwylyo(u)n, Gwynes, Gylyoun, Genelyn*. Ganelon soon became a byword for the foulest treachery: cf. Chaucer's *Book of the Duchess* 1121–3, and the *Monk's Tale* 2389.

**566.** Cf. 310, and note.

**567.** Cf. the *Chanson de Roland* 2610: 'vii anz tuz plens ad en Espaigne estét'.

## Notes

**569. he bett downn þe burghe:** cf. *Pur.* 1292, '& syþen bet doun þe burȝ'.

**570.** According to the *Chanson de Roland*, Marsile had fled from the battle, but his right hand had been cut off by Roland. From this wound he later died, after being told that the Saracen army had been defeated and that Charles had reached Saragossa.

**571.** Cf. *Siege Jer.* 844.

**573 ff.** An allusion to the story of Aymeri de Narbonne. There is no extant English version of his adventures, but he plays a lively part in a cycle of eight *chansons de geste*. See Bédier, *Les Légendes épiques*, i. The story of the siege of Narbonne occurs in the second chanson of the cycle, *Aymeri de Narbonne*.

**574. cite ... sere halfues:** very common, especially in *Morte A.*

**575.** Cf. 398, and note.

**577. To [haue]† and to holde:** cf. W. This was one of the ancient alliterative phrases; it is very common in ME. verse.

**586 ff.** Typical of some of the fabulous tales which gathered round the names of Aristotle and Virgil in the Middle Ages. Aristotle, vaguely understood to be a master of all learning, was naturally credited with a knowledge of alchemy. The most famous reference to this is in the *Secreta Secretorum*, supposed to have been written by Aristotle at the request of Alexander the Great. (See *Secreta Secretorum*, ed. R. Steele, E.E.T.S., E.S. 74 (1898), and the version by Lydgate and Burgh, *Secrees of Philisoffres*, ed. R. Steele, E.E.T.S., E.S. 66 (1894). See also Hoccleve's *De Regimine Principum*, which is drawn largely from this work.)

**588. The grete Alexander to graythe and ȝete golde,** i.e. 'in making and producing gold for the great Alexander': *Alexander* is in the dat. case here. There is no need to adopt Gollancz's emendation [H]e g[er]te. In *hym liste, hym* probably refers to *Alexander: he hym list* in W combines a personal with the old impersonal construction.

**589–93.** For an explanation of these processes in alchemy, see J. Read, *Prelude to Chemistry: Alchemy, its Literature and Relationships* (London, 1936). These lines are another example of the poet's liking for technical terms, shown so strikingly in the hunting and hawking passages. There are no parallel passages on the subject of alchemy in other alliterative poems; Chaucer uses an impressive array of these terms in *The Canon's Yeoman's Tale*.

**594.** The manuscript might read *veruayle* or *vernayle*; I have adopted Gollancz's emendation *ver[r]ayle* (cf. W *veryall*).

**594 ff.** Cf. *Destr. Troy* 49, 'Virgill þe virtuus, verrit for nobill', and 12912, 'Virgell, full verely, þos vertus can tell'. A series of curious and sometimes grotesque legends came to be attached to Virgil in the Middle Ages. One of the many traditions about him is that he made a speaking head of brass. The earliest version of this legend occurs in the *Image du Monde* (c. 1250). Here the story is that the head

## Notes

acted as an oracle, giving an ambiguous answer concerning Virgil's death. For an account of other forms and sources of this story, and a discussion of its origin, see J. W. Spargo, 'Virgil the Necromancer' (*Harvard Studies in Comparative Literature*, vol. x, 60–68 and 132–4).

**599. sett hym by hym one**: i.e. 'set himself apart'. *By hym one*, or *hym one*, is the usual idiom in ME. for 'by himself', 'alone': the dat. pron. is added to strengthen *one*. (Sometimes *al* was used to emphasize *one*—hence *alone*.) Later the possess. pron. is sometimes used, as in W *by his one*.

**600. His Bookes in the Bible.** The reference to Ecclesiastes as a 'clerke' in 638 suggests that the poet meant not the Book of Proverbs and Ecclesiastes here, but rather (as Gollancz suggests) the apocryphal Book of Wisdom and Ecclesiasticus, both of which were often attributed to Solomon in the Middle Ages.

**601. wisdome ... witt wondirfully**: cf. *Wars Alex.* 898, 'His witt & his wisdome wonderly praysed.' 'Wisdom ... wit' is very common.

**605. kynges ... kaysers.** This phrase occurs in OE. verse (and prose) as 'cyningas ... cāseras'. In its ME. version, *kaysers* < ON. *keisari* replaces the OE. form.

**608. Galyan, W golyan.** Probably an allusion to the lady whom Malory calls 'Nyneve', 'Nynyve', the Lady of the Lake: see iv, 1 (Vinaver, 125–6), &c. J. Rhys in his *Studies in the Arthurian Legend* traces this lady to the *Rhiannon*, wife of *Pwyll*, of Celtic mythology. The form Galyan may be an inaccuracy on the part of the poet or (less probably, since both texts have it and there seems to be alliteration on the *g*) a scribal error. In Malory's version of the story, the undignified sequel (for Merlin) is very prominent. But the poet may have been thinking of an episode in one of the *Merlin* romances. In the English prose *Merlin*, the lady is *Nimiane* or *Nimyane*: Merlin comes to her as a fair young squire and makes her an orchard, filled with fruit and flowers, in which to disport with her ladies. So in Lovelich's verse *Merlin*, which evidently follows the same French source. The idea of shutting her away 'that no wy scholde hir wielde', &c., is more prominent in the thirteenth-century French prose *Merlin* (Soc. des Anciens Textes Français, i and ii), where the damsel's name is *Niviene*. There it is told that she asked Merlin to build her a 'manoir' beside the 'lac de Dyane'. He built one, rich and splendid, but made it invisible to the world outside. Eventually, however (as in all the versions, down to Tennyson's *Merlin and Vivien*), she learnt enough of his cunning to rid herself of him by enchantment.

**[gete]**, manuscript *kepe*: cf. *gete* in W, and see Glossary. *OED.* notes that the word is 'chiefly Northern' and occurs frequently in *Cursor Mundi*, in later texts of which *keep* is sometimes substituted.

**611.** This line is repeated at 632. Cf. *Morte A.* 3494, 'I will noghte wonde for no werre, to wende whare me likes.'

**614. Amadase and Edoyne**: two famous lovers, probably as well

## Notes

known in the Middle Ages as Tristan and Iseult. There are many references to their love in ME. literature, but no English romance corresponding to the French *Amadas et Ydoine* is known to exist. (The two ME. versions of *Sir Amadace* seem to be quite unconnected with the romance of *Amadas et Ydoine*.) Perhaps the earliest English allusion to the romance is in the *Love Ron* of Friar Thomas de Hales (no. 43 in *English Lyrics of the XIIIth Century*, ed. Carleton Brown); here these two lovers are coupled with Paris and Heleyne, Tristram and Yseude, 'and alle þeo'. They are mentioned by the author of *Cursor Mundi* in his list of famous lovers about whom 'man yhernes ... for to here', and in Book VI of Gower's *Confessio Amantis*, 875 ff. See, also, the romance of *Emaré* 122–3, and *Sir Degrevant* 1489 ff. A full account of references to this romance in early Dutch and French literature is given in '*Amadas et Ydoine*', *An Historical Study*, by J. R. Reinhard, Duke University Press, 1927.

**616–17. Sir Sampsone ... And Dalyda his derelynge:** the poet thinks of Samson and Delilah as a knight and lady in romance. *Dalyda* is the usual form in ME., from the Greek *Dalida* (in the Septuagint). It occurs in the *Roman de la Rose*, which probably helped to familiarize it.

**617. bo[th]e:** Gollancz also adopts the reading of W here. Death does not 'buy' people; moreover, 'now' suits 'bothe' rather than 'boghte.'

**618–19. Sir Ypomadonn de Poele ... Þe faire Fere de Calabre:** there are three ME. versions, two in verse and one in prose, of the romance of Ipomadon and the Proud One of Calabria (ed. E. Kölbing, Breslau, 1889). These are based on a late-twelfth-century Anglo-Norman romance by Hue de Roteland, who lived at 'Credehulle' (Credenhill, near Hereford). Ipomadon, son of the king of Apulia, has adventures and trials (numerous and in many lands) before he finally wins his lady, the daughter of the Duke of Calabria. Her name is not mentioned in any of the versions, but she is called 'La Fière', 'the Fere', because she had sworn that she would marry only the bravest knight in the world.

**620–1. Generides þe gentill ... And Clarionas þat was so clere:** the only extant English versions of *Generides* are two fifteenth-century texts (ed. W. Aldis Wright, E.E.T.S., o.s. 55, 70 (1873, 1878)), and a few fragments of a sixteenth-century printed version. L. A. Hibbard in *Mediaeval Romance in England*, 231, thinks that the allusion in *Parl.* may be to a lost French version of *Generides*, or to a fourteenth-century English compilation from French versions. Another allusion to these lovers is in Gower's forty-third *Balade*, where he mentions Generides as one who 'sa loialté guardoit'.

**622–3. Sir Eglamour of Artas ... And Cristabelle the clere maye.** There are three fifteenth-century manuscripts of *Sir Eglamour*, and one leaf of a late-fourteenth-century manuscript; besides these there are five sixteenth-century printed versions and a transcript of

## Notes

another early printed version in the Percy Folio MS.: evidence of the popularity of this romance. No French source of the tale is known, but *Sir Eglamour* has a homely and humorous flavour and may be largely an English minstrel's work.

**624–5. Sir Tristrem the trewe ... And Ysoute his awnn lufe.** There are many references to Tristram and Iseult in ME. literature, but only one ME. version of the story, in the N. dialect, is known to exist outside Malory. *Sir Tristrem* (ed. G. P. McNeill, S.T.S. 8, 1886) is a condensed and much less poignant version of the late-twelfth-century Anglo-Norman romance of Tristram by Thomas of Britain. Only fragments of this remain, but it has been possible to reconstruct it from a comparison of the early-thirteenth-century *Tristrams Saga ok Isondar*, which appears to be a close translation of the French. See *The Romance of Tristram and Ysolt*, translated from the OF. and ON. by R. S. Loomis, Columbia University Press, 1951.

**627. Dame Cand[ac]e**: cf. 396, and note. Dido and Candace are appropriately mentioned together here. Their love affairs were rather similar; indeed Candace, while she is waiting for Alexander, 'syngeþ of Dido and Eneas', *Kyng Alisaunder* 7619 (B). Both had taken the lead in their romance, and for both it had ended abruptly.

**628.** pas[sed], manuscript *pasten*; cf. *passed* 421.

**639.** Ecclesiastes i. 2, xii. 8.

**642.** This is quoted by Truth to Mercy in *PP.* B xviii. 149. The reference is to Job vii. 9.

**645 and 647.** Cf. Luke xvii. 14: in the Vulgate, 'Quos vt vidit, dixit: Ite, ostendite vos sacerdotibus. Et factum est, dum irent, mundati sunt.'

**646.** Cf. *GGK.* 1880, 'Þere he schrof hym schyrly & schewed his mysdedeȝ'. *Schirle*: this may mean 'pure(ly)', but 'completely' gives the better sense; cf. *OED.* s.v. *Sheerly* 2.

**648.** Manuscript *ȝe þat*: Gollancz misreads *þat ȝe*, and adds [haue] before *wroghte*.

**654.** Cf. *DL.* 10, 'When Death driueth att the doere ...'.

**656–8.** Cf. *Gol. & Gaw.* 523–4:

> He hard ane bugill blast brym and ane loud blaw,
> As the seymly sone silit to the rest.

**664. There dere Drightyne ... dele vs of thi blysse.** This use of *there* to introduce an optative clause of blessing or cursing is fairly common in ME. (It is not recorded in *OED.*) It occurs several times in Chaucer, as in *Troilus and Criseyde*, iii. 947, 966, 1437, 1456, and *The Merchant's Tale* 1308 ('Writeth this man, ther God his bones corse!'); cf. also *WW.* 124, *Qu. Love* 97. The primary meaning of 'there' in such instances may have been 'in this (that) circumstance', 'in that respect', but generally it is no more than an expletive giving emphasis to the imprecation.

# GLOSSARY

The Glossary is a complete record of the forms used in the Thornton version, but not of all occurrences of each form; where the number of occurrences is incomplete, &c. is added. Forms from the Ware text (prefixed by W) are quoted only when they show a notable linguistic (as opposed to spelling) variation, or when an odd corruption has occurred, as in W *duke pere* or *ducheperis* for *douze per(s)*. In the few instances where an entirely different word has been substituted in W, e.g. *affligid* where T has *flayede*, this is entered separately. Derivations are given only exceptionally, for unusual words or on points of special linguistic interest. An asterisk before a number reference indicates an emended form.

The following points of arrangement may be noted: ʒ follows g; þ is entered under t, with th; initial i = j is separated from i = i; internal y = i is treated as i; initial v = u is separated from v = v; medial u = v is treated as v (e.g. *out* before *ouer*).

Abbreviations which may not be obvious are: AF., Anglo-French; E., English; F., French; (med.) L., (Medieval) Latin; LG., Low German; MDu., Middle Dutch; MHG., Middle High German; MLG., Middle Low German; N., North(ern); Nth., Northumbrian; OF., Old French; ONF., the Northern dialects of Old French; Sc., Scottish; n. = see Note; *MED.*, A Middle English Dictionary (in preparation, ed. H. Kurath and S. M. Kuhn); *OED.*, The Oxford English Dictionary.

## A

a *indef. art.* a 4, 7, 23, &c.; an(e) reg. before *h*, 5, 25, 84, &c.
abaschede *pt. s.* took by surprise, confounded 369; W basshed.
abyde, habyde *v. intr.* to stay, remain, endure 536, 583, 631; abydes *pr. 3 s.* stays, waits 360; habade *pt. s.* lingered 7.
about *adv.* all round, all over 93; aboute, abowte about, round, here and there 46, 76, &c.
adversarye *n.* adversary 311.
affligid *pp.* afflicted, distressed W 428.
affrayede *pt. s.* alarmed, frightened 356.
aftir(e) *adv.* afterwards, then 74, 277, 294, &c.; aftir(e), aftyr *prep.* after, in pursuit of 63, 226, &c.; after 332, 379, &c.; W aftur.

agayne *adv.* again 437; W ayayn.
age *n.* age 164.
agreed *pt. s. refl.* agreed 358.
ay *adv.* always, ever 564; W hay.
ayers *n. pl.* heirs 577; W heyris.
ayther(e) *adj.* either 28, each 512; *pron.* both 456. [OE. ǣgþer; see ouþer]
aldeste see Olde.
alle *adj.* all 49, 149, 177, &c.; *adv.* entirely 26, 119, 122, &c.; ∼ *by-dene*, see by-dene.
alle *n.* all, everything, everyone 57, 92, 184, &c.
als *conj.* as (when, while) 3, 7, 21, &c.; (even) as, like 47, 65, 114, &c.; *adv.* (just) as 271; also 144. See as.
also *adv.* also, as well 167, 511.
amatistes *n. pl.* amethists 127.
amen *interj.* Amen 665.
amende *pr. subj. 3 s.* restore, convert

71

## Glossary

665; **amendes** *imper. pl.* make good, reform 641.
**amerous** *adj.* amorous (of), delighting in W 271; **emerus** W 306, 622; **Emerous** *quasi-n.* W 543.
**ames** *pr. 3 s. refl.* plans, resolves 384, 394, 486; (to go) 493. [OF. *amer*]
**Amorelle** *n.* emir, ruler 515.
**an(e)** *see* a.
**and** *conj.* and 2, &c.; if 106, 189.
**angelles** *n. pl.* angels 215.
**angrye** *adj.* peevish 163. [ON. *angr* grief]
**any** *adj.* any 37, 48, &c.
**anone** *adv.* next, at once, forthwith 74, 86, 539, 554.
**anoþer** *adj.* another 457.
**anoþer** *adv.* differently, otherwise 484.
**appon** *prep.* upon, on 10, 30, 55, &c.; **appone** 574; **vppon** 487.
**araye** *n.* attire, appearance 107, 166, 186, 320.
**arayed** *pt. s.* equipped, prepared 346.
**ardaunt** see **ewe**.
**are** *conj.* before 283; W **or**. [OE. ǣr (? Nth. ār); ON. *ár*]
**ar(e)ste** *adj.* first, most prominent 464, 586.
**armes** *n. pl.*[1] arms 113, 247.
**armes** *n. pl.*[2] knightly warfare 171, 181, 271, &c.; W **armes**; **ermes** 474, 622.
**armes** *pr. 3 s. refl.* arms, equips W 394, 486.
**arsneke** *n.* arsenic 590.
**as** *conj.* as (when, while) 6; as (one who, as if) 57; (even) as, like 5, 27, &c.; as (*correl. with* **als, as** *adv.*) 271, 276; **as** *adv.* as (*correl. with* **als, as** *conj.*) 272, 273, 274, 276.
**askes** *pr. 3 s.* requires, demands 240; **askede** *pt. s.* asked for 160.
**assaye** *n.* 'assay', testing of the deer's flesh 70 n.
**assayllede** *pt. s.* attacked 397; W **saylid** (see **saylen**).
**asseggede** *pt. s.* besieged 574;

**assegede** *pl.* 303; **asegede** *pp.* 356.
**assemblet** *pt. s. trans.* assembled 340.
**assentis** *pr. 3 s.* agrees, complies 63.
**assommet** *pp.* 'summed', with full number of antlers 31. [OF. *assomer*]
**at** *prep.* at 5, &c.; by, from 452.
**athell** *adj.* noble, glorious 345, &c.
**athes** *pr. 3 s.* adjures 499.
**attyrede** *pp.* attired 169.
**aughte** *pt. s.* obtained 392; ruled 406, 465.
**aughtilde** *pt. s.* intended 483; W **athild**. [ON. ǣtla < *\*ahtila*, cf. OE. *eahtian*]
**auntirs** *pr. 3 s. refl.* ventures 375; **aunterde** *pt. s.* 543.
**auntlers** *n. pl.* antlers 28.
**auntoure** *n.* (evil) chance, plight 317; **aventure** risk, peril 451 n.
**a-vowe** *pr. 1 s.* avow, solemnly declare 178; **avowede** *pt. pl.* made vows 365; *pp.* 204.
**a-waye** *adv.* away 80, 504.
**awnn** *adj.* own 392, 406, 451, &c.; **ownn** 177, 304; W **awn** 451, otherwise **ow(e)n**.
**axe** *n.* axe 374.
**axles** *n. pl.* shoulders 113.

D

**babirlippede** *adj.* thick-lipped 158. [? OF. *babine* lip of an animal, protruding lip]
**bade** *pt. s.* asked (for) 390; bade, commanded 559; W **bede, bad**. [OE. *biddan*, early confused with *bēodan*]
**bagge** *n.* money-bag 139; see Björkman, *Scand. Loan-words*, p. 228.
**bak(k)e** *n.* back 200, 272; *one* ~ *adv. phr.* back 369; W **bak, abak**.
**bale** *n.* evil-doing 453; W **bayl**.
**balghe** *adj.* full, rounded 112 n.
**balkede** *pt. s.* ? swerved, stumbled 56 n. [? OE. *balca* ridge]
**ballede** *adj.* bald 158. [? formed on *bal* bail; see *MED*. s.v. *balled*]

## Glossary

**banke** *n.* bank, shore, hillside 7, 509, **bonke** 656; **bankes** *pl.* 14.
**bare, bere** *pt. s.* bore, carried 369, 504; **bere** *refl.* bore (himself), lived 439.
**baron** *n.* baron W 389.
**batelle** *n.* battle array 369.
**be, bi, by** *prep.* by 7, 19, 183, &c.; by (means of) 66, 503; along 128; (indicated) by 40; according to, measured by 164, 269, 308.
**be** *v.* to be 97, 258, 483, &c., **bene** 604; **am** *pr. 1 s.* 650; **arte** *2 s.* 185, 207; **es** *3 s.* 177, 185, 195, &c.; **are** *pl.* 614, 619, 621, &c.; **bene** *pl.* 1, 2, 99, &c.; **be** *fut. pl.* will be 336; *pr. subj. 2 s.* 258; **bene** *pp.* been 49, &c.; **was** *pt. s.* 8, &c.; **were** *pl.* 13, &c.; *pt. subj. s.* 129, 199, 310, 433, 566.
**be-dagged** *pp.* 'dagged', splashed with mud 245 n. [? ON. *döggva bedewe*, sprinkle]
**bedis** *n. pl.* beads, rosary 153.
**be-gynn** *v.* to begin 72.
**belde** *pt. s. refl.* made (myself) a nook 662; see *OED*. s.v. Build, v. II. †8.
**bele** *adj.* beautiful 390.
**be-lyue, by-lyue** *adv.* quickly, straightway 416, 505.
**bellys** *n. pl.* bells 214.
**beme** *n.* beam, the horn from which the antlers grow 26.
**bende** *pt. s.* brought into tension, strung 43; see *OED*. s.v. Bend, v. I, 2.
**benefetis** *n. pl.* favours, kindnesses 143.
**benes** *n. pl.* extra services *or* payments 143.
**beralles** *n. pl.* beryls 123.
**berde** *n.* beard 156, &c.; **berdes** *pl.* 482; W·**berde, byrdes**.
**bere** *see* **bare**.
**bereselet, berselett** *n.* hunting dog, hound 39 n., 69. [AF. *bercelet*; OF. *berseret*, dimin. of *bersier* huntsman; med. L. *bersāre* to hunt]
**beryn(e)** *n.* man, knight 110, &c.; **beryns** *pl.* 395, &c.

**besanttes** *n. pl.* bezants, ornaments resembling small gold coins from Byzantium 123. [OF. *besan*, pl. *besanz*, L. *byzantius*]
**be-syde** *prep.* to one side, hard by 24; *adv.* 85.
**beste** *adj.* best, noblest 391; *as sb.* 297, 458, 480, &c.
**be-tyde** *v.* to happen, befall 596; **be-tydde** *pp.* 596.
**bette** *v.* to beat, storm (a town) 560; **betyn** *pr. 3 pl.* beat up 224; **bett** *pt. s.* 569.
**bettir** *adj.* better 139; **bettir(e)** *adv.* 243, 366.
**bewells** *n. pl.* intestines 69.
**bewes, bowes** *pr. 3 s.* turns, goes 370, 395; **bewede** *pt. pl.* bowed down 490; W **bowis, bowid**.
**bewes** *n. pl.* boughs, branches 662; W **bowes**.
**bi, by** see **be** *prep.*
**Bible** *n.* Bible 424, 600.
**by-cause (of)** *prep.* because (of) 396.
**by-come** *v.* to become 559; **by-comen** *pp.* in *where he was* ~ what had become of him 507.
**byde** *v.* to stay, remain 654.
**by-dene** *adv.* in *alle* ~ all together 364; see *OED*. s.v. Bedene, adv.
**bye** *v.* to buy 147; *imper.* 190.
**by-fore** *prep.* in front, ahead of 37; **before** (*time*) 325; *adv.* in front 75; before (previously) 315, 366.
**by-fore-with** *prep.* before, in front of 549 n.
**by-hete** *pr. 1 s.* promise, avow 178.
**by-hynde** *prep.* behind 54.
**by-lyue** see **be-lyue**.
**bill** *n.* beak 228.
**billet** *n.* ? chaplet *or* girdle W 482; see *MED*. s.v. bilet, n.
**by-luffede** *pp.* beloved 274.
**birche** *n.* birch 39; **birches** *pl.* 662.
**birde** *n.* maiden, lady 390, 453; W **burde, byrd**.
**by-ronnen** *pp.* covered, drenched 62.
**by-segede** *pt. s.* besieged 397, 534.
**by-soughte** *pt. s.* besought, implored 357.

*Glossary*

**bitt** *n.* sharp edge 228. [ON. *bit* sharpness, edge (of blade)]
**bitterly** *adv.* sharply 228.
**by-weuede** *pp.* interwoven 122.
**blake** *n.* black 153, 265.
**blaste** *n.* blazing 593; W **blastyng**.
**[b]launchere** *n.* blancher (in alchemy, one who whitens metals) 593.
**blawnchede** *pt. s.* whitened 285; **blanchede** *pp. as adj.* 156.
**blethely** *adv.* gaily, joyfully 214 n.
**blynde** *adj.* blind 158.
**blyot** *n.* 'bleaunt', a long garment, often richly embroidered at the neck and wrists 482. [OF. *bliaut, blyaut*]
**blysse** *n.* (eternal) joy, bliss 664.
**blode** *n.* blood 55.
**blody** *adv.* with blood 62.
**blonke** *n.* steed 110.
**blossoms** *n. pl.* blossoms 11.
**blowen** *pp.* blown 656; W **blawn**.
**body** *n.* body 22, 32; **bodyes** *pl.* images 595.
**bodworde** *n.* message, behest 558.
**bogle** *n.* bugle 656.
**bolde** *adj.* bold, valiant 110, 370, &c.; **bold(e)ly** *adv.* 558, 595.
**bole** *n.* trunk 39.
**bondemen** *n. pl.* labourers, serfs 143.
**bone** *n.* bone 80; **bones** *pl.* 231, 438.
**bonke** see **banke**.
**booke** *n.* book 407, &c.; **Bookes** *pl.* 600.
**borely** *adj.* massive, strong 26, 32. [OE. *borlīce* adv. admirably, excellently; OHG. *burlīh* lofty, exalted]
**borowes** see **burgh(e)**.
**bosome** *n.* bosom 139.
**bot** *conj.* but (however, yet) 34, 45, 50, &c.; except, other than 117, 165, &c.; unless 289; *adv.* (nothing) but, only 187, 621.
**bote** *n.* boat 509.
**bothe** *adj.* and *pron.* both 55, 266, 329, &c.; **bothen** 13, 276, 629;

**bothe** as *adv.* in both . . . and 22, 285, 333; = as well, too 605.
**boundes** *n. pl.* (farthest) landmarks 334 n.
**boure** *n.* bower 608.
**bowe** *n.* bow 22, 43.
**bowes** see **bewes**.
**bownn(e)** *adj.* ready, equipped 110, dressed 153.
**bownnes** *pr. 3 s.* makes ready, prepares 265; **bownede** *pt. s.* 43.
**brayde** *pt. s.* drew, pulled 69, 371; **brayden** *pp.* embroidered 131. [OE. *bregdan*]
**brayed** *pt. s.* brayed, bellowed 56 n. [OF. *braire*]
**brayne** *n.* brain 446.
**brakans** *n. pl.* bracken 62. [? ON. \**brakni*; cf. Swed. *bräken*]
**brande** *n.* sword 371.
**brasse** *n.* brass 595.
**braste** see **brosten**.
**braunches** *n. pl.* branches 11.
**brawndeschet** *pt. s.* brandished 504.
**brede** *n.* breadth 71.
**breke** *v.* to break 41; **brekyn** *pr. 3 pl.* 231.
**brenn** *v.* to burn 560; **brent(e)** *pp. as adj.* refined (by fire), burnished 131, 191.
**breris** *n. pl.* briars 62.
**breste** *n.* breast 112.
**breues** *pr. 3 s.* tells, treats (of) 424.
**bride** *n.* bride 482.
**bridell, brydell** *n.* bridle 131, 191.
**brighte** *adj.* bright 214, &c.
**bryme** *n.* water's edge, in ~ *syde*, side of a brook, stream 7.
**brynges** *pr. 3 pl.* in ~ *hym to sege*, bring him to a defensive position at the water's edge 224 n.; **broghte** *pt. s.* brought 401, 444.
**brode** *adj.* broad 32, 112; *adv.* with wide-open eyes *or* all around 51.
**brosten** *pr. 3 pl. trans.* crush 231; **braste** *pt. s. intr.* burst 55.
**browes** *n. pl.* eyebrows 156, 285.
**bruschede** *pt. s.* rushed violently 56. [? OF. *brosser* intr. to dash through dense underwood]

## Glossary

**buffetyn** *pr. 3 pl.* buffet 224.
**bullokes** *n. pl.* bullocks 191.
**burgh(e)** *n.* town, stronghold 538, 569; **borowes** *pl.* 560.
**burgons** *n. pl.* buds 11.
**buskede** *pt. s.* arrayed 22.
**butte** *n.* butt, thick end, edge W 228. [? OF. *bout*; or cf. Dan., LG. *but*, Du. *bot* blunt, thickset, stumpy]

### C

**cache** *v.* to catch 33; **caughten** *pt. pl.* took (leave) 362; **caughte** *pp.* 189, 443.
**callen** *pr. 3 pl.* call 425; **callede** *pt. s.* 407; *3 pl.* 151, 545; **called(e)** *pp.* 516, 517, 627.
**calsydoynnes** *n. pl.* chalcedonies 124.
**caprons** *n. pl.* hoods 212, 237. [ONF. *capron*; Central and Mod. F. *chaperon*]
**cares** *pr. 2 s.* carest, art concerned 189; **carede** *pt. s.* 165.
**caris** *n. pl.* cares, anxieties W 377.
**carolles** *n. pl.* dance and song 254 n.
**carpe** *v.* to speak 462.
**carpynge** *n.* conversation 168.
**castelle** *n.* castle 411.
**casten** *v. infin.* or *pr. 3 pl.* cast 212; **keste** *pt. s.* 80; **kest vp** turned over 68 n.
**caughten** see **cache**.
**certayn** *adj.* certain, sure W 635.
**certayne, in ~** *adv.* in truth, certainly 635.
**chambirs** *n. pl.* private rooms (set apart for the ladies' use) 249.
**chaplet** *n.* circlet, garland 118.
**charebocle** *n.* carbuncle 121.
**chawylls** *n. pl.* jaws 72.
**chefe** *pr. 3 pl.* achieve 243; **cheuede** *pt. s.* succeeded, turned out 98.
**chefe** *adj.* specially fine, choice 121; chief, principal, outstanding 255, 520, 538; as *adv.* ? first of all, ? particularly 72 n.; as *n.* chief (knight), leader 531.
**chefe-lere** *n.* head (of hair) 118. [OF. *cheveleüre*]

**chefely** *adv.* above all, especially 89, 235.
**cheres** *pr. 3 s.* encourages, incites 235.
**chese** *v.* to betake oneself, go (to) 255; **cheses** *pr. 3 s.* 538; **chosen** *pr. 3 pl.* 243; **ches(e)** *pt. s.* chose 72, 531; **chosen** *pp.* choice, conspicuous 118, 121; chosen 520.
**chesse** *n.* chess 255.
**cheuede** see **chefe**.
**chynede** *pt. s.* split along the backbone 89. [OF. *eschine* spine, backbone]
**choppede** *pt. s.* chopped 89.
**cite** *n.* city 303, &c.
**clap** *pr. 3 pl.* fondle W 248.
**clene** *adj.* clean, pure 648.
**clere** *adj.* fair, beautiful 621, 623.
**clerke** *n.* sage 638; **clerkes** *pl.* clerks (in the modern sense) 148; scholars, writers 307.
**clyp** *v.* to clasp, embrace 248.
**closede** *pt. s.* made secure, fortified 411.
**clothes** *n. pl.* clothes 188.
**clustrede** *pp.* clustered 124.
**colere** *n.* collar 124.
**coloppe** *n.* 'collop', tasty bit of meat 33; see *OED.* s.v. Collop.
**combrid** *pt. s.* encumbered, hampered W 287.
**come** *n.* coming 336.
**come** *v.* to come 203; *pr. 1 s.* (? or *pt. s*) 246; **comes** *3 s.* comes 583, 631, 636; *with future sense* 293; **comen** *pp.* 355.
**comforthe** *v.* to comfort 248; **comforthed** *pt. s.* 396.
**comly** *adj.* fair, beautiful 627.
**comonly** *adv.* usually 467.
**compaynyes** *n. pl.* companies, gatherings 254.
**compaste** *pt. s.* wrought, devised 409.
**condithe** *n.* conduit, aqueduct 409; W **colonduyte.** [OF. *conduit*, med. L. *conductus*]
**conquered(e)** *pt. s.* conquered 337, 402, 415, &c.

75

## Glossary

**conquerour(e)** *n.* conqueror 441, 458; **conquerours** *pl.* 251, &c.
**conqueste** *n.* conquest 402.
**consell** *n.* advice 195.
**contrees** *n. pl.* countries, lands 492.
**corbyns** *n. gen. s.* raven's 80 n.
**cornells** *n. pl.* battlements, embrasures 411. [ONF. *carnel*, OF. *crenel*]
**Corownne** see **crowne**.
**couche** *n.* bed 165.
**coundythes** *n. pl.* 'cunduts', part-songs 254. [OF. *conduite*, med. L. *conductus*]
**countours** *n. pl.* legal pleaders, serjeants-at-law 148 n. [Cf. AF. *counter* to plead in a court of law, L. *computāre*]
**courbede** see **cowrbed**.
**courte** *n.* court 246, 467; **courtes** *pl.* (legal), manorial courts 148.
**courtly** *adv.* ? in courtly fashion, elegantly W 462.
**couthe** see **kane**.
**couthely** *adv.* clearly, knowledgeably 462.
**couerede** *pt. s. refl.* concealed 42.
**cowchide** *pt. s.* couched, made ... lie down 39.
**cowers** *n. pl.* leather braces (at the back of the hood) 237 n.; W **cours**. [OF. *cuir*]
**cownten** *pr. 3 pl.* tell, relate (or consider, hold to be ?) 307. [OF. *conter, cunter*, L. *computāre*]
**cowpe** *v.* engage in tournament, contend 203. [OF. *couper*]
**cowpe** *n.* cup 401.
**cowples (vp)** *pr. 3 s.* draws (up) 237.
**cowrbed** *pt. s.* bent, bowed down 287; **courbede** *pp. as adj.* 154.
**cowschote** *n.* cushat, wood-pigeon 13. [OE. *cusceote, cuscute*; cf. *cowshot*, &c., in mod. N. dialects]
**crabtre** *n.* crab-apple tree 42. [ON. *krabbi* n. crab; see *OED*. s.v. Crab, sb.²]
**craftely** *adv.* cunningly, with skill 409.
**crakede** *pt. s.* broke 373.
**crede** *n.* creed 161.

**crepite, crepyde** see **krepyn**.
**cried (one)** *pt. s.* appealed (to) 161.
**Cristen, Cristyne** *adj. as n.* Christian(s) 462, 559.
**cristened** *pp.* christened 552.
**croked** *pt. s.* made crooked, deformed 287; *pp. as adj.* 154.
**cronycle** *n.* chronicle 307.
**cropoure** *n.* crupper 132.
**crouschede** *pp.* ? pressed down 64 n.
**crowne, crownn** *n.* crown 466, 517, **Corownne** 553; **crounes** *pl.* 309.
**cruche** *n.* crutch 165.
**cukkowe** *n.* cuckoo 13.
**curssede** *pp. as adj.* accursed 401.
**cuttede** see **kutt**.

### D

**day** *n.* day 6; **daye** 16, 293, &c.; **dayes** *gen. s.* 579, 582, see **tyme**.
**dayses** *n. pl.* daisies 10.
**dalte** see **delys**.
**Dame** *n.* lady, queen 357, &c.
**damesels** *n. pl.* damsels, maidens 249.
**dare** *pr. 1 s.* dare 654; *3 s.* 583, 631.
**daunsen** *v.* to dance 249.
**declares** *pr. 3 s.* declares 638.
**dede** *adj.* dead 65, 258, &c.
**dede** *n.*¹ death 399, 583, 631; W **dede** 312, **deed** 570, 579; a N. variant of **dethe**.
**dede** *n.*² deed, act, feat of arms 452; **dedis, dedys** *pl.* 181, 270, &c.
**deden** see **do**.
**delys** *pr. 3 s.* deals, has to do 264; **dele** *pr. subj. 3 s.* give a share of, bestow 664; **dalte** *pt. s.* shared out, distributed 403.
**demden** *pt. pl.* determined 367; **demed[e]n** pronounced, declared 331; **demed** *pp.* adjudged 472.
**departede** *pt. s. trans.* separated 77.
**dere** *adj.* costly, precious 125; beloved, dear 249, &c.; good, noble 597.
**dere** *v.* to harm 36.

76

## Glossary

**derelynge** *n.* darling 617.
**derke** *n.* darkness 16.
**dethe** *n.* death 233, &c. (Cf. **dede** *n.*[1])
**deuyll** *n.* the Devil 260, 447.
**dewe** *n.* dew 10.
**dyamandes** *n. pl.* diamonds 125.
**dide** see **do**.
**dyede** *pt. s.* died 579.
**digges** *n. pl.* ducks 245; see *EDD*. s.v. Dig, sb.
**dighte** *pp.* set, arrayed 125; ordained, made 597.
**dikes** *n. pl.* ditches (*or* ponds) W 245.
**dynges** *pr. 3 s.* knocks 654.
**dynt** *n.* stroke, blow 447.
**disfegurede** *pt. s.* disfigured 284; **disfygured** *pp. as adj.* 155.
**dispysede** *pt. s.* despised 550.
**do** *v.* to do 294, 521; **doo** 367; **dide** *pt. s.* in ~ . . *pulle doun* 319, see **pulle**; placed 557; ~ *to the dethe* slew 570; **deden** *pt. pl.* did 367; **done** *pp.* over, past 16; done 181; W **do, dud**.
**doers** *n. pl.* men of deeds 461.
**doghetynes, doughtynes** *n.* doughtiness, valour 583, 631.
**dogh(e)ty, dough(e)ty** *adj.* doughty, valiant, worthy 181, &c.; *quasi-n.* 344, 442; **doghtyeste** *superl.* 582.
**dole** *n.* grief, mourning, lamentation 258 n. (*thi* ~, mourning for you), 344, 400, 452. [OF. *doel, dol,* &c.]
**doluen** *pp.* buried 258.
**donkede** *pt. s.* spread moisture 10; see *OED*. s.v. Dank, a.
**dore** *n.* door 292, 654.
**dore-nayle** *n.* door-nail 65.
**doun** *adv.* down 38, 52, 65, &c., **downn** 569.
**doussypers** see **dussypere**.
**douth** *n.* (noble) host, army 348.
**dowkynge** *n.* plunging into water 245. [Cf. LG. *dûken*]
**dowte** *n.* uncertainty 102.
**dragild** *pp.* bedraggled W 245.
**dragone** *n.* dragon 488.

**drede** *pr. 1 s.* dread 292; *pp.* dreaded 488.
**dreghe** *adj.* long 102. [ON. *drjúgr* < *\*dreug-*]
**dreghe** *v.* to undergo, 'try' 3.
**dremed** *pt. s. impers.* dreamed 102.
**dreped, drepide, drepit(t)** *pt. s.* slew 379, 456, &c.
**Dryghtyn, Drightyn(e)** *n.* God 6, &c.; **Drightyn[es]** *gen. s.* 442.
**drynke** *n.* potion 400.
**dryves** *pr. 3 s. intr.* runs, scurries 19; **droue** *pt. s. trans.* drove (on) 6.
**droghe** *pt. s. refl.* withdrew 410; **droghen** *pt. pl. refl.* 381.
**duche** *n.* duchy W 348.
**duellys** *pr. 2 s.* dost dwell 175; **duellyde** *pt. s.* dwelt, stayed 410; **duellyd** *pl.* (they) remained 557.
**Duke** *n.* duke 348, &c.
**dussypere** *n.* one of the twelve peers; usually of Charlemagne, but here applied to one of Alexander's knights 348; **dussypers** *pl.* 403; **doussypers** (of Charlemagne) 521 n.; W **duke pere** 348; **duche peris, ducheperis** 403, 521. [OF. *douze (duze, doce) pers*]

## E

**echecheke** *n.* 'check', a hawking term 243; **ecchekkes** *pl.* 235 n. [OF. *eschec*]
**efte** *adv.* again 436.
**egheliche** *adv.* fearsomely, wondrously 28.
**eghne** *n. pl.* eyes 50, 549; W **Eyen**.
**elde** *n.* age 133, 150, &c.; old age 154, (*person.*) 163, 283, 652; W **eld** 652, **yeld** 283.
**eldeste** see **olde**.
**ell(e)s, ellis** *adv.* else, besides, otherwise 196, &c.
**embroddirde** *pp.* embroidered 123.
**emeraudes** *n. pl.* emeralds 127.
**emer(o)us** in W see **amerous**.
**Emperour** *n.* emperor 345, &c.
**encrampeschet(t)** *pt. s.* contorted

## Glossary

287; *pp. as adj.* 154. [*en*+OF. stem *crampiss-* < *crampir*]
**ende** *n.* end 404, 519.
**endes** *n. pl.* ducks 220. [OE. *ened*]
**enewede** *pp.* driven into the water 245. [OF. *enewer* moisten]
**enymy** *n.* enemy 317.
**ensample** *n.* example, warning 269. [AF. *ensample*, OF. *essample*]
**envyous** *adj.* malicious, spiteful 163.
**erande** *n.* errand, mission 561.
**erthe** *n.* earth, ground 18, 64, &c.; *appon* ∼, *in* ∼, on earth, in the world 298, 581, 603; buried 614, 625.
**es** see **be.**
**ese** *n.* ease 136, 277, 578.
**euen** *adv.* exactly, just, indeed 367, 576.
**euer** *adv.* ever 135, &c.; always, continually 160.
**euer(r)ous** *adj.* eager (for renown, glory) 271 n., 306, 329, 622; *quasi-n.* 543. [? Cf. OE. *gifre* greedy]
**ewe** *n.* in ∼ *ardaunt* ardent spirit (alcohol) 590; W **hewe**. [OF. *eau ardente*]

### F

**face** *n.* face 155, 284.
**fadide** *pt. s.* made pale 284; **fadit** *pp. as adj.* faded, pale 155.
**fayle** *v.* to fail 327, 524; **faylede** *pt. s.* 35.
**fayne** *adj.* glad 388; **faynere** *compar.* more joyous 15.
**faire** *adj.* fair, pleasant 145, &c.; *as sb.* fair lady 357, 552; **fayrere** *compar.* more pleasing 109.
**faire, fayre** *adv.* pleasantly, delightfully 10; well 71, 542; deftly 77, 88.
**faythe** *n.* in *be my* ∼ upon my word 183; faith, religion 548.
**falle** *v.* to fall 12, 38; **fallen** *pp.* fallen, befallen 65, 317, 378.
**fantome** *n.* illusion, vanity 184.
**fare** *n.* behaviour 59.

**fare** *v.* to go 354, 363; **(with) faris** *pr. 2 s.* dealest, hast to do (with) 184; **fares** *3 s.* goes, proceeds 385; **fared** *pt. s.* went 572; *pl.* fared 330; **faren** *pp.* departed 619.
**faste** *adv.* quickly, swiftly 20, &c.; ∼ *to* close to 78.
**fatills** *pr. 3 s. refl.* makes ready 20 n.; **fittilled** *pt. s.* prepared, made ready 542; W **fetuld**. [? Cf. OE. *fetel* girdle, belt]
**faughte** see **fighte.**
**fawkoner(e)s** *n. pl.* falconers 210, 216, 226.
**fawkons** *n. pl.* falcons 222.
**feble** *adj.* poor, weak 195.
**feche** *v.* to fetch, bring 549; **fet** *pt. s.* 378.
**fede** *v.* to feed 69.
**fee** *n.* in *of the* ∼ by inherited legal right 94 n.
**feetur** *n.* growing antler or tine 27 n. [OF. *feture, faiture*]
**fey** *adj.* fated to die, i.e. mortally wounded 485, 496, 498.
**felde** *n.* field (of battle) 382, 485, 496; = the combatants 498.
**fele** *adj.* many 1, &c.; W **fele, feell, felle.**
**felle** *n.* hide 77.
**fellys** *n. pl.* fells, moors 59.
**felowe** *n.* fellow (contemptuous) 183.
**ferde** *n.*[1] company, host 330, 480.
**ferde** *n.*[2] in *for* ∼ for fear; or *pp.* 'because of being afraid' 97 n.; W **for feerde** 429.
**ferde** *pt. s.* went 360; **ferden** *pt. pl.* 578.
**fere** *n.* wife 388; comrade 564; **feris, ferys** *pl.* companions 58, 510.
**ferkes** *pr. 3 s.* goes 20; **ferkede** *pt. s.* went quickly 659.
**ferly** *adj.* strange, wondrous 310, 566.
**ferne** *n.* fern 92.
**ferrere** *adv.* further 47.
**ferse** *adj.* fierce, bold 109, 349.
**fersely** *adv.* eagerly, vigorously 216, 226, fiercely 435.

## Glossary

**feste** *pt. s.* secured, fastened 91.
**festes** *n. pl.* celebrations, festivals 385.
**fet, fete** see **feche, fote.**
**fewe** *adj.* few 187.
**fewles, fewlis** see **foule.**
**fighte** *v.* to fight 301; **faughte** *pt. s.* fought 485, &c.; **foughten** *pl.* 322; **foghten** *pp.* 326.
**filmarte** *n.* foumart, polecat 18. [OE. *fūl+mearþ* marten]
**fynde** *v.* to find, discover 94; **fyndis** *pr. 3 s.* 568; **founden** *pp.* 210.
**fyne** *adj.* excellent, distinguished 587; pure, refined 592.
**fyngere** *n.* finger 81; *n. pl.* in *of two ~ brede* with two fingerbreadths (of fat) 71.
**fynour** *n.* refiner of metal 587.
**fyre** *n.* fire 593.
**firste** *adj.* first 109, 300, 426.
**fiste** *n.* fist 78, 170.
**fittilled** see **fatills.**
**fytz** *n.* son of 476; **fitz** *pl.* 529. [AF. *fitz*, OF. *fiz* son]
**fyve** *adj.* five 31.
**flayede** *pp.* put to flight 428.
**flede, fledden** *pt. pl.* fled 18, 382; **flowen** *pp.* 498; W **floyn.**
**flese** *n.* fleece 338.
**flewe** *pt. s.* flayed 78.
**flye** *v.* to fly 209.
**flyte** *pr. subj. 1 pl.* dispute, argue 264.
**flode** *n.* river 360; **floodes** *pl.* waters, streams 216.
**floreschede** *pp.* lined with fat 71.
**floures** *n. pl.* flowers 8, 119.
**flowen** see **flede.**
**fole(s)** *n.* fool(s) 264.
**foly** *n.* folly 184.
**folke** *n.* men, people 310, 480, 566; **folkes** *pl.* 428.
**fologhed** *pp.* baptized 545.
**folowede** *pt. s.* followed, pursued 435.
**fomen** *n. pl.* foemen, foes W 356.
**fongen** *v.* to get, take 572, 578; **fonge** *pt. s.* took 88, 388, (captive) 544.
**fonnes** *pr. 2 s.* dost play the fool 183. [ME. *fon(ne)* n. fool, der. obscure]
**fonte** *n.* font 545; **founte** 549.
**for** *conj.* for 48, 184, 193, &c.; *prep.* for 242, 257, 557; because of, through, on account of 97, 101, 154, &c.; in spite of 186, 187, 188; about 189; **for to** to 110, 115, 150, &c.
**for-frayed** *pp.* (well) frayed, burnished 27 n. [OE. *for-* (intens.) + OF. *frayer*]
**forfrayede** *pp.* alarmed, terrified 59. [OE. *for-* (intens.) + AF. *(a)frayer*]
**for-sothe** *adv.* truly, indeed 107.
**forthe** *adv.* forth 549.
**for-thi** *conj.* wherefore 641.
**forthire** *adv.* further 269; W **farþer.**
**forward** *adj.* ? to the fore W 485.
**forworþed** *pp.* destroyed, perished W 496.
**fostere** *n.* forester 94. [Contr. form of OF. *forestier*]
**fote** *n.* foot 27, &c.; *dat. pl.* in *hym to ~ at his feet* 490 n.; **fete** *pl.* 77, &c.
**fothire** *n.* cart-load 189.
**fo(u)ghten** see **fighte.**
**foule** *n.* bird 15; **fewles, fewlis, fowlis** *pl.* (the game) 210, 217, 241.
**foundes** *pr. 3 s.* hastens 372; **founden** *pl.* 222, 226; **founded(e)** *pt. s.* 97, 659.
**founte** see **fonte.**
**fourche** *n.* haunch, legs 91 n.; **fourches** *pl.* 88.
**fourme** *n.* form (nest of hare) 20.
**foxe** *n.* fox 18.
**freely** *adv.* readily, eagerly 222.
**freke** *n.* man 109.
**frendis** *n. pl.* friends 354.
**freschely** *adv.* briskly, keenly 372. [OF. *freis*, fem. *fresche*, rather than OE. *fersc*]
**frythe** *n.* woodland 15.
**fro** *prep.* from 76, 77, 87, 88, 212: *that ... fro* whence 246. W **fro** 443, 509, 609; **froo** 246.

## Glossary

**from(e)** *prep.* from, away from 6, 29, 99, 443, 509, 609.
**full** *adv.* full, quite, very 10, &c. (106 times), **ful** 585.

### G

**ģaffe** *pt. s.* gave 198; **ģouen** *pl.* 17 n.
**ģaye** *adj.* gay, gallant, fair 273, 351, 615, 629.
**ģayly** *adv.* gaily 169.
**ģaynly** *adv.* readily 281. [ON. *gegn*]
**ģamnes** *n. pl.* games 255.
**ģane** *pt. pl.* began 12. [OE. *-ginnan*]
**ģane** *pp.* gone, past, ago 460. [OE. *gegān*]
**ģarte** *pt. s.* caused, made 549, 561.
**ģates** *n. pl.* ways 339, 494.
**ģatt(e)** see **ģete**.
**ģedring** *n.* gathering W 340.
**ģentill** *adj.* noble, excellent 422, &c.; **ientille** 338.
**ģentilly** *adv.* nobly 439.
**ģere** *n.* attire, armour 273.
**ģerede** *pp.* attired 122.
**ģesserante** *n.* coat of armour 180.
**ģete** *v.* to get 4, 191, 537; produce 588; **ģatt(e)**, **ģete** *pt. s.* acquired 206, 281; conquered 416, 491.
**[ģete]** *v.* to guard 608 n. [ON. *gǣta*]
**ģirde** *pp.* girt 138. [OE. *gyrdan*]
**ģirdes** *pr. 3 s. trans.* strikes 343; **ģirde** *pt. s. intr.* rushed, leapt 318. [? OE. *gyrdan*, infl. in sense by OE. *gierd* rod]
**ģlayfe** *n.* sword 202.
**ģloes** *pr. 3 s.* glows, shines 188.
**ģloue** *n.* glove 232.
**ģnattes** *n. pl.* gnats 50.
**ģnewen** *pt. pl.* gnawed, bit 50.
**god** *n.* god 196, **God(e)** God 198, 450, 644.
**ģolde** *n.* gold 122, &c.
**ģolyone** *n.* tunic 138; see *OED.* s.v. †Golion.
**ģome** *n.* man, knight 169, &c.
**ģoo** *v.* to go 358, 561; **ģo** *pr. 1 s.* go 653.
**ģospelle** *n.* gospel 644.
**ģoste** *n.* spirit 198.
**ģouen** see **ģaffe**.

**ģrace** *n.* grace 513.
**ģracyous** *adj.* gracious, noble 528.
**ģraye** *adj.* grey 138, 182.
**ģraythe** *v.* to prepare, make 588; **ģraythede** *pt. s.* put, set 85; **ģraythed, ģrathede** prepared (to go) 339, 416; arrayed, prepared 358, *608.
**ģraythely** *adv.* ready 202; promptly, at once 494; aptly 644.
**ģraue** *n.* grave 623, 653.
**ģrauen** *pp.* buried 629.
**ģree** *n.* supreme reward (the Grail), or highest place (the Siege Perilous) 473; see *OED.* s.v. Gree, 5.
**ģrene** *adj.* green 8, 663; *as sb.* 122, 169, &c.
**ģrete** *adj.* large, massive 32, 444; great 588.
**ģret(e)ly** *adv.* greatly 50, 140, 450.
**ģreued(e)** *pt. s. intr.* complained 182, 194; *trans.* grieved, angered 450, 561; *pl.* annoyed, harassed 50.
**ģreues** *n. pl.* groves, thickets 27, 56.
**[Gr]ewe** *n.* Greek 338. [OF. *griu*]
**ģrym** *adj.* cruel, fierce 202, 444.
**ģripis, ģrippes** *pr. 3 s.* grips, seizes, grasps 374, 503; **ģrippede** *pt. s.* pulled, tore 85.
**ģryse** *n.* grass 8 n.
**ģrome** *n.* man W 475. [OF. *gromet*, MDu. *grom*]
**ģronande** *pr. p.* groaning 343.
**ģrounde** *n.* ground 343, 444.
**ģrowen** *pp.* overgrown, covered 8.
**ģrownden** *pp.* ground, sharpened 202.
**ģud** *adj.* good 528, 653, **ģude** 340, 351, 374, &c.; W **ģode** 351, &c., good 340.
**ģude** *n.* goods, possessions 140, 188, &c.; **ģudes** *pl.* 257; W **ģode** 257, **good** 281.
**ģuttes, ģuttys** *n. pl.* guts 82, 85.

### 3

**ȝape** *adj.* lively, active 134, 171, 270.

## Glossary

ʒates, ʒatis *n. pl.* gates 398, 535, 575.
ʒe *pron. 2 pl.* you 106, 266, 267, &c.; ʒow *acc.* 613; *refl.* yourselves 646; ʒow(e) *dat.* 108, 159, 166, &c.; ʒour(e) *poss. adj.* your 268, 290, 634, 641; ʒoure-selfe *pron.* you 635; ʒoure-seluen *pl.* you yourselves 271; W ye, you, yow, &c.
ʒere *n. pl.* years 133, 150, 567; ʒeris 164.
ʒerne *adv.* readily, faithfully 34; carefully 46; eagerly, vigorously 104, 227, 303; thoroughly 183.
ʒernynge *n.* desire 535.
ʒernynge (to) *pr. p.* longing, eager (for) 171; ʒernede *pp.* desired 393.
ʒet(t)e *pp.* surrendered 398, 575, ʒett granted 535. [Late OE. *gē(a)tan*, prob. formed after ON. *játt(t)a*]
ʒit(t) *adv.* yet 450, 610.
ʒolden *pp.* given up 398, 575.
ʒonge *adj.* young 134, 171, 270.
ʒore *adv.* (since) long ago 263.
ʒour(e) see ʒe.
ʒouthe *n.* Youth 134, 652; youth 270.
ʒow(e) see ʒe.

### H

habade, habyde see abyde.
halde see holde.
halfues *n. pl.* sides 574.
hallede (to) *pt. s.* drew (back) 53. [OF. *haler*; see *OED.* s.v. Hale, v.[1]]
halowd *pt. pl.* baptized W 545, 552.
halse, haulse *n.* neck 90, 373.
hande *n.* hand 111, 153, 371, 503, honde 202, 212, 236; in *to* ~ in (my) possession 281; handes, handis *pl.* 309, 533, hondes 287, 433.
hande-while *n.* moment 106, 267.
happen *v.* to happen, befall 5; happenyd *impers.* it happened, chanced 54.
harde *adv.* vigorously 19, firmly, stoutly 201.
hare *n.*[1] hare 19.
hare, here *n.*[2] hair 117, 157.
harmede *pp.* harmed 475.
haspede *pp.* girt, buckled 201. [OE. *hæpsian*]
haste *n.* in *in* ~ speedily, immediately 213, 508.
hastely *adv.* immediately 503. [OF. *haste*; cf. OE. *hǣstlīce* vehemently]
hathelle *n.* man, knight 111, 170.
hatt(e) *n.* hat 117, 179.
hatten see hete.
hauke *n.* hawk 111, 170; haukes, hawkes *pl.* 209, 218, 227.
haulle *n.* hall 253.
haulse see halse.
haue *v.* to have 96, 278; hafe *auxil. s.* and *pl.* have 166, 174, 189, 296, &c., haue 262, 460; haste *auxil. 2 s.* hast 260; hase *pr. 2 s.* hast 186, 196; has *3 s.* 617; haue, hafe *pr. subj. 1 s.* have 289; *3 s.* 447; *3 pl.* 438; *imper. s.* 649; haues *imper. pl.* 653; had(e) *pt. and auxil.* had 49, 117, 315, &c.; *pt. subj. s.* had 48, 49, (would have) 57; W haue 278, &c.; hath *s.* 617, *pl.* 335; han *pl.* 296, 460; had 316, &c., hadde 466.
hawes *n. pl.* hedges 19.
hawtayne *adj.* proud, mettlesome 209.
hawteste *adj. pl.* proudest, most spirited 213.
he *pron. 3 s. masc.* he 31, &c.; hym *accus. and dat.* 33, 34, 35, &c.; *refl.* himself 116, 265, 339, &c.; hym-selfe, hym-seluen *nom.* himself 345, 389, 526, 599, &c.; hym-seluen *accus.* him 429; *refl.* himself 543; *dat.* him 472; (to, for, from) himself 448, 539, 609; (as to, in) himself 624; his, hys *poss. adj.* his 36, 52, 317, &c.
hede *n.* head (including antlers) 25, 66, 90; head 95, &c.
hedis (to) *pr. 3 s.* looks (towards) 508.
hefe *v.* to raise 288; heuede *pt. s.* heaved, dragged 92.
heghe *adj.* tall, stately, noble 25,

*Glossary*

111, 170; high 209, 411; W **highe** 411.
**heghely** *adv.* solemnly 178, 204.
**heghte** *n.* in *appon* ~ aloft, up in the air 215; **highte** in *one* ~ on high 470.
**helde** see **holde** *v.*
**hele** *n.* healing, well-being 177.
**helle** *n.* hell 643.
**helme** *n.* helmet 201, 373, 446.
**helpe** *n.* help 643.
**helpe(n)** *v.* to help 227, 288, 354.
**hem** see **thay**.
**hemmes** *n. pl.* borders 128.
**hendely** *adv.* courteously 267.
**hent** *v.* to seize, get 96; **henttis** *pr. 3 s.* takes 236; **hent** ... *vp pt. s.* took, seized 60; **hent** 66, 373.
**hepe** *n.* heap (prostrate mass) in *one ane* ~ prostrate 57.
**herbere** *n.* arber (first stomach) 74 n. [OF. *(h)erb(i)ere*]
**here** *n.* see **hare** *n.²*.
**here** *v.* to hear 400, 452, 584; **herde** *pt. s.* heard 656.
**here** *adv.* here, in this world 256, 641.
**here-wedys** *n. pl.* battle-attire, armour 201.
**heryet(t)** *pt. s.* dragged 66; *pp.* carried off 427 n. [OE. *hergian*]
**heritage** *n.* in *of* ~ ? possessing heritages W 347 (for *Artage*).
**herken** *v.* to listen (to) 267.
**heron** *n.* heron 223.
**hert** *n.¹* hart, stag 5, 25, &c.; **hertys** *pl.* 17.
**hert(e)** *n.²* heart 177, 248, &c.
**heste** *n.* promise 178. [OE. *hǣs* command, *behǣs* promise]
**hete** *pr. 1 s.* assure 643; **highte** *pp.* promised 204; **hatten** *pass. pt. used as pp.* was called 405; W **hight** 405.
**hethe** *n.* heather 93.
**hethyn** *adj.* heathen 541.
**heuede** see **hefe**.
**heuen** *n.* heaven, sky 6, 162; *gen. s.* 215; *vndir the* ~ on earth 320.
**heuen-riche** *n.* kingdom of heaven 427.

**hewe** *n.* colour, complexion 155, 284.
**hewede** *pp.* coloured 157.
**hewes** *pr. 3 s.* hews 376.
**hid(de)** *pt. s.* hid 92, 95.
**hyghes** *pr. 3 s.* hastens, speeds 508; *3 pl.* fly swiftly 213; **hyen(n)** hasten 59, 210, &c.; **hyede** *pt.s.* 60.
**highte** see **heghte, hete**.
**hilde** *pt. s.* concealed 93.
**hillys** *n. pl.* hills 17.
**hiltys** *n. pl.* hilt(s) 503 n.
**hynde** *n.* hind 5; **hyndes** *pl.* 17.
**hir, hyr** see **scho**.
**hitten** *pr. 3 pl.* hit, strike 223; **hitt** *pt. s.* 54.
**hode** *n.* hood 117, 179.
**hodes** *pr. 3 s.* hoods (in falconry) 236.
**hokes** *n. pl.* hooks, catches 53 n.
**holde** *v.* to hold, keep 148, 237, 577, **halde** 204; **helde** *pt. s.* regarded, thought 164; **halden** *pp.* guarded, kept prisoner 304; **holden** kept, preserved 413; held 467.
**holde** *n.* castle, stronghold 413.
**hole** *n.* hole 84, 92.
**holynes** *n.* holiness 427.
**hologhe** *adj.* hollow 95.
**holte** *n.* wood 57.
**homelyde** *pt. s.* cut 90. [OE. *hamelian*]
**honde** see **hande**.
**hony** *n.* honey 413.
**hoo** *interj.* ho! 223 n.
**hope** *n.* hope 177.
**hopynge** *n.* belief, opinion 164 n.
**horde** *n.* hoard, store W 281.
**horemosse** *n.* hair-moss 93. [ON. *hár* hair, ME. (N. Midl.) *hor, hore*, OE. *mos*]
**hornes** *n. pl.* antlers 95.
**horse** *n.* horse 111, &c.
**hounde** *n.* hound 60.
**houen** *pr. 3 pl.* are poised 215. [? OE. *\*hōfian*]
**how** *adv. interrog.* how 98.
**howghe** *interj.* 'huff' 223 n.
**howses** *n. pl.* houses 142, 279.
**hundrethe** *adj.* hundred 164. [ON. *hundrað*]

82

## Glossary

**hunte** *n.* huntsman 96.
**hurkles** *pr. 3 s.* crouches 19. [OE. *\*hurclian*; cf. MLG. *hurken* to squat]
**hurlede** *pp.* hurled, flung, thrown down 57 (see **hepe**). [? Onomatopoeic; cf. LG. *hurreln* to sling, toss, push]

### I

**I** *pron. 1 s.* I 3, 7, 21, &c.; **me** *accus. and dat.* me, (to) me 24, 50, 106, 108, &c.; *refl.* myself, (for) myself 4, 42, 43, &c.; *with impers. vbs. adj.* 70, 102, &c.; **my** *poss. adj.* my 3, 22, 38, &c.; **myn** (*before aspirates and vowels*) 50, 177, &c.; **my-selfe** *nom.* myself 4; **my-seluen** *accus.* 288; **my-selfe** *dat.* (by myself, i.e. in my own person) 269, **my-seluen** 203, 282.
**iche** *adj.* each, every 15, 27 &c.; **iche a** 420.
**if** *conj.* if 168.
**iles** *n. pl.* islands 334, 420.
**i-liche** *adv.* in like manner 113 n.
**in** *prep.* in 1, 15, 21, &c., **inn** 130, **inne** 197.
**in-to** *prep.* into 4, 64, 67, &c.
**irkede** *v. impers.* grew tired 277. See *OED*. s.v. Irk, v. 3. b.
**it** *pron.* it 75, 78, 80, &c.; *impers.* 5, 98, 215, &c.
**i-wis** *adv.* indeed 276. [OE. *ge-wiss*, adj.; cf. *mid* or *tō gewisse*]

### I = J

**Iapid** *pp.* played the fool W 262; see *OED*. s.v. Jape, v.
**ientille** see **gentill**.
**Iewe** *n.* Jew 426, &c.; **Iewes** *pl.* 422, &c.
**ioyntly** *adv.* firmly, steadily 180. [OF. *joint* + *-ly*]
**ioly** *adj.* excellent, fine 459; gay, gallant 620.
**iugge** *pr. subj. 1 pl.* (let us) consider 422.
**Iury** *n.* Jewry, the Jews W 518. [OF. *ju(e)rie*]
**iustede** *pp.* jousted 180.
**iusters** *n. pl.* jousters 459.

### K

**kayre** *v.* to return 246; **W caris** *pr. 3 s.* turns, goes 395; **care** *3 pl.* return 246. [ON. *keyra*]
**kaysers** *n. pl.* emperors 605 n.
**kane** *pr. 3 pl.* can, are able to 425; **couthe (of)** *pt. s.* had knowledge (of) 511.
**kaple** *n.* horse 189. [ON. *kapall* nag, pack-horse]
**katur** *adj.* four 529.
**keyes** *n. pl.* keys 398, 575.
**kempes** *n. pl.* warriors, champions 251.
**kende** *pt. s.* guided, revealed the way 553. [OE. *cennan*; see *OED*. s.v. Ken, v.¹ †4]
**kene** *adj.* lively, active 13; keen, bold 203, 299, &c.
**kenely** *adv.* eagerly 161; boldly 362.
**kepe** *v.* to keep 608; **keppyn (of)** *v. infin.* or *pr. 3 pl.* snatch (off) 212 n.; **kepide** *pt. s.* detained 353.
**kepyng** *n.* keeping, guarding 443.
**kest(e)** see **casten**.
**keuduart** *n.* ? rascal 68 n. [? OF. *culvert*, *colvert*] See **kiluarde**.
**kyd(de), kiddeste** see **kythe**.
**killede** *pt. s.* killed 309.
**kiluarde** *adj.* infamous, treacherous 516; W **kilward**. [OF. *culvert*, *colvert*, med. L. *collibertus* fellow-freedman; in Middle Ages = 'serf', hence 'abject wretch']
**kyngdomes** *n. pl.* kingdoms 402, &c.
**kyng(e)** *n.* king 33, &c.; **kynges** *pl.* 251, &c.
**kysse** *v.* to kiss 248.
**kythe** *n.* country, people 466; (native) land 493.
**kythe** *v.* to make known, reveal 168; **kyd(de)** *pp. as adj.* renowned 441, 458, &c.; **kiddeste** *superl.* 299.
**knees** *n. pl.* knees 229.
**knelyn** *pr. 3 pl.* kneel 229.
**knyghte** *n.* knight 203, &c.;

## Glossary

**knyghtis** *pl.* 350, 362, 605, k[nyght]es 529.
**knyghtly** *adv.* chivalrously, in knightly fashion 337.
**knowe** *v.* to know, understand 168; **knawen** *pp.* (well) known 458.
**krage** *n.* cave, fissure of a rock 64. [Prob. Celtic]
**krepyn** *pr. 3 pl.* creep 229; **crepite** *pt. s.* crept 42; **crepyde, crept** *pp.* 64, 623; W **crepyn** 229, **cropyn** 623.
**kutt** *pt. s.* cut 68; **cuttede** cut (out) 80.

### L

**lache** *v.* to get, take 211; **laches** to *pr. 3 s.* picks up 239; **laughte till** *pt. s.* seized, took up 52. [OE. *læccan, læhte*]
**lady** *n.* lady 174, 176; **ladys(e)** *pl.* 247, 274.
**laghe** *n.* custom 240; W **Lawe**.
**layde** *pp.* laid 460.
**laye** *n.* faith 197. [OF. *lai*]
**layke** *n.* sport 49. [ON. *leik-r*]
**layke** *v. refl.* to play, amuse oneself 259.
**layne** see **ligge**.
**laythe** *adj.* ugly, repulsive 152. [ON. *leið-r*]
**lanerettis** *n. pl.* lannerets (kind of hawk, male) 220. [OF. *laneret*]
**laners** *n. pl.* lanners (female) 220. [OF. *lanier*]
**langid aftur** *pp.* longed for W 393.
**lappyn** *v.* to enfold, embrace 247; W **lappis** *pr. 3 pl.* coil, fold 238; **lapped** *pp.* 247. [OE. *læppa* fold of cloth]
**large** *adj.* sturdy, broad 115.
**laste** *adv.*[1] least 283; **leste** 259.
**laste** *adv.*[2] for the last time 512; *at the* ~ at last, finally 52, 323.
**laughte** see **lache**.
**launde** *n.* glade, grassy clearing 24, 199.
**laupis** *pr. 3 s.* leaps W 240. [ON. *hlaupa*]
**lede** *n.* man 152, 393; **ledys** *pl.*

(addressed to hearers) 106. [OE. *lēod* (in verse) prince]
**lede** *v.* to lead (experience) 256; **ledys** *pr. 3 s.* leads 352.
**lefte** *adj.* left 54, 240.
**lefte** *v.* see **leue**.
**legge** *n.* leg 75, 76; **legges** *pl.* 115.
**lele** *adj.* (as a vague epithet) fine, handsome 115. [OF. *leël* loyal]
**lelly** *adv.* loyally, faithfully 274.
**leman** *n.* loved one 174. [OE. *\*lēofman*, early ME. *leofmon*]
**lengare, lengere** see **longe**.
**lenge(n)** *v.* to stay, tarry 199, 384; **lenged** *pp.* lingered 655; W **lyng, langid**.
**lenyde** *pt. s.* leant, bent 152 n.
**lepis** *pr. 3 s.* leaps 240; **lepe** *pt. s.* moved quickly 76; W **laupis**, q.v.
**lere** *n.* face W 275. [OE. *hlēor*]
**lessches, lesses** *n. pl.* leashes 211, 238; W **leches**. [OF. *lesse*]
**lesse** *conj.* lest 82.
**leste** see **laste** *adv.*[1]
**lete** *pt. s.* let 38, 61.
**leue** *n.* leave 362.
**leue** *v.*[1] to leave, abandon 235; **lefte** *pt. s.* 506; **leuede** *pp.* 395.
**leue** *v.*[2] to believe 559; *pr. 1 s.* 197.
**leuere** *adj.* dearer (*me were* ~ I would rather) 199; preferable 277.
**leues** *n. pl.* leaves 22, 40, 663.
**lyame** *n.* leash 38, 61. [OF. *liem*, L. *ligamen*]
**life, lyfe** *n.* life 256, 563; **lyues** *pl.* 252, 634.
**lyfe** *v.* to live 256.
**ligge** *v.* to lie (stay, remain) W 542; **layne** *pp.* lain 655; W **lane**.
**lighte** *adj.* gay, cheerful 352; light, bright 663.
**lighte** *v.* to descend, swoop down 222; **lightten** *pr. 3 pl.* 220; **lighte** *pt. s.* alighted, fell 323.
**lightenede** *pp.* dawned 16.
**lightly** *adv.* lightly, gently 38.
**likame** *n.* body 275.
**lykes** *v. impers. w. dat.* pleases 611, 632; **lykede** *pt. s.* 521.
**liste** *pr. subj. 3 s. impers.* (if) it

84

## Glossary

**pleases** (you), if you like 168; *pt. s.* (when) it pleased (him), when he desired it 588 n.
**listen** *v.* to listen to 106.
**lythe** *n.* people, vassals 185, 207.
**littill** *quasi-sb.* little 24.
**loge** *v.* to dwell, stay 542; **lugede** *pt. s.* sheltered 663.
**lokes (to)** *pr. 3 s.* attends (to) 239; **lokes** looks 506; **lokede** *pt. s.* looked 24; **looke** *imper.* 461.
**londe** *n.* land, country 185, 207; **londes** *pl.* 192, 489.
**longe** *adj.* long 28, 113, &c.
**longe** *adv.* long, for a long time 49, 260, 393; **lengare** *compar.* longer 264, 654; **lengere** 613.
**longede** *pt. pl.* belonged, i.e. dwelt 57. [From adj. (*i*)*long*, OE. *ge-long* belonging, depending]
**lorde** *n.* lord, ruler 185, 197, &c.; **lordes** *pl.* 525.
**loste** *pp.* lost 49.
**lothe** *adj.* ugly, loathsome 275; W **lathe**.
**loughe** *adv.* low 460, 658; **lowe** 229, 633.
**louset** see **lowsen**.
**loutted** *pt. s. intr.* bent 52. [OE. *lūtan*, str. v.]
**loue** *n.* love 181; **lufe** 357; **loue**, **lufe** *n.* loved one, lover 392, 393, 625.
**louede** see **luffes**.
**louely** *adj.* comely, fair 247, 275.
**lowde** *adv.* loudly 234, 656.
**lowe** see **loughe**.
**lowly** *adv.* ? dearly W 274. [? OE. *luflīce*]
**lowppes** *pr. 3 s.* loops 238; see *OED.* s.v. Loop, sb.¹ and v.¹ W **lappis**, see **lappyn**.
**lowsen** *v.* to let loose, release 211; **louset** *pt. s.* 61.
**luffes** *pr. 2 s.* lovest 259; **louede** *pt. s.* loved 305, 540; **loueden** *pl.* 612; **luffede** *pp.* 174.
**lugede** see **loge**.
**luyre** *n.* lure (device for recalling hawks) 239 n.; W **lowre**. [OF. *leurre, loerre, loire*]

**lure** *n.* loss, disaster 323; W **lere**. [OE *lyre*]
**lusty** *adj.* lusty, vigorous 474.

## M

**may** *pr. 1 s.* am able to, can 288, 530, 630; *3 s.* 634; **myghte** *pt. s.* might 5; was able to, could 33; *3 pl.* might 431.
**mayden** *n.* maiden 114; **maydens** *pl.* 274.
**Maye** *n.*¹ May 1, 660.
**maye** *n.*² maiden 623.
**maystries** *n. pl.* arts, magical powers 469. [OF. *maistrise*, s.]
**makande** *n.* comfort, ease 278. [ON. *makindi* n. pl. friendly intercourse, *i makindum* at one's ease; cf. Sc. dial. *makint, makintly*]
**make** *n.* mate, wife W 278. [OE. (*ge*)*maca*, ON. *maki*]
**make** *v.* to make 385, 592; *imper. s.* 190; **makes** *imper. pl.* 290; **made** *pt. s.* made, built 279, 342, &c., **makede** 74, 344 n., 408, **maket** 594; **maden** *3 pl.* 105 n.; **made** *pp.* 48, 433, &c.
**man** *n.* man 278, &c., **mane** 347; **men** *pl.* men, people 104, &c.
**manere** *n.* manner, likeness 433.
**many** *adj.* many 125, &c.; *pron.* 221, 295, 571.
**marche** *n.* region, district 151.
**maried** *pt. s. trans.* married 540.
**maryo** *n.* marrow 232. [OE. *mearg, mearh*]
**marlede** *pt. s.* marled (fertilized with marl) 279. [OF. *marle* n.]
**marlelyng** *n.* fertilizing with marl 142.
**materaise** *n. pl.* materials W 592.
**maulerdes** *n. pl.* mallards (wild duck) 221. [OF. *mallart*]
**me**, &c., see **I**.
**medill** *n.* waist 114; **mydle** middle (i.e. the beam) 26.
**Medill Elde** *n.* Middle Age, middle age 151, 278, 649, **Midill Elde** 652.
**mekill, mekyll** *adj.* great 344, 479; W **mykil(l)**.

## Glossary

**mendynge** *n.* repairing 142.
**mendys** *n. pl.* amends, reparation 359.
**mendis** *pr. 3 pl.* increase, fill 146 n.
**mene** *v.* to tell of, relate 630; W **meene** 530 (see **myne**). [OE. *mǣnan* v.¹; see *ment*, below]
**menge** *v.* to mix, mingle 592.
**menskfully** *adv.* gracefully 114. [ON. *mennska* humanity, kindness]
**ment** *pt. s.* moaned, complained 160. [OE. *mǣnan* v.²]
**mercy** *n.* mercy 160.
**mercurye watirs** *n. pl.* mercury-water (aqua regia and corrosive sublimate) 589.
**mere** *n.* mere, lake 500, 502, 508.
**mery** *adj.* pleasant 12.
**meruaylles** *n. pl.* marvels, wonders 487.
**meruayllous** *adj.* marvellous 606.
**metalles** *n. pl.* metals 589, 592.
**mete** *n.* food 52.
**metyn** *pr. 3 pl.* meet 221; **mete, mett** *pt. s.* 342, 495.
**myche** *quasi-sb.* much 276; *adv.* 511, 540; **mo(o), more** *adv.* more 165, 308, &c.; **moste** *superl.* 292, 387, &c.; W **moch**, &c.
**myche-whate** *n.* many things 105.
**myddes, myddis** *n.* middle, centre 29, 87, &c. [OE. *to-middes*, prep. and adv.]
**mydle** see **medill**.
**myghte** *n.* might, strength 479.
**myghte** *v.* see **may**.
**mylde** *adj.* gentle, gracious 665.
**myldely** *adv.* gently, softly 12.
**mynde** *n.* in *hafe* ~ remember, mark well 649.
**myne** *v.* to call to mind, remember 530; W **mynne** 630 (see **mene**). [ON. *minna* remind, *minnask* remember]
**myngyng** *n.* mingling, mixing W 592.
**my[n]tid** *pp.* taken aim 48. [OE. *myntan*; see *OED*. s.v. Mint, v.¹ 4 intr.]
**mirrours** *n. pl.* mirrors 290.

**myrthe** *n.* joy, delight 316 **mirthes** *pl.* 1, 660.
**mys-done** *pp.* done amiss 359 n.
**my-selfe**, &c., see **I**.
**mysse** *n.* sin(s) 641. [OE. *miss* n. loss and *mis-*, prefix]
**mystes** *n. pl.* mists 12.
**mo(o)** see **myche**.
**mode** *n.* mud 433; W **mudde**. [MLG., LG. *mudde*, LG. also *mod*, *mōde*]
**mody** *adj.* proud, bold 302, &c.; **modyere** *pl. compar.* 295.
**molde** *n.* earth 295.
**momelide** *pt. s.* mumbled, muttered 160. [Cf. Du. *mommelen*, Swed. *mumla*, Dan. *mumle*]
**monethe** *n.* month 1*, 660.
**more** *n.* moor 495.
**moste** *adv.* see **myche**.
**moste** *pr. 3 s. impers.* must 653; *pt. s.* must, had to 47.
**mote[d]** *pt. pl.* spoke, argued 105.
**Mounte** *n.* hill, Mount 487, 526.
**mousede** *pt. s.* mused 140.
**moued** *pt. s. refl.* betook (himself), went 546; **mouede** *pp.* moved 48.
**mukkede** *pt. s.* manured 279. [ON. *moka*, Dan. *muge*]
**mukkyng** *n.* 'muck-spreading', applying manure 142.
**multiplye** *v.* to multiply 589.

### N

**naylede** *pp.* nailed 555.
**nayles** *n. pl.* nails 554.
**naymely** *adv.* especially 607.
**nayttede** *pt. s.* practised (indulged in) 607.
**nayt(t)ly** *adv.* exactly 108, 167; dexterously 457; fittingly 554; W **nathly** 457, **natly** 554. [ON. *neyt-r* good, useful]
**name** *n.* name 134, 163; **names** *pl.* 108, &c.
**name** *pt. s.* took 86, 539.
**namede** *pp.* named, told 167.
**ne** *adv.* not 293, &c.; *conj.* nor 179, 187, &c.; **ne . . . ne** neither . . . nor

## Glossary

117, 288, &c.; **ne** ... **noghte** not (emphatic) 583, 631.
**nede** *n.* in *at (the)* ∼ in time of need 327, 524, 565.
**neghede** *pt. s. intr.* approached, came near 573; W **nyghed**.
**nekke** *n.* neck 89.
**nese** *n.* nose in *sett vp the* ∼, i.e. sniffed about 45; **nesse** in *of* ∼, i.e. in scenting 99. [Not OE. *nosu*; cf. MDu. and MLG. *nese*]
**neuen** *v.* to name 108, 297; **neuened** *pp.* 580.
**neuer** *adv.* never 336, &c.
**nygromancye** *n.* necromancy, black magic 607.
**nyne** *adj.* nine 297, 580.
**nynety** *adj.* ninety W 308.
**no** *adj.* no 41, 47, 96, &c.; ∼ *noþer = non oþer*, none other 390; *adv.* no 165, 264, 269, &c.
**nobylnes** *n.* nobleness W 427.
**noble** *adj.* noble, fine, excellent 280, 327, &c., **noblee** 251.
**noghte** *adv.* not, by no means 288, 327, &c., **nott** 536.
**noghte** *n.* nothing 635, 637.
**noyede** *pt. s. impers.* vexed, grieved 573.
**nombles** *n. pl.* numbles 86 n.
**none** *adj.* no, none whatever 186; *pron.* no one 36.
**nones** *n.* in *for the* ∼ for the nonce, indeed 25, 118. [OE. *\*for þam ānum*, early ME. *\*for þan ane +* adv. *-es*]
**noþer** see **no**.
**nott** see **noghte**.
**now** *adv.* now 166, 168, 292, &c., **nowe** 621, 629; *intr.* series of statements, 169.
**nowmbron** *pr. 3 pl.* number, estimate 308.

## O

**of** *adv.* off 68, 79, 89, 212, 373, 551.
**of** *prep.* of: equiv. of gen. 39, 91, &c.; (partitive) of, among 119, 176, &c.; (after numeral) 309; adjectival 1, 2, &c.; (place of origin) 301, 318, &c.; (made) of 120, 130, &c.; (colour) 138; (introd. measurement) 31, 71; (age) 133, 150, 164; of, about, concerning 59, 105, &c.; in 313 n.; (away) from 382; from 665; for 359; on account of 447; in, as regards 270, 300, &c.; ∼ *the fee* 94 see **fee**.
**ofte** *adv.* often 141, 223, &c.
**oke** *n.* oak 95.
**Olde** *adj.* Old 423; **aldeste, eldeste** *superl.* in ∼ *of tyme* earliest in date 300, 464.
**one** *prep.* on 7, &c.; (of) 21; (invocation) 161, 172; in 544, 559.
**one** *pron.* one, a certain 355; one, someone 551; *that* ∼ (the) one 601.
**one** *adj.* alone, only 117, 149; in *by hym* ∼ by himself, apart 599 n.
**onere** *n.* honour 180.
**opynede** *pp.* opened 535.
**or** *conj.* or 5, &c.
**Oryent** *n.* Orient 334.
**oþer, othir** *pron.* the other 15, 512; **oþer, othere, othire** *pl.* others 109, 139, 299, &c.
**oþer, othir** *adj.* other 310, 566.
**oure** see **we**.
**ouþer** *pron.* either 271. [OE. *ā-hwæþer, āwþer, ōwþer*]
**out** *adv.* in ∼ *of =* from 302; **oute** away, apart 98; **oute, owt(e)** out 55, 79, 84, &c.
**ouer** *prep.* over 185, &c.
**ownn** see **awnn**.
**owthir** *conj.* or 472. See **ouþer**.

## P

**paynymes** *n. pl.* pagans 421.
**paleys** *n.* palace 319.
**pappis** *n. pl.* breasts 176.
**paramour(e)s** *adv.* passionately 305, 612; *as sb.* lovers 172, 176, 633.
**parfourme** *v.* to perform, carry out 205.
**parkes** *n. pl.* parklands 145.

# Glossary

**Parlement** *n.* (in title) discussion, debate.
**pase** *n.* way, path 296.
**passe** *v. trans.* to pass (along, over) 296; *intr.* pass, proceed 431; **paste** *pt. s.* passed (from this life), died 325 n.; went 532; **passed** *trans.* surpassed 421, *628; *pp.* passed 296.
**passyoun** *n.* passion, suffering 555.
**pastur(e)s** *n. pl.* pastures 146, 280.
**pawnche** *n.* stomach 82, *84.
**penand** *n.* pennant (flag of the opposing side) W 369.
**penyes** *n. pl.* pennies, money 187.
**penn** *n.* quill (barrel of feather) 232.
**peple** *n.* people 431.
**perche** *v.* to pierce 82; **perset** *pt. s.* pierced 380. [ONF. *perchier*, OF. *percer*]
**pereles** *adj.* peerless 399.
**perilous** *adj.* perilous 470.
**peris** *n. pl.* peers W 365.
**perles** *n. pl.* pearls 120.
**perry(e)** *n.* jewellery 129, 192.
**perset** see **perche**.
**pervynke** *n.* periwinkle 9. [OE. *pervince*, L. *pervinca*; ONF. *pervenke*]
**peteuosely** *adv.* piteously 172. [OF. *pitous*, in ME. infl. by ending *-euo(u)s*, as in *plenteuous*]
**philozophire** *n.* philosopher 587.
**piliole** *n.* penny-royal, a small wild mint 9. [AF. *puliol real*]
**pyne** *n.* torment, grief 555.
**playstere** *n.* healer, salve 176. [OF. *plaistre, plastre*]
**pleynede** *pt. s. refl.* lamented 172.
**ploughe-londes** *n. pl.* arable land 145, 280 n.
**poynte** *n.* point (of knife-blade) 82; feat of arms, deed 380. See *OED*. s.v. Point, sb.¹, C †1.
**polayle** *n.* poultry 144.
**pompe** *n.* pomp 187.
**poo** *n.* peacock 365.
**portours** *n. pl.* bearers, carriers 241.
**pouders** *n. pl.* powders 590.
**powndes** *n. pl.* pounds 129.
**praye** *n.* prey, booty 341.

**prayed(e)** *pt. s.* prayed 430, 436; besought 353.
**praysed** *pp. as adj.* praised, esteemed 387, 449.
**presanttes** *n. pl.* presents 144.
**prese** *n.* press, thick of the fight 368; **presse** in *prowdeste in* ~ 612, a conventional phrase usually applied to knights, here to lovers generally.
**prestis** *n. pl.* priests 646.
**preued** see **prouen**.
**price, pryce, pryse** *n.* price, value 129, 192; worth, excellence 449.
**price, pryce, prise** *adj.* excellent, noble 328, 387, 628.
**pride** *n.* pride 187, 633.
**primrose** *n.* primrose 9.
**prynce** *n.* prince, leader 324, &c.; **prynces** *pl.* 365.
**prise, pryse** see **price**.
**priste** *adj.*¹ keen, quick 618; **pristly** *adv.* swiftly 241. [OF. *prest*]
**priste** *adj.*² esteemed 421. [OF. *pris(i)er, pres(i)er*]
**profers** *n. pl.* vows, promises 205. [AF. *profre*]
**profettis** *n. pl.* profits 146.
**prophecied** *pt. s.* prophesied W 449.
**prophete** *n.* prophet 449.
**proude** *adj.* proud, haughty 305; **prowde** magnificent, splendid 319; **prowdeste** *superl.* proudest, most noble 612.
**prouen** *v.* to prove, make trial of 205, 532; **preued** *pp.* proved (worthy in) 328; tested 478.
**pufilis** *n. pl.* ? small parcels of land 144 n.
**puysonede** *pp.* poisoned 399.
**pulle** *v.* to pull 319 in *dide* ~ *doun* caused . . . to be pulled down, had . . . pulled down; **pullede** *pt. s.* pulled, drew 84.
**purches** *n.* purchase, acquisition 145.
**purches** *v.* to acquire, obtain 192; **purcheste** *pt. s.* 280.
**purse** *n.* purse 146.

## Glossary

**puttes** *pr. 3 s.* puts (down) 633; **puttis** puts 232; **putten** *3 pl.* in ~ *vpe* make (the game) rise from cover 241; **putt** *pt. s.* put 84; **put** *pp.* 324.

### Q

**quelled** *pt. pl.* crushed 233; W **whellid**.
**quene, qwene** *n.* queen 304, 325, 626, &c.
**querrye** *n.* quarry 233; W **whirry**.
**quyppeys** *pr. 3 s. intr.* strikes, slashes (with rod) 234. See *OED*. s.v. Whip, v. I, 1.
**quyrres** *pr. 3 s.* quarries 234 n.; W **wharris**.
**quo[p]es** *pr. 3 s.* whoops 233; W **whopis, whopes** 233, 234. [Cf. OF. *houper* < *houp*, imit. of the cry; poss. infl. by OE. *hwōpan* to threaten]
**quotes** *pr. 3 s.* ? gluts, satisfies 234 n.; W **whotes**. [? OF. *qua(i)-tir* to beat or press down, to force in]

### R

**radde** *adj.* afraid in *for* ~ ? by reason of being afraid, for fear 429 n. [ON. *hrædd-r*]
**raylede** *pp.* arrayed 119, 128.
**raynes** *n. pl.* reins 131.
**rakill** *adj.* rash, headstrong 481. [Obscure; still found in mod. N. and Sc. dialects]
**ranne** *pt. pl.* ran 429.
**rase** *n.* in *at a* ~ in one sweep 73. [ON. *rás* race, infl. by sense of OE. *rǣs* rush, onslaught]
**rathely** *adv.* quickly W 556.
**ratild** *pt. s.* rattled, croaked W 261. [Cf. OE. *hratele, hrætelwyrt*, glossing names of plants; prob. echoic]
**rauȝhte** *pt. s. trans.* grasped 75; **rauȝhten** *pt. pl. intr.* extended 29. [OE. *rǣcan, rǣhte*]
**rawnsone** *v.* to ransom 634; **rawnsede** *pt. s.* ransomed 414 n.; **rawnnsunte** 514.

**receyvid** *pt. s.* W 380 in ~ *hym to deth*, i.e. made him surrender and killed him. See *OED*. s.v. Receive, v. 2 †b.
**reche** *pr. subj. 3 s.* 447 in *the deuyll hafe that* ~ may the devil have him who cares!
**reches** *n. pl.* riches 141, 282, 634.
**rede** *adj.* red 119, 429.
**rede** *v.* to read 250, 425.
**redely, redily** *adv.* readily, promptly 107, 166, 208, 556.
**refte** *pp.* bereft (of) 563.
**reghte** *adv.* in ~ *to* as far as 73, 87; **righte** in *full* ~ straight (away) 339.
**Regum** *n.* (Lat.) Book of Kings 425.
**rek(k)en** *v.* to relate, describe, tell 107, 250; **rekened** *pt. s.* counted, estimated 141; **rekkende** *pp.* described 166.
**releues** *pr. 3 s.* relieves 377.
**Relikes** *n. pl.* Relics 556.
**renke** *n.* knight, man 137, 261; **renkes** *pl.* 253, &c.
**rent** *n.* revenue (from property) 634; **renttes, renttis** *pl.* 141, 186, 282.
**rent** *pt. s.* slit 87.
**rere** *v. trans.* to rouse, dislodge 217; **rerede** *pp.* set in motion, brought about 453.
**rescowe** *v.* to recover, take back by force 341; W **rescewe**. [OF. *rescou-, reskeu-*, &c., stem of *rescoure, -keure*, &c.]
**resorte** *pt. s.* returned 58.
**reuelle** *v.* to revel 253.
**reuere** *n.* banks of a stream 208 n., 217.
**rewed** *pt. s. impers.* regretted 562.
**ryalle** *adj.* royal, noble, magnificent 186, 468; **rialeste** *superl.* 320; **ryally** *adv.* 341. [OF. *rial*, var. of *roial*]
**ryalls** *n. pl.* 'royals', the second branches of the stag's horn, lying above the brow-antler 29.
**riche, ryche** *adj.* rich, splendid, luxuriant 9, 123, 128, &c.; as vague epithet = pleasant 250; of high rank, noble 481, &c.;

*Glossary*

**richeste, rycheste** *superl.* richest, most splendid 119, 320; **richely** *adv.* nobly, splendidly 29.
**ryde** *v.* to ride 110, &c.; **rydes** *pr. 3 s.* rides 494; **rode** *pt. s.* rode 341, 414, 562; overran 514. W rode 341, 414; **rayed** 514, **raied** 562, N. or Sc. forms.
**ryfe** *adj.* abundant, plentiful 282.
**rygalte** *n.* sovereign rule 598.
**rigge, rygge** *n.* backbone 78, 87.
**righte** *adj.* right 75; **right** good, true W 250.
**righte** *adv.* see **reghte**.
**ryngen** *pr. 3 pl.* ring 214.
**ryotte** *n.* merry-making, dissipation 253.
**riste** *n.* repose, rest 572. [OE. *rest*; the -*i*- forms in ME. appear to be N.]
**ritt(e)** *pt. s.* ripped, cut 73, 75.
**roddes** *n. pl.* rods 217.
**rode** *n.* Cross 555.
**rode** *v.* see **ryde**.
**Romance** *n.* romance, (French) tales 250.
**rose** *n.* rose 119.
**rosett(e)** *n.* 'russet', a reddish-brown, coarse woollen material 137, 261. [OF. *ro(u)sset*]
**rothelede** *pt. s.* ? croaked, railed 261 n.
**rowmly** *adv.* amply, corpulently 137.
**rownnde** *adj.* round 468.
**rubyes** *n. pl.* rubies 128.

S

**sadde** *adj.* firm, solid 333.
**sadill** *n.* saddle 130, 173.
**sadly** *adv.* firmly, vigorously 322. [OE. *sæd* sated > heavy > firm > stout, vigorous, &c.]
**saye** *pr. 1 s.* say 649; **sayd(e)** *pt. s.* said 161, 183, 195, &c., seyde† 173; **sayde** *pp.* 263.
**sayled** *pt. s.* sailed 489; W **sailed** 489; **salid** glided, sank 658. [OE. *segl(i)an*]

**saylen** *pr. 3 pl.* assail, attack 225; **sayled(e)** *pt. s.* 534, *pl.* 303. W **sailed** 534, **saylid** 397, **salid** 303. [Shortened < OF. *as(s)aillir*]
**Sayn(e)** *adj.* Saint 487, 557, 579; **sayntes** *n. pl.* saints 162.
**sal-ieme** *n.* sal-gem, a pure rock-salt 591. [med. L. *sal-gemma*, lit. gem-like salt]
**sall** see **schall(e)**.
**salpetir** *n.* saltpetre, i.e. potassium nitrate 591. [OF. *salpetre*, prob. = L. *sal-petrae* salt of stone]
**same** *pron.* in *of the* ~ of the same colour 157; *fared of the* ~ suffered the same fate 330.
**samples, sampills** *n. pl.* proverbs 263, moral tales, parables 602.
**sanke** *pt. s. trans.* sank 437.
**saphirs** *n. pl.* sapphires 126.
**sattillede** *pt. s.* settled (flowed back) 437. [OE. *setlan*, *sætlan*]
**saule** *n.* soul 103; **soule** 195, 198, 266.
**sauage** *adj.* fierce, terrible 616.
**sawes** *n. pl.* wise sayings, proverbs 602.
**sawtries** *n. pl.* psalteries 162; here = psalters, psalms.
**schadowe** *n.* foreshadowing 291.
**schall(e)** *v. auxil. 1 and 3 s.* shall, will 103, 107, 179, 256, &c., **sall** 168; **schalte** *2 s.* shalt 257; **schall** *2 pl.* 648; **scholde** *pt. s.* should, would, was to 36, 82, 94, &c.
**schame** *n.* shame, disgrace 471.
**schapen, schapyn** *pp.* shaped, formed 114, built 137.
**schawes** *n. pl.* copses, thickets 4, 661.
**schelfe** *n.* (grassy) bank (or poss. ledge of rock) 661.
**schepe** *n. pl.* sheep 443.
**schewe** *v.* to see, look at 115, 275; to show 585, 646.
**schewere** *n.* mirror 291.
**schirle** *adv.* completely, thoroughly 646 n.
**scho** *pron.* she 540; **hir, hyr** *refl.*

## Glossary

**herself** 20, 608; *accus.* her 540, 609; *poss.* her 20, 623.
**scholde** see **schall(e)**.
**scholdire** *n.* shoulder 54; **scholdirs** *pl.* 79, 112.
**schorte** *adj.* short 258; **schortly** *adv.* briefly 585.
**schote** *v.* to shoot 43.
**schotte** *n.* shot 4.
**schryue** *v.* to shrive, confess 646.
**schunte** *imper. pl.* shrink (from) 291. [? OE. *scunian*]
**schurtted** *pt. s. refl.* amused (myself), passed the time 661. [OE. *(ge)scyrtan* to shorten]
**schutt** *v. refl.* to conclude 585.
**seche** *v.* to seek, look for 546; **sekis** *pr. 1 s.* 269 n.; **seches** *3 s.* gives chase (to) 63; **soughte** *pt. s.* sought 83; **soghte** went 537; **soughten** *pl.* went 434.
**seconde** *adj.* second 136.
**see** *n.* sea 333, &c.
**see** *v.* to see 70, 98, &c., look (at) 150; **seghe** *pr. 1 s.* see 263; *pt. s.* saw 25, 103, 135, &c., **sawe** 512; **see** *pt. subj. 3 s.* saw, (should) see 501; W **se(e)** 263, &c., **sye** 512.
**sege** *n.* in *to* ~ 'to siege' 224, a term used of herons, = 'to a defensive position by the water side'; ~ *perilous* the Siege Perilous 470, the seat made by Merlin for King Arthur.
**segge** *n.* man 135, &c.
**seghe** see **see**.
**sekire** *adj.* certain, assured 635.
**sekis** see **seche**.
**selcouthes** *n. pl.* marvels, wonders 501. [OE. *seld-, sel-cūp*]
**semblen** *pr. 3 pl. intr. refl.* assemble 322; **semblete** *pt. s. trans.* gathered 83.
**semely** *adj.* fine, handsome 30; fair, noble 417, 470; **semely[este]** *superl.* 135.
**semyde** *pt. s. impers. w. dat.* (it) seemed (to me) 70; (he) seemed 150.
**semys** *n. pl.* the embroidered stuff along the seams 126.

**sendys** *pr. 3 s.* sends 558; W **sendith**.
**serchid** *pt. s.* searched, looked out (for) W 661.
**sere** *adj.* divers, sundry 162, 254, 489; separate 574. See *OED.* s.v. †Sere.
**serely** *adv.* individually, separately 218, 225, 322. [ON. *sér-liga*]
**seruede** *pt. s.* deserved 570.
**seruen** *v.* to serve 218 (in falconry = help to drive the quarry out of covert for the hawk); **seruet** *pt. s.* served, attended 34.
**sesid** *pt. s.* ceased, lost W 286. [OF. *cesser*]
**sesyn** *pr. 3 pl.* seize 225; **seside**, **sessede** *pt. s.* seized, captured 417, 419.
**sesone** *n.* season 2.
**sett** *pr. 1 s.* set 269; *pt. s. refl.* set, seated (myself) 98; in ~ *vp the nese* took scent, sniffed about 45; *refl.* sat (up) 173; set (himself) 599; set, placed 470; ~ *vp* arose 432; *pp.* in ~ *of* furnished with 31; set, inlaid 126; set down (written) 602; set (of the sun) 658.
**set(t)e** *n.* seat 100, 136.
**seuen** *adj.* seven 567.
**sewet** *n.* suet (term in venery for the fat of the deer) 83.
**sewet** *pt. s.* followed, pursued 34, 45, 58, **suede** 382, 567.
**sewte** *n.* pursuit, chase 63.
**sexty** *adj.* sixty 150.
**shift** *v. refl.* to change (the subject) W 585.
**shiverd** *pt. pl. intr.* divided, broke W 383. [Cf. MDu. *scheveren*, MHG. *schiveren*]
**siche** *adj.* such 317, &c.
**syde** *n.* side 7, 28, &c.; *one a* ~ aside, apart 98; **sydes, sydis** *pl.* sides 30, &c., flanks 88, 91.
**syghede** *pt. s.* sighed 172.
**sighte, syghte** *n.* sight 96, 286.
**sykamoure** *n.* sycamore 130.
**syled** *pp.* sunk 658. [Cf. Norw. and Swed. dial. *sila* to flow, to pour with rain]

## Glossary

**silke** *adj.* silk 131.
**siluere** *n.* silver 238, 592.
**synys** *n. pl.* signs 48.
**synn** *n.* sin 665.
**Sir** *n.* (as polite form of address) Sir 195; as title before names of knights 300, &c.; **sire** sire, father 650, 652; **Sirres** *pl. voc.* Sirs 266.
**sythen** *adv.* since 335, 413, 460; *conj.* since, seeing that 631.
**sitt** *v.* to sit, crouch (of the hare in her form) 20; lie, be placed 179; sit 471; **sittis** *pr. 3 s.* 651; **satt(e)** *pt. s.* sat 100, 130, 136.
**skayled** *pp.* dispersed 383. [? Scand.; or cf. OF. *escheiller*]
**skaterede** *pp.* scattered 383.
**skyftede** *pp.* moved, divided 383. [ON. *skifta*]
**slayne** see slo(u)ghe.
**slaughte** *n.* slaughter, murderous deed 314. [? OE. *sleaht* (cf. gen. pl. *wælsleahta*), a variant of *sliht, sleht*, &c.]
**sleghe** *adj.* sly, cunning 36; **sleghely** *adv.* deftly 81, cunningly 314; W slyly. [ON. *slæg-r*]
**sleghte** *n.* sleight, cunning 36, 445, 511. [ON. *slægð*]
**slepe** *n.* sleep 36.
**slepeles** in *for* ~ because of sleeplessness, for lack of sleep 101 n.
**sleues** *n. pl.* sleeves 125.
**slynge** *n.* sling 445.
**slyppede** *pt. s.* slipped 81.
**slitte** *pt. s.* slit *70 n., 81.
**slome** *adj.* heavy (for lack of sleep) 101. See *OED*. s.v. Sloomy, a., and Sloom v.²
**slomerde** *pt. s.* slumbered 101. [OE. *slūmerian*, cf. *slūma*]
**slo(u)ghe** *pt. s.* slew 445, 533; **slayne** *pp.* slain 314.
**smale** *adj.* small, slender 662.
**smote** *pt. s.* smote, struck 53.
**so** *adv.* so, in this way 76; *intensive* so 100, 169, &c.
**socoure** *n.* succour 537.
**sodaynly** *adv.* suddenly 636.
**softe** *adj.* mild, pleasant 2.
**some** *pron.* some 243.

**somere** *n.* summer 2.
**sonde** *n.*¹ sand 333.
**sonde** *n.*² dispensation, ordinance 442. [OE. *sand, sond* < *sendan*]
**sondere, sondire, sondree** *adv.* in *in* ~ apart, asunder 90, 231, 383.
**sone** *n.*¹ son 650, 651.
**sone** *n.*² sun 100, 658.
**sone** *adv.* at once 58, &c.; soon 296, &c.
**soppe** *n.* sop 438.
**sore** *adv.* bitterly, exceedingly 194, &c.
**sothe** *n.* truth 103, &c.; merging into the *adv.* **for-sothe** (cf. 107) in *for* ~ for a fact, with certainty 159, 643; *adj.* true (or *n.* 'the truth') 263.
**sothely** *adv.* truly, indeed 568.
**sotted** *pt. s.* dulled, blurred 286. [OF. *a(s)soter* < *sot* n. fool]
**sottes** *n. pl.* fools 266.
**so(u)ghte** see seche.
**soule** see saule.
**Sowdane** *n.* sultan 533, 568.
**sowed** *pt. s. intr.* was sorely pained, grieved 286 n.
**sownnde** *adj.* safe, unharmed 434.
**sowre** *n.* 'soar', a buck or hart in its fourth year 34 n., 45, 58. [OF. *saur, sor*, L. *saurus*]
**sowssches** *pr. 3 pl.* beat up 218 n.
**spanyells** *n. pl.* spaniels 244.
**sparede** *pt. s.* saved, hoarded 260.
**speche** *n.* speech, words 366.
**sped(d)** *pt. s. intr.* succeeded, prospered 366; *refl.* sped, hastened 541; **spede** *pr. subj. 3 s. trans.* help 260.
**spedely, spedily** *adv.* in a lively manner 244, speedily 541.
**speke** *v.* to speak 265, 595; **spoken** *pp.* spoken, uttered 366.
**spend** *v.* to spend 260.
**spilles** *pr. 2 s.* art destroying (thyself), coming to ruin 193.
**spitte** *pt. s.* spat 550.
**spournede** *pt. s.* kicked 550.
**spryngen** *pr. 3 pl.* spring, leap 244.
**staffe** *n.* staff 289.

## Glossary

**stale** *n*. in ~ **stonden** ? be of any use 289. See *OED*. s.v. Stall sb.¹ †2, †b.
**stalkede** *pt. s.* stalked 41, **stelkett** advanced cautiously 51.
**stalkynge** *n.* stalking 21.
**stalles** *n. pl.* stalls, stables 190.
**standerte** *n.* standard 376.
**standes** see **stonde(n)**.
**starede** *pt. s.* stared, gazed 51.
[**start**] *pt. s.* sprang 502.
**stede** *n.*¹ place 21.
**stede** *n.*² steed 190, &c.; *gen. s.* 200, 272.
**stele** *adj.* steel 446.
**stele-wede** *n.* armour 200 n.
**stelkett** see **stalkede**.
**sterapis** *n. pl.* stirrups 116. See 'Language', p. xviii, 9.
**stiewarde[s]** *n. pl.* stewards 147 n.
**stiffe, styffe** *adj.* firm, unyielding 272, 376.
**stikkes** *n. pl.* sticks, twigs 41; bits, pieces 376.
**stille** *adv.* still, firmly W 289.
**stillen** *v.* to quieten 268.
**stilly** *adv.* quietly 41.
**stynte** *v. trans.* to stop 268.
**stirkes** *n. pl.* heifers 147, 190.
**stirre** *v.* to stir, move 47.
**stoken** *pp.* enclosed 200; see *OED*. s.v. Steek v.¹
**stonde(n)** *v.* to stand 47, 289; **standes** *pr. 3 s.* exists 604; **stode** *pt. s.* stood, was standing 21, 47, 116.
**stone** *n.* stone 446.
**stong**† *pt. s.* struck, pierced 446.
**storye** *n.* story 306, 423.
**storrours** *n. pl.* store-keepers 147 n.
**stotayde** *pt. s.* paused, came to a standstill 51. [? Cf. OF. *estoteier* to upset, throw into disorder, Du. *stuiten* check, stop]
**stourre** *n.* battle, conflict 272.
**streghte** *pt. s.* stretched 116.
**strenghte** *n.* strength 532; **strengthes** *pl.* 205.
**stryffe** *n.* strife, quarrelling 268.
**strikes** *pr. 3 s.* strikes 228; **striken, stryken** *3 pl.* strike 219, 221.
**suede** see **sewet**.

**surely** *adv.* stoutly, confidently W 322.
**surryals** *n. pl.* 'surroyals', the branches of the antler above the 'royals' 30.
**swange** see **swynge**.
**swapped** *pt. s.* struck, smote 551. [? echoic; cf. OE. *swāpan* to sweep]
**swerde** *n.* sword 500, &c.
**swete** *adj.* sweet, fair 11, 176.
**sweuynn** *n.* dream, vision 102.
**swiftely, swyftely** *adv.* swiftly 500, 551.
**swyne** *n. pl.* swine 99.
**swynge** *v.* to swing, hurl 500; **swange** *pt. s.* hurled 502.
**swith** *adv.* quickly 502, **swythe** exceedingly, greatly 369.
**swithely** *adv.* quickly, swiftly W 500, 551.

## T, Þ

**table** *n.* table 468.
**tachede** *pt. s.* fixed 67.
**tayle** *n.* tail 73.
**taysede** *pt. s.* took aim (at) 44. [OF. *teser*, pr. 3 s. *teise*]
**tayttely** *adv.* nimbly, swiftly 219. [ON. *teit-r* glad, merry]
**takes** *pr. 3 s.* captures 547, takes 556; **toke** *pt. s.* took 79, **tuke** captured 313, 569.
**tale** ? *adj.* lively, bold (of speech) 105 n. [? OE. *ge-tal, ge-tæl*]
**tale** *n.* estimate (of number) 308. [OE. *talu*]
**tame** *adj.* tame, subdued 342.
**tary** *v. trans.* to keep waiting, delay 613; **taryen** *pr. 3 pl. intr.* wait 242; **taried(e)** *pt. s.* tarried, lingered 23, 361.
**tartaryne** *n.* rich silk stuff (imported from the East through 'Tartary') 132.
**teches** *pr. 3 s.* teaches 601, 644.
**techynges** *n. pl.* teachings 604.
**telys** *n. pl.* teals (small fresh-water ducks) 219. [Not in OE.; cf. Du. *taling, teling*]

## Glossary

**telle** *v.* to tell, relate 103, &c.; **tell** *pr. 1 s.* tell 159; **telles, tellis** *3 s.* 306, 423.
**tendith** *pr. 3 s.* makes his way, goes W 321.
**tenefull** *adj.* full of woe, querulous 159.
**tenyn** *pr. 3 pl.* harass 242; **teneden** *pt. pl. intr.* felt anxiety, grief 321.
**tentid** *pt. s.* was tending, seeing to 313.
**tentis** *n. pl.* tents 361.
**tercelettes, -is** *n. pl.* tercelets, male falcons 219, 242.
**Testament** *n.* Testament 423.
**thay, þay, they** *pron. pl.* they 13, 214, 215, &c.; **thaire, theire,** once **þaire** *poss. adj.* their 107, 166, 303, &c.; **thaym, þam** *accus. and dat.* them 67, 226, &c.; *refl.* themselves 105, 381, &c.; **thaym-seluen** 498. W has, as well as **th-, þ** forms, **hir** 237, 536, **hem** 226, 227, 233, 234, 242, 369.
**þan** *conj.* than 15, **than** 109, &c.;
**than(e), þan, then,** once **þen** *adv.* then, thereupon, next 38, 43, 74, &c.; *intr. a statement* now, and further 405.
**that, þat** *adj. demonstr.* that, the 15, 21, 63, &c.; as *def. art.* in ~ one 601; *pron.* that 379; *rel. pron.* that, which, who(m) 34, 35, 45, &c.; that which, what 204, 260, 359; him who 447; *conj.* that 16, 431, 500, &c.; so that 36, 55, 94, &c.; = because 317; *till* ~ = until 180.
**the, þe** *def. art.* the 1, 2, 3, 4, &c.
**thedir** *adv.* thither 19.
**the(i)s** see **this**.
**ther(e),** once **þare** *adv. demonstr.* there 23, &c.; *indef.* there 34, &c.; *rel.* where 8, 64, 335, &c.; used idiomatically with opt. clause 664 n.; **ther(e)-aftir(e),** once **þer-aftir** afterwards, then, next 86, &c.; **þer-fore** therefore 151; **there-fro** thence 97; **ther(e)-inn,** once **þer-in** therein 304, &c.; **þer-to, ther(e)-to** in addition,

as well 32, &c.; **ther-vndere** underneath (it) 42; **ther(e)-with** with (it) 259; thereupon 657.
**thies** see **this**.
**thik** *adj.* stout, valiant W 384.
**thikke** *adv.* abundantly 124.
**thynges** *n. pl.* things 606.
**thynke** *v. impers. pr.* in *me* ~ it seems to me, I think 637; **thynkes** *pr. 3 s.* thinks 484; **thoghte** *pt. s.* thought 21.
**thirde** *pron.* third 152; *adj.* 472.
**thirtene** *adj.* thirteen 262.
**this** *adj. demonstr.* this 149, &c., *pron.* this 256, &c.; **this, the(i)s, thies** *adj. pl.* these 109, 173, 182, 220, &c.; **theis** *pron. pl.* 610.
**þoghe** *conj.* though 243.
**tholede** *pt. s.* suffered 403.
**thorowe** see **thurgh**.
**those** *adj. pl.* those 556.
**thou(e), þou** *pron.* thou, you 175, 184, &c.; **the** *dat.* (to) thee 178, (for) thee, thyself 190, 191, 192; **thi, thy(n)** *poss. adj.* thy, your 27, 177, &c.; *obj.* of thee 181; **thi-selfe** *gen.* (of) thee thyself 651.
**thre** *adj.* three 104, &c., *pron.* 421.
**threpe** *n.* argument, dispute 268.
**threpen** *pr. 3 pl.* contend in song (or poss. 'scold') 14 n.; **threpden** *pt. pl.* disputed 104; **threpid** *pp.* 262.
**threuen** *pp.* grown to manhood 133.
**thryfte** *n.* thrift 262.
**thrynges** *pr. 3 s.* makes his way, pushes forward 368.
**thritty** *adj.* thirty 133.
**thro** *adj.* keen, determined 104.
**throly** *adv.* vigorously 14, excellently 133; fiercely W 326.
**throstills** *n. pl.* throstles, thrushes 14 n.
**thurgh(e),** once **thorowe** *prep.* through 56, 91, 238, &c.; by (means of), because of 593, 594.
**thus** *adv.* thus 404.
**tyde** *v.* to befall 471; *pr. subj. 3 s.* 37; **tydde** *pt. pl.* 660.
**tighte** *pt. s.* drew 79. [OE. *tyhtan*]
**tighte vp** *pt. s.* set firmly (in posi-

## Glossary

tion) 44; pitched, set up 361. See *OED*. s.v. †Tight, v.² 3.
**tylere** *n.* stock (of cross-bow) 44. [OF. *telier*, orig. a weaver's beam, L. *tela* web]
**till** *prep.* 52, see **laughte**; *conj.* until 180, 485. [OE. (Nth.) *til*, ON. *til*]
**tyme** *n.* time, age, day 293, 300, &c.; *at his dayes* ~ at his appointed hour 579; *in thaire dayes* ~ in their day 582; **tymes** *pl.* times 162.
**titly** *adv.* quickly 613. [ON. *titt*, neut. of *tiđ-r*]
**to** *adv.* 53 see **hallede**.
**to** *conj.* until 336, 496.
**to** *prep.* to 3, &c.; towards 24, 508; against 39; at 150; upon 220; for 482.
**to-gedir(e)** *adv.* together 83, 230, 331, &c.
**to-gedirs** *adv.* together 600. [OE. *tō-gædere*+adv. *-es*]
**toke** see **takes**.
**tolid** vp *pt. s.* ? pitched, set up, W 362. [? OE. *teldan, teldian*]
**tonge** *n.* tongue 68.
**totheles** *adj.* toothless 159.
**toþer** *pron.* in *the* ~ the other 602 (false division of OE. *þet oþer*).
**toure** *n.* tower 408.
**to-warde(s)** *prep.* towards 23, 360, &c.
**townn** *n.* town (perh. village) 659.
**towre** *n.* soaring flight 213 n.
**trayfoyles** *n. pl.* trefoils 120. [AF. *trifoil*, OF. *trefeu*(i)*l*]
**traylede** *pt. s.* trailed 132.
**tree** *n.* tree 23.
**trenchore** *n.* knife 79.
**tretes** *pr. 3 s.* treats (of), deals (with) W 424.
**trewe** *adj.* faithful, trusty 326, &c.; as vaguely approbatory epithet 408.
**trewloues** *n. pl.* true-love knots 120.
**tried** *pp.* tried, tested 301; **triede** *pp. as adj.* fine (of proven quality) 120; **tryed** proved (of valour), valiant 525.

**triste** *adj.* trusty 565, 624; W **trusty**. [OE. *\*trȳstan* or ON. *\*trýsta*, beside *treysta*]
**tristyly** *adv.* faithfully, valiantly 326.
**troches** *n. pl.* the tines at the summit of the deer's horn 67 n.
**trouthe** *n.* troth, plighted word 290, 499.
**trowede** *pp.* believed 604.
**tuke** see **takes**.
**tulke** *n.* man 313.
**turned(e)** *pt. s. intr.* turned 23; *trans.* turned 67.
**twayne** *adj.* two, both 30, 432.
**twelue** *adj.* twelve 402, 440.
**two** *adj.* two 71, 525.

### V = U

**vmbe** *adv.* around 657; see *OED*. s.v. † Umbe.
**vmbycaste** *v.* to cast about, look for scent 61.
**vnburneschede** *pp.* unburnished 26 n.
**vncertayne** *adj.* uncertain, unexpected 636.
**vnclosede** *pp.* unconfined, released 336.
**vndide** *pt. s.* destroyed 311.
**vndir** *prep.* under 320.
**vndire-ʒode** *pt. s.* undermined 283. [OE. *under-gān*, pt. *-eōde*]
**vnpereschede** *pp.* undestroyed, unharmed 431.
**vnsele** *n.* misfortune 438.
**vn-to** *prep.* unto 386, 558.
**vp** *adv.* up 43, &c.; **vpe** 240, 241.
**vppon** see **appon**.
**vp-rightes** *adv.* upright 116.
**vs** see **we**.
**vttire** *adv.* out, into the open 66, 381.

### V

**vayne** *adj.* vain, futile 640.
**vanyte** *n.* vanity 640; **vanytes** *pl.* 640.
**ver[r]ayle** *adv.* in truth, verily 594.
**vertus** *n. pl.* supernatural powers 594.

## Glossary

**vertwells** *n. pl.* varvels, rings 238 n.
[OF. *vert(e)velle*, later *vervelle*,
L. *vertibulum* joint]

### W

**waggynge** *n.* stirring 40.
**wayes** *n. pl.* paths, tracks 37.
**wayte** *v. trans. and intr.* to guard,
keep 99; **waitted** *pt. s.* watched,
observed 40; **waytted(e)** looked
46, 657; *pp.* awaited 49.
**wake** *v.* to keep vigil 257; **woke** *pt. s.*
35 n.
**wakkened** *pt. s. intr.* awoke 657.
**walle** *n.* wall 433; **walles** *pl.* 318.
**wandrynge** *n.* restlessness, anxiety
257 n.
**wan(n)e** see **wynne**.
**ware** *adj.* prudent W 455.
**waryed** *pp. as adj.* accursed 536.
**warme** *adj.* warm 100.
**warned** *pt. s.* warned 35.
**warnestorede** *pt. s.* stored with provisions 412. [ONF. *warnesture* n.
< *warnir*]
**watirs** *n. pl.* waters 589; see
**mercurye**.
**we** *pron. pl.* we 264, 422; **vs** *acc. and
dat.* us 664, 665; **oure** *poss. adj.*
our 384, &c.
**weddis** *pr. 3 s.* weds 386.
**wedres** *n. pl.* winds, breezes 2.
**wele** *n.* wealth, riches 149, 637; joy,
delight 175.
**wele** *adv.* well 263, 570.
**wele-neghe** *adv.* wellnigh, almost
193.
**welthe** *n.* wealth, prosperity 252.
**wende** *v.* to go, turn 611, 632, 653;
**wendes** *pr. 3 s.* goes 505; **went**
*pt. s.* went 3, 37, &c.
**werdes** *n. pl.* fate, chances 3.
**were** *n.*[1] man 581.
**were** *n.*[2] war 313 n., 455, 544.
**wery** *adj.* weary 571.
**werke** *n.* deed 505; **werkes** *pl.* 311,
481; W **warkes** 481.
**werlde** *n.* world, earth 149, &c.,
**worlde** 332, 610.
**whare** see **w(h)ere**.

**what, whatte** *pron. interrog.* what
294, 461; **whate** *rel.* 103, 596,
649; **whate, whatt** *adj. interrog.*
293, 501.
**whedir-wardes** *adv.* whither 294.
**when** *adv. rel.* when 1, 35, &c.
**w(h)ere, whare** *adv. rel.* where 175,
294, &c.; *adv. interrog.* 185, 626.
**while** *n.* time, while (adverbially)
23, 101, &c.; *no* ~ at no time,
never 291.
**while** *conj.* while 256, 270; until
398, 535, 575.
**whileme** *conj.* while W 256. [OE.
*hwīlum*]
**whills** *conj.* while 604, 641; **whils**
until 490. [OE. (*þā*) *hwīle* (*þe*)+
adv. *-es*]
**whitte** *adj.* white 156, 285.
**who** *pron. indef.* whoever, if anyone
33.
**wy** *n.* man, fellow 193; (any) man,
person 298; knight 609; ~ *vn-to*
~ each knight to his lady 386;
**wyes, wyghes** *pl.* men 571, 584.
**wiche** *adj. interrog.* which 293.
**wielde** *v.* to possess 609.
**wies(e)ly** *adv.* carefully, prudently
40, 412.
**wylde** *adj.* wild 99.
**wyles** *n. pl.* wiles, cunning 312, 315.
**will** *n.* will, pleasure 406, 465; *with
a lighte* ~ gaily, gladly 352.
**will** *pr. 2 pl.* will (expressing mild
request) 106, 267; as auxil. of
*fut. 2 and 3 pl.* shall, will 584, 604;
**willen** *3 pl.* are eager (to) 209;
**wolde** *pt. s. auxil.* would 191,
&c.; desired, wished 278, 548.
**wilnede** *pt. s.* desired (to be) 386.
**wynde** *n.* wind 35, 40.
**wyndide** *pt. s.* sniffed the air, took
scent 46.
**wynges** *n. pl.* wings 230.
**wynne** *v.* to win, gain 609; **wynnen
(to)** *pr. 3 pl.* get at, catch hold of
230; **wan(n)e** *pt. s.* won, gained
276, 338, 473, conquered 332;
**wanne, wonnen** *pt. pl.* 252, 463.
**wynter** *n. pl.* years (with numeral)
262.

## Glossary

**wirchip(e)** *n.* honour, renown 175, 252, &c.
**wisdome** *n.* wisdom 601.
**wyse** *adj.* clever, cunning 99; wise, prudent 455; **wyseste** *superl.* 584; *as sb.* 603, 610.
**wysede** *pt. s.* sent 451; W vised.
**wiste** see **wot**.
**with** *prep.* with 8, 22, &c.; by, among 274, 458, 605.
**with-inn** *prep.* within 472.
**witnesses** *pr. 3 s.* bears witness, testifies 412.
**witt** *n.* mind, thought, intelligence 149, 603, 610, &c.; (right) mind, senses 193; reason, understanding 601.
**wittyly** *adv.* cautiously 46.
**wodde** *n.* wood 3.
**woke** see **wake**.
**woman** *n.* woman 315.
**wondes** *pr. 3 s.* hesitates 611, 632.
**wondirfully** *adv.* wonderfully 601.
**wondres** *pr. 3 s.* wonders 505.
**wondure** *adv.* wondrous(ly) W 488.
**wonne** *imper. s.* stay, remain 193 n.; **wonnede** *pt. s.* dwelt, lived 603.
**wonnen** see **wynne**.
**woo** *n.* woe 257.
**wordes** *n. pl.* words 173, 182, 261.

**worlde** see **werlde**.
**worthe** *adj.* worth 129.
**worthen** *v.* to become 648; **worthes** *pr. 3 s.* turns (to), becomes 637; **worthen** *pp.* become 461, 485, 496.
**worthy** *adj.* worthy, distinguished 455; **worthieste** *superl. as sb.* most excellent 404.
**wot** *pr. 1 s.* know 293; **wiste** *pt. s.* realized 283, knew 298, 507; *pp.* known 581.
**wothe** *n.* danger 37. [ON. *váði*]
**woundede** *pt. s.* wounded 312; *pp.* 571.
**wrien** *pr. 3 pl.* twist W 230. [OE. *wrigian*]
**wryghede** *pp.* accused, exposed 97. [OE. *wrēgan*]
**wrythen** *pr. 3 pl.* cross, twist 230. [OE. *wrīðan*]
**wroghte** *pt. s.* wrought, performed 487; *pl.* did 648; *pp.* devised 315.
**wronge** *n.* wrong, evil 648.

## Y

**ye** *adv.* yea, yes W 266.
**yeve, yoven** *pp.* given W 398, 575. See **gaffe**.

# INDEX OF NAMES

*Examples are quoted from the Thornton text only*

**Achilles** Achilles 311.
**Affrike** Africa 418.
**Alexander(e)** Alexander the Great 382, 586 (*gen.*), 588 (*dat.*); **Alysaunder** 332; **Alixander** 345, 394; **Alyxandere** 384.
**Alexaunder** Alexandria 417.
**Amadase** Amadas 614 n.
**Amenyduse** see **Emenyduse**.
**Antecriste** Antichrist 336.
**Antyoche** Antioch 515.
**Antiochus** Antiochus 456 n.
**Appolyne** Apollonius 456 n.
**Arestotle** Aristotle 586.
**Arraby** Arabia 418.
**Artage** ?Arcadia 347 n.
**Artas** see **Eglamour**.
**Arthur(e)** King Arthur 464, &c.; **Arthures** *gen.* 483.
**Askanore** Escanor 476 n.
**Aubrye** Aubrey 523 n.

**Babyloyne** Babylon 395, 627.
**Bade-rose** Bauderis 389 n.
**Balame** Balan, the father of Ferumbras 546 n., 548.
**Bawderayne** Baudrain 370 n., 389 n.
**Bedwere** Bedivere 479.
**Berarde de Moundres** Berard of Mondisdier (Mons desiderii), 527 n.
**Bersabee** Bathsheba 453.
**Betys** Betis, a son of Gadifer of Larris 391.
**Bolenn** see **Godfraye**.
**Bretayne** Britain 407; Brittany 490.
**Bruyte** the 'Brut' 407 n.
**Burgoyne** see **Gy**.

**Calabre** see **Fere de C.**
**Calcas** Colchis 337.

**Cand[ac]e** Candace, a queen of Media 396 n., 627 n.
**Carlele** Carlisle 467.
**Car(r)us** Clarus, king of India 355, &c.
**Cartage** Carthage 626.
**Cassabalount** Cassivellaunus 415.
**Cassayle** Cassiel 389.
**Cassamus** Cassamus, brother of Gadifer of Larris 353, &c.
**Cassander** Cassander 401.
**Caulus** Caulus, one of Alexander's knights 350.
**Cherlemayne** Charlemagne 520, 538.
**Cherlles** Charles (Charlemagne) 531.
**Clarionas** 621 n.
**Clyton** Cliton, one of Alexander's knights 350.
**Corborant** 516 n.
**Cristabelle** 623 n.
**Criste** Christ 161, &c.

**Dalyda** Delilah 617.
**Dares** Dares Phrygius 331 n.
**Dauid** David 442, 448.
**Deauneys** see **Ogere**.
**Denys, Sayn(e) D.** Saint-Denis (near Paris), 557, 579.
**Dido** Dido, Queen of Carthage 626.
**Dioclesyane** the Emperor Diocletian 597.
**Dittes** Dictys Cretensis 331 n.
**Dovire** Dover 410.

**Ecclesiastes** 638.
**Ector(e)** Hector of Troy 300, &c.
**Edease, Edyas** Edias, one of the daughters of Antigonus and niece of Fesonas 364 n., 390.
**Edoyne** Idoine 614 n.
**Egipt** Egypt 418.

# Index of Names

**Eglamour of Artas** Eglamour of Artois 622 n.
**Egremorte** Aigremore, a Saracen stronghold 547.
**Elayne** Helen of Troy 304.
**Ely** Elias 335 n.
**Emenyduse** Emenidus, the slayer of Gadifer of Larris 342; **Amenyduse** 359; **Meneduse** 347.
**Emorye** Aymeri de Narbonne 576.
**Emowntez, katur fitz E.** the Four Sons of Aymon 529 n.
**Ennoke** Enoch 335 n.
**Ercules** 329 n., 334 n.
**Errake fytz Lake** Erec fitz Lake 476 n.
**Ewayne** Ywain 476 n.

**Facron** a river 360 n.
**Ferambrace** Ferumbras 544.
**Fere de Calabre** 'La Fière' of Calabria 619 n.
**Fesome** 'Epheson' 354 n.; cf. **Fozayne**.
**Filot** Filot(e), one of Alexander's knights 349.
**Flagott** the river Flagot (in Spain) 542.
**Florence** the name given to Ferumbras after his baptism 545.
**Florydase** Floridas, one of Alexander's knights 349, 372.
**Floripe** Floripas, sister of Ferumbras 552.
**Fozayne** 'Epheson' (cf. **Fesome**), 356 n., 363, 385.
**Fozome** Fesonas, daughter of Gadifer of Larris 356 n.; **Fozonaze** 357, 363, 388.
**France, Fraunce** France 520, &c.

**Gadefere** Gadifer of Epheson, son of Gadifer of Larris 374.
**G[a]derayns** people of Gadres (? Gaza) 340.
**Gadyfere** Gadifer of Larris, a leader of the people of Gadres against Alexander \*340, 343.
**Gadres** ? Gaza 339.
**Gaynore** Guinevere 629.
**Galade** Galahad 473.

**Galeys** see **Perceualle**.
**Galyan** 608 n.
**Garsyene** Garsene (Graciēn), one of Alexander's knights 351.
**Gascoyne** Gascony 491.
**Gawayne** Gawain 475.
**Generides** Generides 620 n.
**Genyone** Ganelon, the stepfather of Roland 561 n.
**Gy de Burgoyne** Guy of Burgundy 528 n.
**Gyane** Guienne 491.
**Glassthenbery** Glastonbury 494.
**Godfraye de Bolenn** Godfrey of Bouillon 513 n.
**Golyas** Goliath 444.
**Grece** Greece 302, &c.
**Gregeis** Greeks 318.

**Idores** one of the daughters of Antigonus and niece of Fesonas 364 n., 392.
**Inde** India 355 (see Tolkien, *M.E. Vocabulary*, s.v. *Ynde*).
**Indyans** Indians 375, 381.
**Inglande, Inglonde** England 406, &c.
**Ypomadonn de Poele** Ipomadon of Apulia 618 n.
**Ysoute** Iseult 625 n.
**Israelle** Israel 428.

**Iazon** Jason 338.
**Iene** see **Raynere**.
**Ier[u]salem** Jerusalem 518.
**Ihesu(s)** Jesus 430, 436.
**Iosue** Joshua 426, &c.
**Iudas Machabee** Judas Maccabeus 454.
**Iulyus** Julius (Caesar) 405.

**Kay** Kay 477.

**Launcelot de Lake** Lancelot of the Lake 474.
**Lyncamoure** Lincamour *or* Lincanor, one of Alexander's knights 352.
**Londone** London 408.

**Machabee** see **Iudas**.

## Index of Names

**Marie** Mary 665.
**Maundevyle** 540 n.
**Mawltryple** Mautrible 546 n.
**Meneduse** see **Emenyduse**.
**Menylawse** Menelaus 302, 316.
**Merchill** Marsile 558 n., 569.
**Merlyn** Merlin 469, 606.
**Michaells, Sayn M. Mounte** St. Michael's Mount (in Cornwall) 487.
**Mordrede** Mordred 479, 495.
**Morgn la Faye** Morgan le Fay 511.
**Moundres** see **Berarde**.
**Mounte Ryalle** see **Sampsone** 526.

**Naymes** Naimes of Bavaria 524 n.
**Neptolemus** Neoptolemus, son of Achilles 327.
**Nerbone** Narbonne 573.
**Nychanore** Nicanor 457 n.
**Nioles** 539 n.

**Ogere Deauneys** Ogier the Dane 523 n.
**Olyuer** Oliver 523 n., &c.

**Palamedes** Palamedes, a Greek hero in the Trojan war 328.
**Pantasilia** Penthesilea, a queen of the Amazons, who was fighting on the Trojan side 325.
**Paresche** Paris, son of Priam 305.
**Penelopie** Penelope, wife of Ulysses 628.
**Perceualle de Galeys** Perceval of Galles (Wales) 478.
**Pharaoo** Pharaoh 428, 435.
**Poele** see **Ypomadonn**.
**Polborne** ? Paderborn 532 n.
**Porus** Porrus, son of Clarus 365, &c.
**Priamus** Priam, King of Troy 324.

**Raynere of Iene** Reiner of Gennes (? Genoa) 522 n.
**Romayne**, a province of Rome (i.e. Gaul ?) 414; **Romanye** 514 n.; the Roman Empire 598.
**Rome** Rome 598.
**Rowlande** Roland 522 n., 563.
**Rowncyuale** Roncesvalles 562.
**[R]oystone** the giant slain by King Arthur 481 n.

**Salamadyne** Salamadin 533 n.
**Salomon** Solomon 599.
**Sampsone** Samson (of the Book of Judges) 616.
**Sampsone . . . of the Mounte Ryalle** Samson of the Mount Royal 526 n.
**Saragose** Saragossa 568.
**Sarazenes** Saracens 567.
**Sathanas** Satan 438 n.
**Sessoyne** Saxony 419, 537.
**Sezere** (Julius) Caesar 405.
**Spayne** Spain 541.
**Surry** Syria 419.

**Terry** T(h)ierri 525 n.
**Tristrem** Tristram 624 n.
**Troye** Troy 301, &c.
**Tro(y)gens** Trojans 301, 321.
**Troylus** Troilus 326.
**Turpyn** Turpin 525 n., 565.

**Vlixes** Ulysses 329.
**Vrye** Uriah 451.

**Virgill** Virgil 594.

**Wawayne** Gawain 497 n., &c.
**Witthyne** Widukind (Guiteclin, Guitelin) 536 n.

**Y-** *forms*, see **I-**.

The manufacturer's authorised representative in the EU for product safety is Oxford University Press España S.A. of El Parque Empresarial San Fernando de Henares, Avenida de Castilla, 2 - 28830 Madrid (www.oup.es/en or product.safety@oup.com). OUP España S.A. also acts as importer into Spain of products made by the manufacturer.
Printed and bound by CPI Group (UK) Ltd, Croydon, CR0 4YY

20/03/2026

02075339-0011